The
CULDEES
of the
BRITISH
ISLANDS

CONTENTS.

---

a 2

THE

CULDEES OF THE BRITISH ISLANDS,

AS THEY APPEAR IN HISTORY:

WITH

AN APPENDIX OF EVIDENCES.

BY

WILLIAM REEVES, D. D.,

LL. D. EDINB.; MED. BAC. DUBL.; HON. MEMB. SOC. ANTIQ. SCOT.; HON. MEMB. SOC. ANTIQ. ZURICH;
HON. FELLOW OF THE KING AND QUEEN'S COLLEGE OF PHYSICIANS IN IRELAND;
SECRETARY OF THE ROYAL IRISH ACADEMY;
VICAR OF LUSK; VICAR-CHORAL OF ST. PATRICK'S CATHEDRAL OF ARMAGH.

Small-paper reprint 1994
Llanerch Publishers, Felinfach.
ISBN 1 897853 29 7

DUBLIN:
PRINTED BY M. H. GILL,
PRINTER TO THE ROYAL IRISH ACADEMY.

1864.

PREFACE.

HAVING occasion, when discussing the primitive constitution of the monastery at Hy, in the " Life of St. Columba," which was published by the Irish Archæological and Celtic Society, to advert to the solitary passage in the page of history which records the existence of Culdees in that island, I ventured to express the hope that I should have " an early opportunity of dealing with the Culdee question in a special dissertation ;" and, accordingly, at the close of 1860, I endeavoured, in two papers which I had the honour to read before the Royal Irish Academy, to put forward, not so much my own views upon the subject, as a comprehensive statement of trustworthy materials upon which to form a sound and philosophical opinion. These communications, which the Council have done me the favour of admitting to the " Transactions " of the Academy, form the matter of the following Essay, concerning which I may be permitted to make a few premonitory observations.

Fully persuaded that pretensions to originality are often at the very outset a fetter upon legitimate investigation, and that indulgence in speculation has brought great detriment to the cause of Irish history and antiquities, I made it my business to gather together, in a compact and methodical form, all the scattered evidence upon my subject which I could discover in external as well as domestic records, and by acting the part of a literary apparitor to bring up to court, as it were, all the Irish, Scotch, and English witnesses who were qualified to bear testimony,—both those who were walking in the open day of print, and those who were hiding in the secret recesses of manuscript retirement ; that, on examination had, an impartial public might take the place of judge, sum up evidence, and give judgment accordingly.

We all know how long and widely public opinion was distracted upon the case of the Round Towers,—how a question, which was originally plain and simple in its bearings, became complicated and embarrassed by the interference of ingenious theory, wild speculation, and contempt of authority, often accompanied by defective learning and disinclination to research ; and what labour the master mind who righted the question in the Transactions of the Royal Irish Academy was put to in clearing off the incumbrances of his subject, before he was permitted to address himself to the real merits of the case, and finally, by his incontrovertible conclusions, place it beyond the reach of all legitimate controversy.

In the present instance many obstructions of a like nature exist, with the addition of the prejudices arising from professional bias and ecclesiastical predilections, making the Culdee question a party one, and subsidiary to religious strife.   To enter upon the polemical arena I was neither disposed from the nature of the case in hand, nor, if disposed, was I permitted by the constitution of the body to whose indulgence I owe the delivery and publication of my statements.   There is, however, one weakness, if it be a weakness, to which I must plead guilty, and that is, earnestness in the cause of Ireland's ancient dignity ; but I do so under the protection of the great Ussher, whose apology for adverting to the successful issue of the English claims for precedence at the Council of Constance, in virtue of their Irish title, was " because it maketh something for the honour of my country, to which I confess I am very much devoted."   At the same time I have endeavoured, in dealing with the points at issue, whatever my private sentiments may be, to hold them back, and keep in view the precept of the great master, which English usage has in a measure transferred to the witness box, " omnis homines qui de rebus dubiis consultant, ab odio, amicitia, ira, atque misericordia, vacuos esse decet."

In the following pages it will be found that I have accepted the interpretation of the term Céle-Dé which has been proposed by O'Donovan and some lexicographers, and have referred its origin to the prevalence, through Latin Christianity, of the expression *Servus Dei*, in its limited and technical sense. I am aware that in so doing I have adopted a secondary and somewhat unusual signification of the word *céle*, and that Toland, O'Reilly, and Curry have preferred the more obvious and general one of " spouse ;" but I have done so advisedly, first because there is an incongruity in the expression " Spouse of God;" and, secondly, because the nature of the compound does not require such an interpretation. The Church, no doubt, is, in Scripture imagery, the Spouse ; and ecclesiastical language has even descended so far as to individualize the epithet *Sponsa Dei* in sparingly adopting it as another form for *monialis* or *ancilla Dei*. But I have not been able to discover an instance where *Sponsus* or *Maritus Dei* has been used as an equivalent for *monachus* or *servus Dei*. It is true that the Irish may have taken into account the celibacy of their ancient monks, their seclusion from the world, and their entire devotedness to religion ; and in this sense have employed the expression, " Spouse of God," to denote a class who owned no other master, no other love, no other companion but God ; and this notion may possibly have suggested to Giraldus Cambrensis, when adverting to the Colidei, his emphatic *cœlibes*, and to Jocelin his *singulares clerici*,—the companions of God, to the exclusion of all earthly ties ; living a life of utter poverty, in reliance upon His unconditioned supplies ; members of such a class as that to whom, as Probus relates, our Apostle was directed by the angelic precept—" Vade ad plebem Dei. id est eremitas et solitarios nudis pedibus." And possibly such an application among the Irish may

have been an anticipation of the mendicant orders, which long after came
formally into existence in other regions of Europe ; and the Four Masters
may have so regarded it, when they spoke of the Dominicans of Sligo as a
society of Céli-Dé.   But it is always to be remembered that this is a refine-
ment of the term, which does not seem, among its earliest recorded instances,
to have had reference to any particular attribute, especially such as was common to ecclesiastics of the time, but to have been employed in the general
comprehensiveness of the received expression *Servus Dei*.   Again, the term
céle, like *puer* and *comes* in Latin, and *gilla* in Irish, naturally admits of the
secondary meaning of subjection or devotedness, where the relation of master
and servant exists ; so that to a mind imbued with the spirit of such gracious
declarations as " Henceforth I call you not servants : but I have called you
friends," the adoption of *Servus Dei* in the encouraging sense of companionship
would be likely to suggest such an equivalent as Céle-Dé.   It is also to be
remembered that the word *céle* enters into combination, as a proper noun,
with certain names and terms, in the same manner that *mael* and *gilla* do,
where the sense of servant or devotion is manifestly implied.

This preface, which by a common ὕστερον πρότερον, has been written since
the subsequent pages were printed, affords me an opportunity of adding some
particulars in illustration of my subject that have lately come under my observation, and are worthy of being recorded.

Mr. William M. Hennessy, in a recent visit to Oxford, found among the
Irish manuscripts of the Bodleian Library a tract having the colophon—Iτeατ
annrin epιrτιl ιmmαpαlαιτ ιτep Qlαχαnυep pι an υomαιn αcur Dιnnιm pιϛ na
mbpαϛmαnυα, " These, then, are the epistles which passed between Alexander,
king of the world, and Dinnim, king of the Braghmans."   (Rawlinson, 512.)
In the course of the tract the following passage occurs : Nι υo αιττpebταιb

ın beṭha ḟḟecnaıṗc ouınnı, ol Oınnım, aṗbeṗıṗıu, a Qleṙanoaıṗ, acht aṗ Céuı Oé aṭancomnaıc ıṗın.   Nı ʒabam ḟoṗba naċh oıleṗ ıṗın bıṭ, aṗ aṭa aṗ naṭhaṗoa aṗ áṗ cınn .ı. nem, cona ṗoṗṭaıb acuṗ ḟoċhṗacaıb; ḟobıṭh aṗ nınbṗaıṗıṭ cınaıo na ṭaṗʒabala ʒaıṭe no eṭhıʒ, no ḟoṗ ecın ṗamlaıo, " Not of the inhabitants of the present world are we, I tell thee, O Alexander, said Dinnim ; but Céli-Dé is our title.   We do not accept land, unnecessary in the world ; for our patrimony is before us, namely heaven, with its abodes and rewards.   Because guilt stains us not, nor the offences of theft or falsehood, nor any similar injustice." (fol. 60 a).   The Dinnim here mentioned is the Dandamis of Plutarch and Arrian, and the Mandanis of Strabo ; whose spirited replies to Alexander, when he visited Taxila, are recorded by these historians.   Christian writers of subsequent times, such as Palladius, the pseudo-Ambrose, and an anonymous Latin author, amplified the statements previously made of the habits of the Indian philoso-phers, and drew a picture of their religion and practices which looks as if it had been regarded as the type of strict monastic life.   The last mentioned of these writers, whose tract " De Bragmanis" was printed from an unique manuscript by Edward Bisse (4to Lond. 1668), represents a correspondence by letter " Alexandri Magni Regis Macedonum et Dindimi regis Bragmano-rum," in which, at the opening of the second reply, is found the passage upon which the preceding Irish extract is modelled : " Nos, inquit Dindimus, non sumus incolæ hujus mundi, sed advenæ : nec ita in orbem terrarum venimus, ut in eo libeat consistere, sed transire : properamus enim ad larem patrium nullis delictorum ponderibus prægravati, nec aliquibus illecebrarum taberna-culis commorantes, nec flagitiorum cauponibus obligati," &c. (p. 98 a).   The Bragmani of the Latin are the bṗaʒmanoa of the Irish writer; and Dindimus, by the assimilation of the medial consonants, becomes Oınnım with the latter. It is remarkable to find the term Céle-Dé applied to a Brahmin chief, who

b

lived in the year 326 before Christ ; but the anticipation is accounted for by
the supposed resemblance of these Gymnosophists to the Christian ascetics of a
later day,—their profession being, as Palladius represents it, Ἡμεῖς Θεὸν τιμῶμεν,
ἀνθρώπους φιλοῦμεν, χρυσοῦ ἀμελοῦμεν, θανάτου καταφρονοῦμεν, ἡδονῶν οὐ φρον-
τίζομεν. Θεῷ ὕμνους ἄδομεν, καὶ τὰ μέλλοντα ἐπιθυμοῦμεν. (Bissæus, pp. 17,
26.) What is expressed by advenæ in the original, as denoting " strangers
and pilgrims," is more technically rendered in the Irish by Céli-Dé, and it is
worth observing that in one case Colgan gives this very Latin word as the
translation of the Irish term. (See pp. 3, 4, *infra*.)

In the Supplement to the reprint of O'Reilly's Irish Dictionary, recently
published by James Duffy, the following articles from the late Dr. O'Donovan's
manuscript additions are found:—" Céile, a vassal, a tenant, a liegeman ; ᴅᴀᴇꞃ
céile, a base or unfree vassal: ᴍᴀ ꞃucuꞃᴛᴀꞃ ın céile ƀeᴀn nᴀ ꝑlᴀċᴀ. *Rawlinson*, 506, fol. 25 *bb* [Bodleian Library, Oxford]. *See* Ceilꞃıne. *Catalogue*
[of MSS. in Trin. Coll. Dubl.]; plural, ceilıᴅe. H. 3. 17, col. 200 [Trin. Coll.
Dubl.] Ceile ᵹıᴀllnᴀ, a base vassal ; ꞃᴀeꞃ céile, a free vassal. H. 3. 18,
p. 3 *a*. ƀeᴀn ᴠınᵹṁᴀlᴀ nᴀ ꝑlᴀċᴀ ᴀᵹ ın ceilı. H. 3. 18, p. 124."

" Céile-ᴅé, a culdee. *See Ann. Four Masters*, Ann. 1031, 1072, 1076, 1132,
1170. *Rawlinson*, 487, O'Donovan's Transcript of the Brehon Laws, 2024."

" Céillꞃıne, service, vassalage. *Rawlinson*, 487. Transcr. of Brehon Laws,
2072. Ro ƀᴀ ƀıᴄhᴠılꞃı ᴀ ceilꞃıne ꞃe ꞃᴀoᵹᴀl nᴀ coṁᴀꞃbᴀ ᴠo ᵹꞃéꞃ, " the
service would be continued during the existence of the heirs for ever." H. 3. 17.
Transcr. of Brehon Laws, 572."

It is probable that " Comgan the Céle-Dé," who is mentioned at p. 9, *infra*,
is the subject of the following entry in the Annals of Ulster, at the year 869
(Four Masters, 868): " Comgan Fota [the Tall], anchorite of Tamlacht,

pupil of Maelruain, rested in Christ." The connexion of Aengus the Céle-Dé with the monastery and teaching of St. Maelruain is known (see p. 8, *infra*); and it is interesting to find the only other individual in hagiology who expressly bears this epithet, under the same head and in the same society.

The statement concerning the intermittent celebration of mass by the Keledei of St. Andrews, which is borrowed, at p. 38, *infra*, from the Great Register of that church, bears a striking resemblance to Mabillon's account of St. Pancratius' church at Rome:—" Hanc prius occupabant sæculares clerici, sed ita negligenter rem divinam tractabant, ut sæpe nec die dominico sacra missarum sollemnia ibidem celebrarent." (Annal. Bened., tom. i. p. 231). St. Gregory the Great, being dissatisfied with the irregularity and neglect of the secular priests, in 594 transferred the cure of this church to a society of monks. (Epist. iv. 18, Opp. tom. ii. col. 696. ed. Par. 1705.)

THE LIBRARY, ARMAGH,
November 16, 1864.

A MEMOIR

ON

THE CÉLI-DÉ, OR CULDEES, OF IRELAND AND GREAT BRITAIN.

PART I.—PRELIMINARY OBSERVATIONS.

SECTION I.—ORIGIN OF THE NAME.

THE devotion and self-denial which characterized monastic life upon its introduction into the Latin Church procured for those who adopted it the special designation of *Servi Dei*, which in process of time acquired a technical application, so that *Servus Dei* and *Monachus* became convertible terms ; *Ancilla Dei* was understood to signify " a nun;" and *servire Deo*, " to lead a monastic life." This usage prevailed so early as the days of St. Augustin, in whose writings we frequently find the above-mentioned expressions, and of whom his biographer relates that " factus presbyter, monasterium intra ecclesiam mox instituit, et cum Dei servis vivere cœpit secundum modum et regulam sub sanctis Apostolis constitutam."[*] Henceforward the term Servus Dei was admitted into the familiar language of the Church; and we observe it, in this limitation of sense, running through the works of the Latin Fathers, the acts of councils, and the biographies of saints.[†] To Pope Gregory the Great it naturally descended, and the extreme popularity of his writings tended to give it wider diffusion, and to recommend it to the remote parts of western Christendom, especially to Ireland, among whose ecclesiastics the eloquence of this

---

[*] Possidius, Vita S. Augustini, cap. 5; Opp. S. Augustini, tom. x. App. col. 260 (Venet. 1729).

[†] EVIDENCES, A.

distinguished Father was in such high repute, that with his name was commonly coupled the title of *Bel-oir*, " the Golden-mouthed."

Familiarized, therefore, to the expression *Servus Dei*, it is only reasonable to suppose that the Irish would adopt it in their discourse, and find a conventional equivalent for it in the language of their country. To this origin we may safely refer the creation of the Celtic compound *Céle-Dé*, which in its employment possessed all the latitude of its model, and, in the lapse of ages, underwent all the modifications or limitations of meaning which the changes of time and circumstances, or local usage, produced in the class to whom the epithet was applied. Of this we have an interesting example in the Irish Annals of so late a period as 1595, at which year the Four Masters apply the term *Céile-nDé* to the Dominican Friars of Sligo, members of an order which was not formally instituted till the year 1215.* The Book of Fenagh, a compilation of the sixteenth century, on the other hand, anticipates the actual introduction of the term, and in applying, by a prolepsis of some centuries, the word *Celedei* to St. John the Evangelist, necessarily employs it in the general sense of devotional sanctity, and probably poverty.†

Two earlier manuscripts, the Book of Leinster and the Book of Lismore, preserve a legend of St. Moling, in which that ecclesiastic classes himself among the *Céle-nDé*, and implies that his associates were chiefly to be found among the miserable, to wit, the sick and lepers.‡ Now, St. Moling, the founder of Tech-Moling, which is known in modern times by the name of St. Mullins, in the county of Carlow, was the contemporary of St. Adamnan, and died in the year 697. He was not only an abbot but a bishop, and was successor to St. Moedoc in the episcopal see of Ferns.

Passing over to Scotland, whither the term had been imported with the language and institutions of the Scotic immigrants, we find, about the middle of the thirteenth century, certain ecclesiastics, entitled, *Keledei sive Canonici.* In fact, during the range of time in which the term is of record, we discover the greatest diversity in its application,—sometimes borne by hermits, sometimes by conventuals; in one situation implying the condition of celibacy, in another understood of married men; here denoting regulars, there seculars;

* EVIDENCES, F, No. 15.   † Ibid., E, No. 4.   ‡ Ibid., E, Nos. 1, 2.

some of the name bound by obligations of poverty, others free to accumulate property ; at one period high in honour as implying self-denial, at another regarded with contempt as the designation of the loose and worldly-minded.

Some, who would contend for the uniformity of an order bearing the name of *Céli-dé*, endeavour to reconcile these incompatibilities by supposing the existence of two classes in the order, the one of stricter, the other of laxer discipline : but this expedient is unsupported by record authority; and when at last *Céle-dé* does become a distinctive term, it is only so as contrasting those who clung to the old conventual observances of the country with those who adopted the better organized and more systematic institutions of mediæval introduction,—in fact, as denoting an old-fashioned Scotic monk in an age when the prevalence of such surnames as Mac Anaspie, Mac Nab, Mac Prior, Mac Intaggart, Mac Pherson, Mac Vicar, Mac Clery,[*] indicated a condition of clerical society not exactly in accordance with the received notions of ecclesiastical discipline.

The earliest instance in which I have observed the adoption of the Latin term by an Irish writer is in TIRECHAN's memoirs of St. Patrick, written in the early half of the eighth century, where the bishop, from whom Killespugbrone in the county of Sligo derives its name, is called *Bronus filius Icni, servus Dei, socius Patricii.*[†] Had the Tripartite Life translated this into Irish, as it has most of TIRECHAN's narrative, we should in all probability be supplied with an important testimony as to the origin of our vernacular *Céle-dé ;* but unfortunately it transfers the Latin sentence as it stands into the body of its own recital. We have, however, in another part of this ancient and valuable compilation an example of the Irish term, which is one of the earliest instances of it that I have yet found. Speaking of St. Patrick in reference to a lad who had lost his life, it goes on to say—ꝼoꞃoꞃchonᵹaꞃꞇ ꝼoꞃ céli nꝊé ꝺia muinꞇiꞃ .i. Ɱalach bꞃiꞇꞇ a ꞇhobiuꞃcu,[‡]—" He ordered a céle-dé of his family, namely, Malach the Briton, to restore him to life:" where COLGAN incorrectly renders

---

[*] That is, Son of the Bishop, Son of the Abbot, Son of the Prior, Son of the Priest, Son of the Parson, Son of the Vicar, Son of the Cleric.

[†] Book of Armagh, fol. 11 *ba.*   [‡] MS. Brit. Mus., Egerton, 93, fol. 13 *ba.*

the term in question by *cuidam advenæ*,* instead of *monacho* or *servo Dei*, the more reasonable translation.

Section II.—Analysis of the Name.

And now that the term has come before us in its primitive form, it is time to examine its component elements, céle and Oé.

The word céle is of frequent occurrence in the earliest Irish manuscripts, and is the usual gloss on the words *socius* and *maritus*, where they occur in the Wurtzburg copy of St. Paul's Epistles, and the St. Gall Priscian ; it further supplies the grammarian Zeuss with the paradigm of an old declension of a noun in his first series. In like manner, céle ιηϛιne (i. e. *socius filiæ*) is the gloss on *gener*, and cocéιlϼine on *societas*. From this it passes into the pronominal sense of *alius, alter*, and the adverbial of *seorsum*. The cognate Welsh word *cilid* (*gelyd* of later time, now *gilydd*), the Cornish *gele*, and the Breton *gile*, are only found in this secondary use.†

More rarely the word céle has the sense of *servus :* thus the Wurtzburg Epistles gloss *libertus* by ϼoιϼmuϛ, ϼoιϼchéle, that is " freed slave." In O'Davoren's Glossary chéle is explained by ϛιlla, that is "a servant," and with this interpretation it is found in modern Irish and Gaelic dictionaries.‡ We also meet with the term in the composition of a few proper names, combined in the same manner that the commoner elements mαel and ϛιlla are found ; as, Celecleirech, Celeclamh, Celecrist, Celedabhaill, Celedulaisi, Celeisa, Celepetair, Celetighernaigh."§

The other component, Oé, is the genitive of Oιa, " God," and is occasionally found as a kind of religious intensive in combination with certain monastic terms, as αncoϼ Oé, *anchorita Dei ;* cαιllech Oé, *monialis Dei ;* ʋeoϼαιʋh Oé, *peregrinus Dei :* and a man was said to renounce the world αϼ Ohια " for God," when he exchanged the secular for the monastic habit.

Taking, therefore, into consideration the true form of the term, it may safely be pronounced that the Scotch charter of the twelfth century, which represents

---

* Trias Thaumaturga, p. 156 *b*.   † Evidences, B.
‡ Ibid.   § Evidences, C.

it by *chelede*,[*] and the biographer JOCELIN, who latinizes it *calledeus*,[†] and the generality of Scotch records, which have it in the form *keledeus*,[‡] are more correct than the York Chartulary, Giraldus Cambrensis, and the Armagh records,[§] which presume some affinity between the Irish céle and the Latin *colo*, when they represent the term by *colideus* and *cœlicola ;* in fact, making céleoé the Celtic equivalent for the familiar *deicola*. By a similar process Eudeus, the Latin form of Єnᴏɑ or Єnnɑ, is derived, quasi *En-Deus ;* and Ath-firdiadh, " ford of Firdia," now Ardee, is latinized *Atrium Dei* in the old records of Armagh. The man's name Dicuill is turned into *Deicola*,[||] though the two words have not an element in common, save a similarity of sound. So, Célechrist, " servant of Christ," is rendered *Christicola ;*[¶] and thus, as in the case of *colideus*, while sound and sense very nearly approximate, an etymological fallacy is still suggested. We therefore wonder when we find COLGAN, who was a master of the Irish language, say· concerning *Kele-De*, " quæ vox latinè reddita Deicolam, seu Amadeum designat."[**]

In Scotland, HECTOR BOECE, followed by GEORGE BUCHANAN, gave currency to the term *culdeus*, out of which grew, in that country, the vulgar form, *culdee*, which has come into general acceptance, and has been the subject of so much speculative error and historical mystification.[††]

---

[*] EVIDENCES, P, No. 14.   [†] See Part iii., sect. 1.

[‡] EVIDENCES, M, &c.   [§] EVIDENCES, I, K, L.

[||] DU CANGE gives one instance of this word as used in the sense of *Monachus*. The following example is found in S. Columbanus' Instructio ii.: " Quicumque ergo se habitaculum Dei effici voluerit, humilem et quietum se facere contendat, ut non verborum aviditate, et corporis flexibilitate, sed humilitatis veritate cognoscatur esse Deicula : cordis enim bonitas non verborum fictis indiget religionibus." Fleming, Collectanea, p. 47 *b*. See also Holstenius, Codex Regularum, tom. ii., p. 116 *b* (ed. Brockie).

[¶] Christicola is employed by Prudentius and others in the general sense of Christianus; and DU CANGE cites one case from Martene, where it is used in the limited sense of *monachus*. Adamnan styles one Petrus *deicola*, and describes him as " vitam ducens solitariam." De Locis Sanctis, lib. ii., cap. 26. He also applies the same term to St. George, *ib*. iii. 4 (Mabillon, Actt. SS. Ord. S. Bened., Sæc. iii., pars ii., pp. 466, 467, 471).

[**] Acta Sanctorum Hiberniæ, p. 580 *a*, cap. 5. " S. Ængussius cognomento Cele dé, id est, Deicola." Ib. p. 5 *b*, cap. 8.

[††] EVIDENCES, D.

PART II.—THE CÉLI-DÉ IN IRELAND.

Section I.—Strangers.

That the class of persons denoted by the term *Céli-dé* were not supposed by the Irish to be peculiar to this country we learn, not only from the passage of the Tripartite Life of St. Patrick above cited, which represents Malach, a Briton, as a Céle-dé among the saint's companions, but also from two very curious entries in the Annals of the Four Masters, though the source whence they were derived is uncertain.(*) At 806, which is 811 of the common era, they relate that—" In this year the Céile-dé came across the sea with dry feet, without a vessel; and a written roll was given him from heaven, out of which he preached to the Irish, and it was carried up again when the discourse was finished. This ecclesiastic used to go southwards across the sea, every day when his preaching was finished."† *F 1·5*

Setting aside the marvellous part of this statement, which ill assorts with the matter of fact entries among which the compilers have inserted it, one can easily perceive that it records the arrival of a foreign monk, whose object was to bring about some reformation in morals, or change in discipline, among the natives, and whose exhortations possessed pretensions or force sufficient to invest his message with a heaven-sent character.

Again, at the year 919, the same annalists record that " Maenach, a Céle-dé, came across the sea westwards to establish laws in Ireland."‡ The Celtic form of this individual's name suggests North Britain as the quarter whence he came, it being a common practice with the ancient Irish to style Scotland " the eastern country." Or else we may suppose him to have been an Irish settler on the Continent, who came back charged with some temporary commission regarding ecclesiastical discipline.

---

* The former is to be met with also in the *Leabhar Gabhala* of the Four Masters (p. 200, MS., Royal Irish Academy, L. i.), but where they found it, unless in the original authority of the Chronicon Scotorum, has not been discovered. See O'Donovan, Four Mast., vol. i. p. 417, *note* ª.

† Evidences, F, Nos. 1, 5.   ‡ Ibid., No. 2.

Section II.—Tamhlacht-Maelruain.

The close of the eighth century, if we may credit certain Irish records, presents to us the term Céle-dé in a definite sense, and in local connexion with a religious class or institution. St. Maelruain, founder, abbot, and bishop of the church of Tamhlacht, now Tallaght, near Dublin, gathered round him a fraternity, for whom, amidst the prevailing corruption of religion and laxity of monastic discipline, he ordained certain rules of stricter observance, which consisted partly of precepts for conventual and sacerdotal guidance, but were especially distinguished by the principles laid down, and the regulations prescribed, for religious worship and the exercise of devotion. Of his history we know nothing beyond a few broad facts. A religious rule, ascribed to him, is preserved, in manuscript, in the Leabhar Breac, entitled Riaȝail na Celeꝺ-nꝺe, óⅯoelꝑuaın cecınıc, that is, "The Rule of the Céle-ndé, from *the poem which* Moelruain composed." The language in which it is written is Irish; and though its age, as it now stands, is proved by the orthography and grammatical structure to belong to a date not earlier than the twelfth or thirteenth century, it may be fairly regarded as a modernized, and perhaps amplified, version of a much earlier document. The length of the tract allows of great variety in the subjects of which it treats; but its contents are greatly deficient in arrangement, and are in many places obscure. Though of importance in the illustration of the subject in hand, its insertion here would break the continuity of this memoir, and introduce matter foreign to the immediate discussion. It is therefore reserved for the Appendix, where it will be found, with a literal translation from the pen of my friend, Dr. O'Donovan.[*] It is sufficient to observe in this place that the subjects of its precepts are in various places styled Céle-nDé, either in an application limited to a particular order so called, or, what is more likely, in a sense allied to that of "ascetics," or "clerics of stricter observance." Besides this, there is a religious poem of twelve stanzas preserved in another venerable manuscript, having the superscription, Ꝺo Chelıu Ꝺe ınꝛo ꝛıꝛ, "Of the Céli-Dé down here," or, "as follows," and chiefly devoted to precepts

---

[*] Evidences, H.

Metrical Rule of CD ?

regarding Divine worship, according as the subjects of them might be clerics, readers, or laymen.* This poem forms the seventh division in a metrical composition of 145 stanzas, which is ascribed to St. Carthach or Mochuda of Lismore, and immediately succeeds a division containing nineteen stanzas on the duties of a monk. If this be a genuine composition, or even a modernized copy, it will follow that the Céli-dé were a separate class, previously to the year 636. when St. Carthach died, and that they were distinct from the order called monks.†

St. Maelruain died on the 7th of July, 792 ; and his death is thus recorded, at 791, in the Annals of Ulster: " *Maelruain Tamlachta episcopus et miles Christi in pace dormivit.*" In his fraternity there lived an ecclesiastic, somewhat his junior, called Aengus, surnamed from his father, Mac Oengobann, and from his grandfather, Ua Oiblen, whose poetical compositions obtained great celebrity among the Irish, yet of whom, either as regards his life or death, there is not the slightest notice in our Annals, and of whose history the sole chronological notes which we possess are his connexion with St. Maelruain and one or two other contemporaries, his pedigree, and his obital day in the Calendar. This distinguished writer, having spent the early part of his monastic life at Cluain-eidhnech, now Clonenagh, in the Queen's County, and having founded a church in the neighbourhood, called after his name, Disert-Aenguis, now Disertenos, was afterwards induced by the celebrity of Maelruain's institution, and what was probably a stronger attraction, the congeniality of its discipline to his peculiar habits, to attach himself to the congregation of Tamhlacht. " Audiens nempe," as COLGAN observes, " S. Malruani Abbatis nomen, monastici instituti rigore, et eximia vitæ sanctimonia eo tempore inter Hibernos longe celebre; iter suscepit versus Tamlactense Monasterium tertio miliario a Dub-

---

* EVIDENCES, G.

† It is worthy of observation that in the early Irish notices of the Céli-dé the superior is generally styled cenn " head," not abb " abbot," or pրion " prior." See EVIDENCES, F, 6, 10, 11, 12, 13.; and Four Mast., 1143, cited in § 6, *infra*. This distinction is also observed in some of the Scotch records, where the superior of the Keledei is called *Præpositus.* There are two instances, however, where he is termed *Abbas.* In Brechin he appears as *Prior ;* but the term is qualified at Monymusk, *Prior vel Magister.* In the case of Armagh, it was declared that the name *Prior* only indicated precedence, and in 1550 it was advisedly changed to *Magister aut Rector* (§ 3 *infra*).

linio urbe, ubi magnum monachorum cœtum S. Molruanus Regularis disciplinæ eximius restaurator et pietatis promotor, sanctissime regebat."* Here he is said to have composed his metrical calendar, or Felire, and to have taken part in compiling the Martyrology of Tamhlacht. Besides these works, the author-ship of various religious poems and tracts of a liturgical and historical character is ascribed to him; and the title by which he is invariably designated is that of *Céle-dé;* so that "Aengussius Keledeus" in Latin, and "Aengus the Culdee" in English, is a name familiar to every one at all conversant with Irish history.

As a member of the community for whom the title Céle-dé has been espe-cially claimed, he may have borne it rather as denoting his order than for any peculiar quality which he possessed ; or, as Colgan supposes, his personal holiness procured him, *par excellence,* the title of Céle-Dé in the sense of "a lover or worshipper of God:"† to which Dr. Lanigan adds, as a "surname peculiar to himself."‡ A better view to take of it in the case of Aengus is to suppose that it was a received term denoting rigid monastic observance, especially in the order of divine service, and to have been applied to him as one who both contributed to the devotional compositions of the church, and also lived according to the straitest sect of his religion. From the manner in which it is mentioned in the Annals and the Rules, there can be no doubt that it was a common term ; and we even find it, in one instance, coupled with the name of an obscure individual : Comʒan céle-ɒe, "Comgan the Culdee," is commemorated in the calendars of Tamhlacht, Marianus Gorman, and Donegal, at the 2nd of August, but without any comment concerning his date or place. It may appear strange that the title is not oftener applied to saints of conven-tual distinction, amidst the host of names which crowd the Irish Calendar; but it is to be remembered that the term only came into use with any thing like a determinate application towards the end of the eighth century, when the Irish Calendar was nearly closed.

The church of Tamhlacht was founded about twenty-four years after the institution by Chrodegang of the order of canons, in his church of Metz, to whom the title of *Fratres Dominici* was given, and afterwards that of *canonici.*

---

* Acta Sanctor. Hib., p. 579 *b*, cap. 4.   † Ibid., p. 580 *a*, cap. 5.
‡ Ecclesiastical History of Ireland, vol. iii., p. 248, *note* 96.

They were an intermediate class between monks and secular priests, adopting to a great extent the discipline, without the vows, of the monastic system, and discharging the office of ministers in various churches.   At the Council of Aix-la-Chapelle in 817, a new rule and additional regulations were enacted for them. Possibly the institution of Maelruain may have borrowed from, or possessed some features in common with, the order of canons : for certain it is that in after ages both the Keledei of Scotland and the Colidei of Ireland exhibited in their discipline the main characteristics of secular canons.

SECTION III.—ARMAGH.

The next church on record as having a fraternity of Céli-dé in connexion with it is that of Armagh; and here we have a great range of time for their continuance, namely, from the commencement of the tenth century to the Reformation.

At the year 920, or 921 of the common era, the Annals of Ulster relate that " Ardmacha was pillaged on the Saturday before St. Martin's day, which was the 10th of November, by Gofrith, grandson of Ivar, and his army, who saved the houses of prayer with their people of God, that is Céli-dé, and their sick,* and the whole church-town, except some houses which were burned through neglect."† The Four Masters record the same event at the year 919 of their reckoning.‡

The remarkable feature in this passage is that there is no mention of abbot, subordinate officers, or monks, of Armagh, although it possessed several churches, and was from an early period very fully provided with all grades of conventual ministers.   It must be owned, however, that at this period there is a great hiatus in the succession of its ecclesiastical functionaries.   Maelbrighde Mac Tornain, the abbot, died in 927; but he was of the Cinel Conaill, or Donegal race, and successor of Columcille and Adamnan, that is, abbot of Hy and Derry, from which we might infer that his connexion with Armagh was more titular

---

* COLGAN renders the latter clause thus: " *pepercit tamen Ecclesiis, Colideis, et infirmis.*" Trias Thaum., p. 296 *b.*

† EVIDENCES, F, No. 4.   ‡ Ibid., F, No. 3.

than real. There seems to have been no *secnab* or prior, no bishop, no *fer-leghinn* or lecturer, no anchorite, nor any of the usual officers of a great monastery at this date. In fact the Norse pillagings and burnings of the years 830, 839, 850, 867, 879, 890, 893, and 914, as recorded by the Four Masters, had so desolated the ancient establishment, that we can conceive it reduced to a condition in which scarcely any but the most devoted and self-denying ministers of its churches and hospitals would remain in it. Hence we can understand how the annalist despatches all the religious of the place under the term "people of God," or, more technically, Céli-dé, who would seem to have been the officiating attendants of the choir and altar, and in close connexion with whom were the receptacles for the sick and poor. In this view the Céli-dé of Armagh would denote the ministerial portion of the old conventual society.

This is the first and last time that the Irish annals notice the Céli-dé of Armagh; and it is not till the year 1366 that they reappear upon the page of history. In the interval, the Norsemen having ceased from their depredations, and Armagh having recovered her normal condition, the chief local clan acquired a religious as well as a secular ascendancy, and the six hereditary successions of lay abbots occurred, together with other abuses, which grew out of an enervated state of the conventual system. During this period we may suppose, however, that while the wealthier portion of the community became so much secularized, the officiating priests continued to discharge the duties of the sacerdotal office, as in former times, living in community, and it may be, like the Céli-dé at Clonmacnois, or the Keledei of Scotland, occasionally entering the married state. The laxity of their discipline was the probable cause which rendered the introduction of regular canons into Armagh a desideratum; and we can easily understand how the public recognition of this order in 1126 would greatly tend to diminish the influence and importance of the secular corporation, who henceforward took rank in the diocese *after* the regulars, though they represented the original clergy of the place.

The exact date when the cathedral economy was recast is not recorded, but it probably took place in the interval between the retirement of Malachi O'Morgair and the conquest of Ireland, during the episcopate of Gelasius: and then the normal cathedral staff of dean, chancellor, treasurer, archdeacon, and canons, hitherto unknown in Ireland, but now borrowed from English or

Continental usage, was introduced. In other dioceses a different process took place, as in Down, where Malachi O'Morgair, in 1138, founded a priory of regular canons, leaving the cathedral church to its old corporation of secular canons, who, I presume, were akin to the Céli-dé, and who continued to conduct its services till 1183, when John De Courcy turned them out, and Anglicized the church by bringing over Benedictines from St. Werburgh's of Chester to be its future chapter. Two years after, the memorable *Invention* was published, which made amends to the native feeling of the district. Again, in Meath, there has never been a cathedral establishment of any kind, and the Céli-dé who formerly served the church at Clonard, merged, with their privileges, in the parochial clergy of the diocese.

But, to return from this digression, when the new capitular constitution was introduced into Armagh, the ancient system was not altogether superseded, as elsewhere, but, owing to some influence or motive at present unknown, the old society of the Céli-dé, who now began to be called, after the Latin fashion, by the name *Colidei*, were continued in their endowments and religious functions, only in a less prominent position. Their ministrations in the "great church" proceeded as hitherto, and their head or prior (which was a title of precedence, but not authority) fell into the place, though not the name, of the ordinary præcentor, while his fraternity of Colidei performed the office of vicars in the choir. They continued to be a several corporation, and never merged in the chapter, their prior only having a place and voice in capitular meetings. Hence the formal communications from the archbishops ran thus—" Decano, Priori Colideorum, et aliis de capitulo, necnon Colideis ;" or, " Decano, Priori Colideorum, omnibusque et singulis Canonicis et Colideis ecclesiæ nostræ Armachanæ."

The first place that the name appears in the records of Armagh is in the Register of Primate Sweteman, at 1367, where that prelate remonstrates with Ohandeloyn [O'Hanlon] for the injuries that he had offered to the " Decanus et omnes alii Canonici et Colidei." In the same year Cristinus,* a Colideus, was the bearer of a letter from the primate to the dean. Odo M'dynim, or M'doynym, the prior of the Colidei, was despatched to Rome, in 1366, as the

---

* A latinized form of *Gillacrist* or *Cælecrist.*

primate's proctor in a case pending there ; and he is also styled "Prior communitatis nostri capituli Armachani." In his absence he was elected to the office of chancellor in the cathedral, which had precedence, and was better endowed.[*]

During the course of this and the following centuries there is repeated mention of the Colidei and their priors in the Registers,[†] and from the incidental notices we collect the following particulars regarding their constitution and office:—1. The body consisted of a prior and five brethren. 2. The celebration of divine offices was discharged by them ; and skill in music as well as eloquence in preaching were considered necessary qualifications for the office of prior, which, subject to these conditions, was in their election. 3. The office of Colideus was accepted as a title for holy orders. 4. The repair of the fabric of the church was in their hands ; and among them was frequently found the office of " Magister operis Majoris Ecclesiæ," and of Apparitor. 5. License to appoint a confessor was granted to them by the primate under certain conditions. 6. Their consent was not required for the ratification of the primate's official acts. 7. They had no voice in the election of the diocesan, except so far as their prior, in virtue of his præcentorial position, had a vote in the chapter. 8. They took no part in the custody of the spirituals of the diocese *sede vacante.* 9. In the order of precedence, as a body, they ranked third in the diocese; the dean and chapter being first, the convent of regular canons of St. Peter and St. Paul being second, they third, and the clergy at large fourth. 10. Their inferior position was implied in the title of *canonici majores,* which was applied to the non-dignified members of the chapter ; while the secular character of their head distinguished him from the *prior claustralis,* who was an officer among the regular canons. 11. Their prior ranked in the cathedral next after the chancellor. 12. Rectories or vicarages with cure of souls were generally held by the priors, and occasionally by the inferior members, as the rectories of Achlunga [Aghaloo], Carnsegyll [Carnteel], and the vicarages of Twyna [Tynan], Onellan [Kilmore], and Drumcrygh [Drumcree]. 13. In 1427 they were possessed of the rectory and certain townlands in the parish of Derenoysse [Derrynoose]. 14. At the dis-

---

* EVIDENCES, K. † Ibid., K.

solution they were found to have been seized of seven townlands, now in the parish of Lisnadill, consisting of 1423 acres; the rectories of seven parishes, with the vicarages of three ; and some small holdings, all in the county of Armagh. 15. The archbishop had a residence among them ; for in 1462 Primate Bole speaks of his accustomed abode "in loco Collideorum vulgariter nuncupato." And this connexion was probably a vestige of their ancient relation, when the " Successor of Patrick" was abbot, and their predecessors his brotherhood.

In Primate Mey's Register* is entered a long and detailed account of certain proceedings which took place relative to the title of one of the vicarages above mentioned; and as this involved an examination into the nature of the office of Colideus, we possess in the record an amount of contemporary evidence which is of great importance in the discussion of this question.

In the year 1430, David M'Gilladé, prior of the Colidei of Armagh, died, and Donald O'Kellachan, a canon of the church, was unanimously elected by the college of Colidei to succeed him, who was thereupon duly installed. On the 17th of May he presented himself to Primate Swayne, at his residence in Drogheda, for confirmation, which was readily granted, inasmuch as he was, to use this prelate's words, " in expositione verbi Dei, et aliorum exponendorum plurimum facundus," and also qualified to conduct divine service as being " cantilena peritus." The primate further, with the approbation of the dean and chapter, granted him a dispensation for holding the perpetual vicarage of Tynan whereof he was then possessed, in conjunction with the said priorate, which office, by reason of its slender emoluments, was insufficient in itself for his respectable maintenance, his predecessors having, in long succession, held benefices together with their cathedral appointment. But towards the close of 1442, Donald M'Kassaid, a priest of the diocese of Clogher, having misrepresented the case at the court of Rome, by stating that the office of prior was incompatible with a benefice having cure of souls, obtained a decree that the vicarage of Tynan, which Donald O'Kellachan had held for twelve years, and was estimated at the annual value of five marks sterling, was now unlawfully occupied, and therefore void, and, by virtue of a canon of the Council of

* EVIDENCES, I.

Lateran, devolute to the see of Rome. Accordingly a bull of Eugenius IV. was obtained, dated February 28, 1443, directed to the dean and Arthur and John McCathmayll, canons of Armagh, empowering them, or any of them, to evict Donald O'Kellachan from his benefice, and induct McKassaid therein ; to whom, " propter defectum natalium, utpote de soluto et soluta natus," a dispensation was granted, together with license to hold two or more vicarages, or two prebends or canonries, and liberty of exchange; as also an express faculty to hold the rectory of Teachtalan [Tehallan], in the diocese of Clogher. Whereupon Arthur McKathmayll, as one of the commissaries, proceeded to execute the said mandate, declaring the vicarage empty, and Donald the prior amote and to be expelled as an unlawful intruder. Donald McKassaid, on bended knee, received investiture, and was decreed into corporal possession. At the same time sentence of canonical censure was pronounced against all contraveners, not excepting the diocesan himself. Having no seal of his own, the commissary borrowed that of Eugenius, abbot of St. Peter and Paul's of Cluaineysse (now Clones), and the whole transaction is stated to have occurred at Ceandaird (now Caledon), in the house of Johannes Flavus O'Neyll.

Thus aggrieved, the prior appealed to the court of Rome directly, and to that of Armagh tuitorially, employing John White as his proctor, who died at Rome on the 13th of October, 1445, before he was able to execute his commission. A delay consequently occurred in the prosecution of the suit, and, owing to the poverty of the prior, as well as the detention of the vicarial revenues by the friends of Donald McKassaid (Patrick McKassaid, a kinsman, being herenach of Tynan), he was unable to employ a fresh proctor till the close of the following year, when Thomas O'Kellachan, a clerk of Armagh, was despatched by the prior and Colidei. In his journey he was waylaid near Carryk, in Meath, by certain *malandrini,* and robbed of his money and credentials. The appeal, however, was proceeded with, and, pending the decision, the primate sat in court in Armagh cathedral, on the 24th of July, 1445, to receive evidence and pronounce judicially on the matter of fact whether the priorate of the Colidei was an " office" or " dignity with cure." The following parties were examined on oath:—Charles O'Mellan, the dean ; Salomon McCreanayr, the chancellor ; Arthur McCathmayll, official of Tullaghog; Thomas McGillacrany, Nicholas McGillamura, Donatus O'Hallian, and John McGeerun,

Colidei; Philip M‘Kewyn, herenach of Dareynoysse; William O’Moryssa. prior claustralis; John O’Goddane, canon regular; O’Coffy, O’Martanan, and M‘Gillamura, captains of their clans; who, with one consent, at the relation of the dean, declared, as well on the authority of records a hundred years old, as from all that they had been told by their seniors, that the *Prioratus Colideorum* never had cure; that divers priors, at successive periods, peaceably enjoyed benefices having cure, on which they did not reside, but, for the honour of the cathedral church, and the due celebration of divine service, they dwelt with the other Colidei; that the priors as such had no cure, but the chief seat at table, and the rank of præcentor in the regulation and conducting of divine worship. Further, that the *Colideatus* was only an office for celebrating service, being a *ministerium*, and no way charged with cure. And, what was of still greater weight, the ancient chronicles of holy fathers, and the annals of antecedent generations, having been examined, the same evidence was fully confirmed. The primate thereupon delivered judgment that the priorate was not incompatible with a benefice in cure. Meanwhile the prior’s appeal was pressed at Rome, and a bull of Nicholas V., dated 1447, was issued, stating that the petition of Donald O’Kellachan, vicar of Tynan, had been received, setting forth that the “ Prioratus collegii *secularium presbyterorum, Colideorum vulgo nuncupatorum*,” was a simple office, and praying that the accidental delay in the appeal might not bar his rights. The rescript empowers the primate and the abbot of St. Peter’s and St. Paul’s of Armagh, or either of them, to hear the appeal, and to affirm or annul the antecedent decision, as the ends of justice might demand. This was lodged with the primate on the 23rd of March, 1448, by Thomas O’Kellachan, the prior’s proctor; and after some preliminary hearings, the archbishop sat, on the 7th of November, in the house of the Friars Minor of Armagh, outside the town, which was chosen for safety’s sake, as the plague was raging within. After various adjournments, the appellant produced in court a “ liber notabilis de antiquis cronicis,” and proceeded to examine witnesses, among whom was William O’Moryssa, a canon regular and prior claustralis, who swore that the priorate was not a dignity, but only a precedence among the Colidei, and that at the time he himself “ intravit religionem,” David M‘Gilladé, prior of the Colidei and vicar of Onellan, was his kind master, but that he incurred his displeasure by entering a regular order instead of becoming a Colideus. Nicholas O'Hernaid swore that the prior was only " inceptor in executione divinorum." On the 16th of November, 1448, the primate gave definitive sentence, declaring McKassaid's title null and void, and decreeing the said priorate to be merely an office, and tenable with a beneficed cure ; at the same time condemning McKassaid in all the costs and fees of court incurred by reason of his temerary vexation. On the 16th of December letters refutatory were despatched to the pope, refusing to admit McKassaid's further appeal, as being frivolous. Thus was delivered from the gravest ecclesiastical tribunal in the land an authoritative definition of the office and functions of the Irish Culdee in the middle of the fifteenth century.

There are occasional notices of the Colidei in the Armagh registers during the succeeding century, after which they become silent ; but the Antiphonary of Armagh, which came into the possession of Archbishop Ussher, and is preserved among his manuscripts in the library of Trinity College, Dublin, contains some obituary entries, which are of importance in confirmation of what has been now advanced.[*]

A. D. 1549, January 28, died. at an advanced age, Edmund McCamyl, dean of Armagh, and prior of the Collidei or convent of the greater metropolitical church of Armagh.

A. D. 1556, August 16th, died master John McGillamura, late master of the works, and Collideus of the metropolitical church of Armagh.

A. D. 1570, June 9th, died Roland M'Gillamura, formerly rector of Clonmore, vicar of Ardee, bachelor in sacred theology, lecturer in the same, and Collideus of the metropolitical church of Armagh.

A. D. 1574, September 26th, died Nicholas McGillamura, late master of the works, and Collideus of the metropolitical church of Armagh : he was a blameless priest, and a great proficient in the art of music.

These entries are all subsequent to the Act for the suppression of Religious Houses, and seem to imply that, notwithstanding the inquisition which had been taken, in 1541, on the priory of the Colidei of Armagh, means had been

---

[*] Evidences, L.

found to evade its operations. This was in a great measure effected by annexing the office of prior to that of the dean, thus divesting the corporation of that appearance of severalty which it had hitherto possessed, and by the primate's subjecting its revenues to his own more immediate control. On the death of Edmund M°Camyl, who was both dean and prior, Terence Danyell succeeded to the deanery; and on the 31st of May, 1550, received a commission from Primate Dowdall to exercise the rule and government of the Colidei and other ministers of divine service in the college, "sub nomine Magistri aut Rectoris collegii, et non Prioris,"[*] but was at the same time inhibited from the alienation or disposal of any lands, rents, tithes, or other emoluments belonging to the said Colidei, without his and their consent. The religious changes which soon after took place broke up the corporation, and the succession of the Colidei was interrupted, so that before 1600 they were found to have entirely died out. The Crown, however, neither took possession, nor made any grant of their estates, but they continued to be farmed by the primates and others for the use of the cathedral till 1625, when Charles I. ordered an Inquisition of Discovery concerning their possessions as unlawfully concealed or detained. Whereupon it was found that, previously to the year 1541, there had been a priory or religious house incorporated at Armagh under the name of "Prior et Collodei," Anglice, "the prior and vicars choral of Armagh." Two years after the king granted a charter incorporating a prior and five vicars choral, to be called "The College of King Charles in the cathedral church of Armagh." In this instrument he confirmed to them all the original estates of the Colidei, excepting the rectories and vicarages of parishes which had been consolidated under James I. And it is a curious historical fact that the ancient title survived the Reformation, and existed in the year 1628, when a deed was executed in which the lessor was "Edward Burton, prior of the cathedral church of Armagh, on behalf of the vicars choral and Colideans of the same."[†] The corporation was soon after increased to eight, but the office of prior was suppressed, there being now a præcentor in the capitular body. Their endowments also were augmented, without disturbing their old estate, which continues in their possession

---

* Liber Niger, DOWDALL, p. 126.   † Original, in the Primate's Record Room, Armagh.

to the present day, and contributes towards the maintenance of a body who, within the same walls, discharge the same duties in person, or by representation, which the Colidei did six hundred years ago.

SECTION IV.—CLONMACNOIS.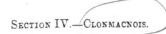

The most distinguished ecclesiastic connected with this ancient and celebrated church, in the early part of the eleventh century, was an individual called Conn, who, from his liberality to the poor, was commonly styled *Conn na m-bocht,* that is, " Conn of the paupers." He was descended, through a long line of ancestors, all of whom held some office at Clonmacnois, from Torbach, an abbot of Armagh, who died in 812, and who was the son of one Gorman, an abbot of Louth, who had died on a pilgrimage at Clonmacnois in 758. Joseph, the father of Conn, was *anmchara,* or " spiritual adviser," in the monastery. The Four Masters contain a notice of this Conn at 1031, which is the earliest passage in which the Céli-dé of Clonmacnois are mentioned, but from which we may infer that a body so called had been for some time in existence there. " Conn na-mbocht, head of the Céle-ndé, and anchorite of Clonmacnois, the first who invited a company of the poor of Clonmacnois to Iseal-Chiarain,* and who presented twenty cows of his own to it."† He lived till 1059, at which year the Four Masters record that Conn-na-mbocht, the glory and dignity of Clonmacnois, died. He left behind him several sons: Maelfinnen, who died in 1056, and whose son Cormac became abbot of Clonmacnois ; Maelchiarain, who was abbot from 1070 to 1079; Gillacrist, who died in 1085 ; Cormac, reversionary abbot, who died in 1103 ; and Ceilechair, whose son, Maelmuire, was the writer of the Leabhar na hUidhre, now in our library. The Four Masters relate that during the presidency of Maelchiarain, in 1072, Murchadh O'Melaghlin made a forcible descent upon the institution at Iseal-Chiarain, and maltreated the Céili-Dé, and that the superintendent of the poor was killed on the occasion.‡ The Annals of Clonmacnois couple the name of the son of Conn-na-

---

* That is, " Ciaran's low ground." It was a tract near Clonmacnois, which was under tillage in the founder's time. See Martyrology of Donegal, *Ciaran,* Sept. 9.

† EVIDENCES, F, No. 6.   ‡ Ibid., F, No. 7.

mbocht with the sufferers in this outrage, whom they designate as "the family
of Moylekyeran, son of Conn-na-moght."* Thus we perceive a close connexion
subsisting between the Céli-dé and an hospital, of which father and son were
successively the guardians. In 1089, Cormac, another son of Conn-na-mbocht,
purchased Iseal-Chiarain, in perpetuity, of O'Flaithen, and Donnell O'Melaghlin,
king of Meath. He also, though it is not expressly stated, was probably connected with the Céli-dé of the place. Forty-three years afterwards, that is, at
1132, the Four Masters record the death of " Uareirghe O'Nechtain, head of
the Céle-ndé of Clonmacnois, and its venerable senior."† From him the office
was transmitted to his son, as we gather from the obit in same chroniclers, at
1170, of " Maelmordha, *son of Uaireirghe,* a learned charitable senior, the prosperity and affluence of Clonmacnois, and head of its Céle-dé."‡ He again was
succeeded by his son; for we are told in the same annals, at 1200, of the death
of Uaireirghe, *son of " Maelmordha, son of Uaireirghe O'Nechtain,* one of the
noble sages of Clonmacnois, a man full of the love of God and every virtue, and
head of the Céle-dé of Clonmacnois."§ Thus we perceive that, whatever these
Culdees of Clonmacnois were, their presidency was for a time hereditary in
one family.

Section V.—Clondalkin.

Two monuments still remain to attest the former importance of Cluain
Dolcain, a church situate about five miles south of Dublin, namely, its round
tower, and its antiphonary, which is preserved in the library of Trinity College,
Dublin. It was founded at an early period by St. Mochua, or Cronan, whose
festival is the 6th of August; and the names of two bishops and a series of
abbots, who presided over this church from 776 down, are recorded in our
native annals. We are informed by them that, in the year 1076, a body of
the southern clergy, headed by Mac Maoildalua,‖ came in force to Cluain-

---

* Evidences, F, No. 8.   † Ibid., F, No. 10.
‡ Ibid., F, No. 12.   § Ibid., F, No. 13.

‖ This Mac Maoildalua died in 1095, at which year he is styled by the Four Masters " chief
anmchara of all Ireland." His opponent, Fiachna O'Ronain, was airchinnech of Cluain-Dolcain,
and died in 1086.

Dolcain to obtain satisfaction for injury done to this ecclesiastic, and that they expelled O'Ronain, who had usurped the abbacy. Further, that a church, with its land, was granted to Céle-dé in perpetuity.* After 1086 the name disappears from the annals; and the only surviving document of antiquity connected with it is a charter of Mac Gilleholmoc and his wife Dervorgaill, which recites its endowments.

SECTION VI.—MONAHINCHA.

A church was founded in the eighth century on an island in a lake near Roscrea, in the county of Tipperary, which formerly bore the name of Loch Cré, but is now called Monaincha† (Móin na hinnre, " Bog of the island"). St. Elair or Hilary, the founder, who is described as an "anchorite and scribe," died on the 7th of September, 807. We may infer that there was a conventual establishment here in 1143, from the words of the Four Masters, who record " the death of Macraith O'Fidan, head of Loch Cré." Other notices of the place in the annals show that it was regarded as one of the minor monastic establishments of Ireland. But GIRALDUS CAMBRENSIS affords us a glimpse of its condition towards the close of the twelfth century: " Est lacus in Momonia Boreali, duas continens insulas, unam majorem, et alteram minorem. Major Ecclesiam habet antiquæ religionis. Minor vero capellam, cui pauci cœlibes, quos Cælicolas vel Colideos vocant: devote deserviunt."‡ This passage seems to imply that the chapel on the smaller island was not equal in antiquity to the church on the larger, and that these *cœlibes* were in holy orders. In his account of Bardsey, in Wales, the same writer employs similar language, describing its occupants as " monachi religiosissimi, quos cœlibes vel colideos vocant." His use of the term Colideus is interesting, as showing that even in his day it was, though etymologically different, the received Latin equivalent for the Irish Céle-dé. As regards the two neighbouring establishments, the case was probably this: the original church of St. Elair was on the larger island, which

* EVIDENCES, F, No. 9.

† Ordnance Survey, *Tipperary*, sheet 18. For a description of the spot, see LEDWICH, Antiquities of Ireland, p. 113 ; and note ¹, in Cambrensis Eversus, vol. i., p. 123 (Celtic Society, 1848).

‡ Topographia Hiberniæ, Dist. ii., cap. 4 (CAMDEN's Anglica, &c., p. 716).

during a long period was occupied by monks of some old Irish order.   Their
ascetic habits, and the exclusion of women from their settlement, gave rise to
the legend which GIRALDUS records, that no female of man or beast could live
on the island.   In process of time the monastery was converted into one of
regular canons, who became possessed of the island, and enjoyed the endowments ; while the little fraternity of secular priests, of whom GIRALDUS speaks,
and who represented the earlier occupants, withdrew to the smaller island, and
established themselves there.   Thus, as in the case of Armagh and Devenish, we
find corporations of regular canons and Colidei in similar juxtaposition ; but
in the long race the smaller fraternity of the Insula Viventium yielded to their
more powerful neighbours ; and the result was that, after the dissolution of religious houses, their memory had perished, and it was found by inquisition, in
the year 1568, that the monastery of canons regular of the Virgin Mary, in the
Island of the Living, otherwise called Inchenebo* was seized of the island, which
contained three acres of moor, wherein were two chapels, with sundry holdings
at Corbally and elsewhere.

SECTION VII.—DEVENISH.

The island of Daimh-inis, in Loch Erne, was celebrated for its monastery,
which St. Molaisi founded in the sixth century, out of which grew that striking
memorial of pristine importance, the noble round tower which still remains
there in its original proportions.   In the twelfth or thirteenth century a body
of regular canons superseded the ancient community of the island, and became
possessed of their church and endowments, allowing, however, a small society
of secular canons, probably the representatives of the original occupants, to
remain, but in a subordinate position.   The notices of Devenish in the Annals
of the Four Masters contain the names and offices of various individuals connected with its monastery ; but there is only one which specifically mentions the
fraternity under consideration, in which they record, at 1479, the death of
Piarus (or Piers), the son of Nicholas O'Flanagan, who had been a canon chorister, a parson, and prior of Céle-ndé, a sacristan at Devenish, and an official

---

* Iniꞃ na m-beo, " Island of the living."

of Loch Erne.* Here, as in the case of Armagh, we observe the musical qualifications in the prior of the Céli-ndé. He was a canon choral of the cathedral of Clogher, in whose diocese Devenish is situate, and of which the parish of Devenish still constitutes the corps of a prebend.

The O'Flanagans were the chiefs of Tooraa, a district on the west side of Loch Erne, and for several generations furnished incumbents to the parishes of Devenish† and Inismacsaint. Nicholas, father of the above-mentioned Piers, was parson of Devenish, and died in 1450. A son of the same Piers, also called Nicholas, who died in 1520, was also parson of Devenish. Thus we again perceive that the office of Céle-dé did not necessarily require a single life, unless we make an exception in favour of Piers O'Flanagan and the O'Neachtains of Clonmacnois on the score of their being priors, and therefore entitled to the exemption enjoyed by heads of houses in the universities of Oxford and Cambridge.

At the dissolution of monasteries there were two conventual societies on the island,—one a priory of regular canons, and the other described as " the late priory or house of *secular priests of Collidea* in the same island, with an orchard thereunto belonging, and four tathes of land possessed by Rory Ballogh O'Corcon as corbe; the tithes of which were possessed by the prior O'Flanagan of the abbey."‡ In a patent of James I. the buildings are described as " a cell or chapel called *Callidea* alias *Colldea*, in said island, to said abbey near and belonging."§ In the table annexed to the Martyrology of Donegal, Michael O'Clery thus writes in 1630:—" Ubi prioratus saecularis Colideorum, pertinens ad templum magnum ecclesiæ parochialis S. Molassi (ita antiquitus), et vicaria ejusdem ecclesiæ."‖ The house of these secular priests appears to have been a relic of

---

* Evidences, F, No. 14.

† The name of Bartholomeus O'Flanagan, Prior de Daminis, appears on an inscription at Devenish, with the date 1449. Archdall, Monasticon Hibernicum, p. 260; Statistical Survey of Ireland, vol. ii., p. 194.

‡ Inquisitions of Ulster, p. xxxv., Appendix, *Fermanagh*, p. 26 *b*.

§ Patent Rolls of James I., p. 83 *b*; Erck's Repertory, vol. i., pp. 234, 275.

‖ Under " Molaissi, abbot of Daimhinis." A little to the N. E. of the round tower stood a small stone-roofed chapel, called St. Molais's House, and beyond this the priory, with its graveyard. South-east of the round tower is the abbey, with its grave-yard. Ord. Survey. *Fermanagh*, sheet 22. A description of these buildings is to be found in Archdall, Monasticon Hib., p. 259; Ledwich's Antiquities, p. 517; especially Ulster Journal of Archæology, vol. iv., p. 178.

the ancient establishment of St. Molaisi, who were superseded by the regular canons, and to whom they stood in the same relation that the Colidei of Armagh did to the cathedral chapter.

SECTION VIII.—CLONES.

Archbishop USSHER, when treating of the Culdees, makes the following statement :—" In majoribus certe Ultoniensium ecclesiis, ut in metropolitica Armachana, et in ecclesia de Cluan-ynish Clochorensis diœceseos, ad nostram usque memoriam, presbyteros qui choro inservientes divina celebrabant officia Colideos, eorumque præsidem priorem Colideorum appellatum esse novimus."[*] There is no church in the diocese of Clogher which bore the name Cluain-ynis, so that Cluain-eois, now Clones, must be the one intended.[†] The Four Masters, at 1486, enumerate the preferments of an ecclesiastic who died in that year thus :—" Philip, son of the coarb (i. e. James, son of Rury, son of Ardghal) Mac Mahon, a canon chorister at Clogher, coarb of Clones, and parson of Darty, &c.," where we may reasonably suppose the Colideate to be included in the *et cetera.*

SECTION IX.—PUBBLE.

In the parish of Enniskillen, in the county of Fermanagh, there is a townland called Pubble, having a cemetery, with the remains of a church.[‡] Here there existed before the Reformation a small society of secular priests, as we learn from the sole notice of the church on record. In 1603, the commissioners for surveying the county found that there was the " chappell of Popull, *alias* Collidea, having two tathes of land, and that it was possessed by Gille ro O'Huine as corbes."[§]

---

[*] Britann. Ecclesiar. Antiqq., cap. xv. (Works, vol. vi., p. 174).

[†] This is proved by the statement in SPELMAN's Glossary (voc. *Culdei*), which embodies a communication made to him on the subject by USSHER, " et Ecclesia de Clunish sive Cluain-ynish Chlochorensis Diœceseos;" as also by Sir JAMES WARE, " Erat item Prior Colideorum apud *Cluain-Inis* in agro Monaghanensi." Antiqq. Hib., cap. xvii. § 4.

[‡] " Old church and grave-yard," Ordnance Survey, *Fermanagh*, sheet 23.

[§] Inquisitions of Ulster, p. xxxvi.

SECTION X.—SCATTERY ISLAND.

This island, called in Irish Inis-Cathaigh, is situated in the River Shannon, near its mouth. A church was founded upon it by St. Senan, son of Gerrcind, about the year 540. In reference to him an Inquisition taken the 27th of October, 1604, states, that "Shinan M'Girrygyne, formerly bishop of Iniskaha, enjoyed sixteen quarters of land called Tarmon Shinan, which lands were given by him to the fraternity and society of thirty-three chanons and their successors in Iniskaha, to the intent that the said chanons and their successors, from time to time for ever, might serve God and perform divine service in the said place."* This foundation came to an end when the see of Inis-Cathay was annexed to that of Killaloe, about the close of the twelfth century, and the lands were transferred to the bishop. In 1599, a deed was executed by Maurice, bishop of Killaloe, to Teige M'Gillahanna, or Gillchanna, prior of Inis-Cathay, the representative of the ancient society, who was married, and whose son and daughter were living in 1667. Bishop Worth, in his rental of Killaloe, drawn up in that year, recites the above inquisition, and adds as a note on the thirty-three canons, "these in Ulster are called Culdees, q. Dei Cultores."†

PART III.—THE CÉLI-DÉ OF SCOTLAND.

SECTION I.—GENERAL REMARKS.

HAVING examined the origin of the name Céle-dé, and traced its application in the country where it took its rise, I now proceed to notice its appearance in British records, in connexion with foundations, which either were direct offshoots of the Irish Church, or were to a great extent influenced by it. In this inquiry I shall have to do with Scotland extendedly, and with England and Wales in the single cases of York and Bardsey, respectively.

* See ERCK's Irish Ecclesiastical Register, p. 209.
† COTTON's Fasti Ecclesiæ Hibernicæ, vol. v., p. 66.

The primitive history of the Church of Scotland is essentially Irish in its character ; and during a long period our annals afford the most trustworthy materials for the chronology of that country, as our less systematic records do for the investigation of its ancient polity both civil and ecclesiastical.

Situate in the west, St. Columba's great monastery of Hy exercised a religious influence which was felt in every quarter of Scotland. In the extreme north the Orkneys were rendered safe to the devout pilgrim by St. Columba ; in the far south Melrose attained its greatest celebrity under Eata, one of St. Aidan's twelve disciples ; and in the eastern extremity of Pictland, Drostan son of Cosgreg accompanied the indefatigable Columba, when he founded the churches of Aberdour and Aberlour, becoming their joint patron saint, and perpetuating in Buchan the remembrance of fraternal attachment, in a church whose name of Deir, that is, "tear," commemorated their parting scene, and whose after history, now preserved in the oldest book of Scotland, as well as the sole relique of its early literature,* gave proof of the fulfilment of the promise which was made to them who "sow in tears." Even the nunnery of Coludi, or Coldingham, is introduced to notice by the father of English history, to illustrate his narrative of one Adamnan, a Scot of Ireland.

There were, it is true, two ecclesiastical establishments in the south-west which were not of Columbite origin. Rosnat, the Whithorn of Saxon, and the Candida Casa of Latin history, was founded by St. Ninian, prior to St. Columba's date ; while the episcopal see of Glasgow owes its origin to St. Kentigern, a Muna Strathclyde Briton. But Ninian, though British by race, and Roman by education, was intimately associated with many Irish ecclesiastics of his day,† and, if we may credit his Irish life, as cited by Archbishop USSHER, finished his course in a monastery which he had founded at Cluayn-Coner in the modern county of Kildare.‡ St. Kentigern, or Munghu, as he was familiarly called,

---

* Mr. Whitley Stokes, in an exquisite article in the Saturday Review (Dec. 8, 1860, p. 734), has, with a master's hand, cleared the way for the publication of this precious book.

† Under the name *Nennio qui Mancennus dicitur,* he is stated in the Lives of Eugenius of Ardstraw, Tighernach of Clones, Enna of Aran, and Finian of Moville, to have been the preceptor of these saints in his monastery of Rosnat.

‡ He is commemorated in the Felire of Ængus and other Irish calendars on the same day as in Scotland, namely, the 16th of September. Ængus calls him Moinenn ; and the Martyrology of

was consecrated, after the Irish fashion, by a single bishop, who had been brought over from Ireland for the purpose ; and Rhydderch Hael, his regal patron, had been baptized by St. Patrick's disciples in Ireland.

In the history of St. Kentigern, as compiled by JOCELIN, we have the earliest Scottish record of the name and discipline of the Céli-dé. For, although this piece of biography was not written till the close of the twelfth century, it was compiled from much earlier authorities, and embodied the traditional persuasion of the day. The passage is as follows :—" Vir* Dei itaque perplures ut diximus discipulos adunaverat. Quos divine legis sacris literis erudiens, verbo et exemplo ad vite sanctitatem instituit. De quibus cooperarios in messem dominicam destinare proposuerat. Hii omnes emulabantur Dei emulatione vitam et doctrinam ejus; jejuniis et vigiliis sacris assueti, psalmis et orationibus, et divine legis meditationi intenti, victu et vestitu mediocri contenti, labore manuali certis temporibus et horis occupati. More namque primitive ecclesie sub apostolis et eorum successoribus, nichil proprium possidentes, satis sobrie juste et pie et continentissime viventes ; in singulis tamen casulis, ex† quo etate et sapientia maturaverant, sicut et ipse sanctus Kentegernus, commorabantur.‡ Unde et singulares clerici a vulgo Calledei nuncupabantur."

Thus we learn that the Céli-dé, or, as the name is latinized, *Calledei,* were understood by the Scotch, in the twelfth century, to have been a religious

---

Tamlacht has " Mo-nenn, i. e. *Ninianus episcopus Candide case.*" His Irish church is Cluɑɪn-Conɑɪpe, now known as Cloncurry.

* This extract is taken from a MS. of JOCELIN's Life of St. Kentigern, preserved in Primate. Marsh's Library, Dublin, V 3. 4. 16., fol. 29 *b*, among the MSS. which Bishop Stearne of Clogher bequeathed to that collection. It is written on vellum, in a hand of about the latter part of the thirteenth century. The volume, which is in quarto, contains at the beginning the Life of St. Servanus; and may be the small volume containing the lives of St. Kentigern and St. Servan, which belonged to Glasgow cathedral in 1432. In many places, where it differs from the Cotton MS. of St. Kentigern's Life, printed by Pinkerton (Vitæ Antiquæ SS. Scot., pp. 195–297), its readings are preferable, and rectify the *sics* of Pinkerton. This passage is in chap. 20, p. 236, of Pinkerton.

† " Exquierant et sapientiam maturaverant."—*Pink.* But this reading is incompatible with *commorabantur,* which follows.

‡ " Commorabantur, unde et Clerici Singulares et vulgo Calledei nuncupabantur."—*Pink.*

order of clerks who lived in societies, under a superior, within a common enclosure, but in detached cells, associated in a sort of collegiate rather than cœnobitical brotherhood,—solitaries in their domestic habits, though united in the common observances, both religious and secular, of a strict sodality. Such was the nucleus of the great city of Glasgow. With St. Kentigern's death its church and monastery disappear from history till 1116, when David, prince of Cumbria, and brother of King Alexander I., ascertained by an inquisition of the seniors and sages of Cumbria* what were the ancient possessions and jurisdiction of the see ; and, having probably cut off the hereditary entail of its estates, caused his tutor, John, to be consecrated under the long dormant title of bishop of Glasgow. This, it is to be observed, was just the time when Malachi Omorgair, in Ireland, found the once famous abbey of Bangor, a kindred institution, in lay occupation, and its church in ruins : an evil result which in both countries had grown out of the universal prevalence of the monastic, as distinguished from the diocesan system. And here I may observe, as the principle which, if borne in mind, will solve many enigmas in the ecclesiastical history of Scotland as well as of Ireland, that the distribution of the country into dioceses and parishes was practically unknown in the Scotic Church till the beginning of the twelfth century.† The whole ecclesiastical fabric was constructed on the monastic foundation, and its entire economy regulated by the discipline of conventual life. This was the system which for ages placed the episcopate in a subordinate position, exalting the office of abbot to the pinnacle of church preferment, and subjecting all other relations to its social weight, until, in the lapse of time, it lost much of its sacred character, and became compatible with a secular life. Sometimes the abbot was in holy orders, sometimes not ; and at all times the monastic profession was respected above the ministerial calling.

---

* This interesting record was printed by Sir James Dalrymple (Hist. Collect., p. 337); by Gibson (History of Glasgow); by Pinkerton (Enquiry, vol. i., p. 516); but most correctly in the Registrum Episcopatus Glasguensis, edited by Cosmo Innes, vol. i., pp. 3–5.

† The reign of David I. (1124–1153) is celebrated by historians as the period when the Scotch dioceses became permanently defined. The Synod of Rathbreasil, at which the first attempt was made to effect a like arrangement in Ireland, only preceded his accession by fourteen years. A spirit of order was evidently developing itself in both countries about the same time, and it would be an interesting subject of inquiry to ascertain the immediate influences which produced it.

Thus the useful ferleghinn, or lecturer, and the contemplative anchorite, often in our annals take precedence of the bishop. The essential officer was the abbot, but the presence of the bishop was an accident ; and hence, even in the best times, his office was intermittent, so that in the worst it became defunct, and with it, in many instances in Scotland, the entire religious character of a monastery perished except in name ; and a species of lay property called an *Abthein,* or Abbacy, is presented to view in the twelfth century,* embracing the site of a primitive abbey, accompanied, it may be, by a cemetery and holy well, the annual resort of a whole country side, and held in prescriptive right, by the tenure of a bell or bachall.

Where secularization was only partial, a shadow of the old society continued to exist, and, under greater or less laxity of discipline, the representatives were known as *Kele-dei,* a title which, with portions of the church property, in some cases descended from father to son, and in others was practically entailed to members of certain families.

In any districts where secular influence led to the erection of a stated diocese, the principal monastery therein became the episcopal see, and the appointment of the bishop, as of old, was exercised by the conventual body who had hitherto been the officiating clergy of the place. Thus the diocese of Dunblane, on its creation, was made conterminous with the earldom of Stratherne, the nucleus being the ancient monastery of Dun-Blaan, which was founded by, and derived its name from, Blaan, an Irish ecclesiastic of the sixth century. Now, although Dunblane was so ancient a foundation, the first recorded bishop is of the date 1160, after the restoration of the see under David I., when little more seems to have been done than secure an endowment, and define the limits of jurisdiction.

Sometimes a bishop's see was erected, as at Aberdeen, in a town of growing importance, where there had not previously existed a monastic foundation of any celebrity. Here, as might be expected, we discover no trace of Kele-dei.

---

* See an able article written by Joseph Robertson, Esq., in the Quarterly Review, vol. lxxxv., p. 117, where a list of such denominations is given. Abbaine is the general form in Irish for "abbacy," or "abbotship;" but in the Annals of Innisfallen we find apchaine (An. 801, 920, 1017, 1035), apchan (977), and abchaine (822, 968), which very nearly approach the Scotch form of the word.

Again, we meet with churches which possessed Keledei, but were never raised to the rank of episcopal sees. This was owing to some secular influence or peculiarity of position. And these merely retained their conventual character, with diminished importance, as being inside the jurisdiction of more favoured churches, until, in the course of events, their societies were suppressed or died a natural death. In Ireland, in like manner, churches such as Bangor, Movilla, and Lusk, though of great celebrity as seats of learning and sanctity, and possessing long catalogues of abbots, bishops, and other functionaries, never rose above the level of monastic distinction ; while churches of much inferior claims, as Kilkenny, Kilfenora, Killaloe, and Aghadoe, or of recent origin, as Dublin, Limerick, and Waterford, became the seats of bishops and the centres of ecclesiastical jurisdiction.

In fact, the generality of monasteries, both in Scotland and Ireland, were in a state of decrepitude at the beginning of the twelfth century, and those which survived for any length of time owed the continuation of their existence either to the superaddition of a bishop and chapter, or to their reconstruction on a new model. Most of the old religious communities were Keledei, till the changes just mentioned took place, and then the name became limited for their brief future to those institutions which adhered to the original discipline as contradistinguished from those which were remodelled or created in the new.

It was in the reign of David I. (1124–1153) that the great change in the framework of the Scottish Church took place. His biographer states that he found three bishoprics in Scotland, but left nine. By which we are to understand that he revived, and perpetuated the succession of bishops in, six decayed communities, securing to them a mensal provision, or assigning to them respectively a defined diocese.

In his restorations he merely added a bishop to the existing societies at Brechin, Dunblane, Ross, and Caithness ; while in the earlier sees of St. Andrews and Dunkeld, he superseded the Keledei by instituting chapters of regular canons. His English education and connexions, no doubt, weakened his attachment to the institutions of his native country; and Robert, the bishop of St. Andrews, an Englishman born, seems to have quickened his distaste for the old-fashioned Keledei. The encouragement of their lax and impotent system would have ill accorded with the vitality and reforming spirit which pervaded all his measures; and further, as the representatives of the Celtic clergy, they were little likely to be acceptable to a prince who wished to infuse the Saxon element into the Scottish Church. Among the names of Keledei which are on record we meet with *Gillefali, Mathalan, Macbeth, Malbride, Cormac, Malpol,* and *Malcolm,* which in the subscriptions of charters stand out in native relief among such forms as *Willelmus de Bosco, Hugo de Sigillo, Robertus filius Edgari,* &c.

JOHN PINKERTON, whose sagacity and candour far outweighed any national or religious bias, came to the conclusion that, " The Culdees were surely only Irish clergy. In the gradual corruption of the monastic order, they married and left their Culdeeships to their children: and, after the havoc introduced by the Danes, usurped the rank of secular clergy. In short, they were merely corrupted monks, such as abounded in all the countries of Europe till the eleventh century, when the popes were forced to institute canons regular, whom the princes gradually introduced into the chief monasteries, instead of the old depraved monks."[*] Similar sentiments are expressed by CHALMERS in his Caledonia, who, as well as his rival, had discernment enough to see through the mist which DALRYMPLE and others had diffused over the simple question, and in which, even to the present day, the subject, in the minds of the vulgar, is to a great degree enveloped.

In one point, however, even the ablest of modern writers on the Culdees has fallen into the national error of supposing them to have been a peculiar order who derived their origin from St. Columba; in other words, that they were Columbites, in the same sense that we speak of Benedictines. It is true that, after the lapse of centuries, Culdees were found in churches which he or his disciples founded; but their name was in no way distinctive, being in the first instance an epithet of asceticism, and afterwards that of irregularity. Among the numerous references to Hy in the Irish annals there is only one notice of Céli-dé as existing there, and this solitary example is of so late a period as 1164. The Irish, who find the name employed in their own country in connexion with societies which had not a shadow of Columbite relationship, naturally dismiss the notion as an unreasonable assumption, and find in a modern

---

[*] Enquiry into the History of Scotland, vol. ii., p. 272 (ed. 1814).

Bollandist a fair exponent of their view : " Cæterum et nos quoque ejus sumus opinionis ut nullam inter Columbianos monachos et Culdeos cognationem intercessisse credamus."[*]

Among the Cotton manuscripts in the British Museum is preserved a catalogue of the religious houses of England and Wales, at the end of which is a list of the Scotch sees, and the orders of their respective societies.[†]   It is annexed to Henry of Silgrave's Chronicle ; and as that compilation comes down to the year 1272, and is in the same handwriting as the catalogue, the latter cannot reasonably be referred to an earlier date.   USSHER,[‡] LLOYD,[§] and TANNER[||] regard this catalogue as the work of Silgrave.   I select from it those names which are to the present purpose :—

KILRIMONT/ST ANDREWS	Episcopatus S. Andree.	Canonici nigri.	Keldei.
DUNKELD	Episcopatus Dunkeldre, S. Columkille.	Canonici nigri.	Keldei.
BRECHIN	Episcopatus de Brechin.		Keledei.
	Episcopatus de Ros.		Keledei.
DUNBLANE	Episcopatus de Dublin.[¶]		Keledei.
	Episcopatus de Katenesio.		Keledei.
	Episcopatus de Argiul.		Keledei.
IONA	Abbatia in Insula.[**]		Keledei.

These are the only instances where the term Keldei, or Keledei occurs in the record.   The *Canonici nigri* are regular canons of St. Augustin, and are

---

[*] Josephus Van Hecke, Acta Sanctor., Octob., tom. viii., p. 166 *a.*

[†] COTTON, Cleopat. A. xii. 1, fol. 56.   The Scotch portion was printed in the Scalacronica, edited for the Maitland Club, by Rev. Jos. Stevenson (Edinb. 1836), p. 241.   The editor, however, does not seem to have been aware of the authorship assigned to the Catalogue, and errs in stating that it is in a hand *circa* 1200.   It probably records a state of things anterior to its own date.

[‡] " Meminit etiam circa annum MCCLXXII. Keldeorum sancti Andreæ Henricus Silegravius, in domuum religiosarum Britanniæ catalogo."   Brit. Eccl. Antiqq., cap. 15, Works, vol. vi., p. 197.

[§] Historical Account of Church Government, cap. 7, p. 142.

[||] Bibliotheca Britannico-Hibernica, voc. *Silegrave,* p. 672.

[¶] The mark of contraction over the *u* is inadvertently omitted in the original; but the name intended is Dunblane.

[**] That is, Hy, or Iona.

(handwritten marginalia at top: "(cowan) p2 26 Turriff on 'older Columban type' mon. site (as Iona) fer-léginn")

represented as existing in St. Andrews and St. Columba's of Dunkeld collaterally with Keledei. The societies at Mureve (Moray) and Glascu are styled
Canonici seculares.

To these may be added, from charter sources, some non-cathedral monasteries, namely :—

The church of Lochlevin in Kinross.
The church of Abernethy in Perthshire.
The church of Monymusk in Aberdeenshire.
The church of Muthill in Perthshire.
The church of Monifeith in Forfarshire. *(handwritten: "an enigma" is cowan Diet of Scoth 4 Th)*

(handwritten marginalia at left: "What about Aringask??")

This list might be considerably enlarged, if such churches as Scone, Melrose, Montrose, Abirlot, Dull, Ecclesgirg, and others, which are presumed to
have resembled the foregoing, were admitted ; but my object at present is to
treat only of those in which we have record evidence that Keledei did exist.
These, however, are twice as numerous as the analogous societies which are on
record as existing in Ireland,—an anomaly which is best accounted for by supposing that the term Céle-dé was not so generally applied in Ireland, or, if it
was, that it was more in conventional than literary use.

Without attempting the hopeless task of determining the priority of foundation among the Scotch Keledean houses, I shall now proceed to treat of them
briefly in the order of the foregoing lists.

SECTION II.—ST. ANDREWS.

This church, whose Celtic name was Cill-Righmonaigh, appears, like most
of the early Scottish foundations, to have been of Irish origin. St. Cainnech,
the patron of Kilkenny and the diocese of Ossory, whose labours in Scotland
were followed by the wide diffusion of his celebrity in that country, died in
600, and is commemorated in the Scotch as well as Irish calendars at the
11th of October, in the latter of which, two churches only are associated with
his memory, namely, Achadh-bo, now Aghabo, in Ireland, and Cill-Righmonaigh in Alba. His British connexion, however, has long been forgotten
at St. Andrews ; and the name by which the old church of St. Andrews was

known among the Gaelic population was Kilrule, denoting the " Church of Rule," that is, of St. Riaghail, in Latin Regulus, who appears in the Scotch calendars at the 17th of October, and is conjectured to be the same as our Riaghail of Muic-inis in the expansion of the Shannon called Loch-Derg, who is commemorated with us on the preceding day ; though the Scottish legend represents St. Regulus as coming from the East with the reliques of St. Andrew, about the year 800, and changing the name of the place from Mucros to Kil-remonth.*

The probability is that the ancient but inconsiderable church which existed here from primitive times, and of which we have one notice in the Irish Annals, at the year 747,† was, about the beginning of the ninth century, extended and endowed by the Pictish sovereign, under the title of St. Andrew the Apostle, and that, to shed lustre on the proceeding, the story was circulated that the relics of the saint, consisting of three fingers of the right hand, the humerus and patella of the same side, and one tooth, were stolen from Patræ, and brought

---

* The orientation of a portion of Scotch hagiology is remarkable. St. Servan, in his legend, is represented as the son of a noble king in Chanaan by the daughter of a king of Arabia. St. Boniface, or Kiritinus, is made an Israelite by nation. St. Monanus, or Monance, comes from Pannonia, and his master Adrian from Hungary. The first two may have been pilgrims in the east, whose travels were converted into descent. A remarkable instance of the transformation of sex occurs in the Scotch calendars. At Mar. 13, they have a *Sancta Kevoca*, who was venerated as the patroness of Kyle. In Ireland *she* is, at the same day, known as Caembog (pronounced *Keevóg*), more generally called, with the familiar prefix, Mo-Chaemhog. This saint's name is Latinized *Pulcherius;* and *he* was founder and abbot of Liathmor, which, with the addition of his name, was afterwards called Leamokevoge. He was a celebrated Irish saint, and his Life is printed by COLGAN. His death is recorded in our annals at 655. Now, the history of his metaphysis is easily explained. The termination *og* is grammatically feminine, so much so that the Irish peasantry consider St. Dabheog of Loch Derg a woman. Under the same influence they couple the pronoun *she* with the Irish words for *stallion* and *bull*. And if we were not possessed of record evidence concerning the sex of St. Dabheog, we can very easily conceive how a legend writer who was guided by popular conceit would create a *Sancta Davoca*. The Gaelic-speaking Scotch of the middle ages, not knowing the antecedents of St. Caemhog, changed his gender, and the hagiologist accepted the name upon the terms. *Glycerium* of Terence, and *Eustochium* of St. Jerome, would sorely embarrass the grammatical sensitiveness of a Celt. St. Fintan, or Munna, is in one Scotch charter called *Sancta Munda*. (Orig. Parch. Scot., vol. ii., p. 72.)

† Tuathalan, abbot of Cenn-Righmonaidh, died, *Tighernach*, 747. See REEVES's Columba, p. 385.

by Regulus to this place, where they were deposited, and, by their supposed importance, helped to procure for the church which possessed them a degree of distinction which resulted in its becoming the seat of the Scotch primacy. The unhistorical nature of the legend is shown by its representing the emperor Constantius as the contemporary of Athelstan, Hungus, and Regulus, an anachronism of nearly five centuries, which stamps the whole story of the origin of St. Andrews with the character of a gross and comparatively modern fabrication. Authentic history pretends to no earlier bishop at St. Andrews than Cellach, or Fothadh, in the tenth century.

The early condition of the see appears to have been similar to that of the principal monasteries in Ireland, wherein the bishop was incorporated with the brotherhood, at first in a subordinate position as regarded local jurisdiction, but gradually gaining more and more official importance till he emerged from the society as its chief, and eventually depressed it by his influence.

The names of the first twelve bishops of St. Andrews are Celtic in form, and indicate an undisturbed possession of the see by native ecclesiastics for a period of above two centuries. Under Cellach, the first of these, king Constantine, son of Aedh, being, as an ancient chronicle states, "in senectute decrepita, baculum cepit, et Domino servivit."[*] That is, in the language of the day, " he took the pilgrim's staff, and became a monk."[†] A record copied from the Magnum Registrum of the priory of St. Andrews associates his retirement with the ancient monastery of that place: " Hic dimisso regno sponte, Deo in habitu religionis, abbas factus Keledeorum S. Andreæ, quinque annis servivit, et ibi mortuus est et sepultus."[‡]

---

[*] Innes, Critical Essay, tom. ii., p. 786. Pinkerton, Enquiry, vol. i., p. 496.

[†] This selection of St. Andrews by the ex-monarch seems to indicate some preeminence in the society, and probably conferred upon it additional distinction. The story of the king's becoming abbot looks like an incipient or established secularization in the chief office.

[‡] Innes, Critical Essay, tom. ii., p. 802. Fordun, in almost the same words, says, at 942: " Regno sponte dimisso, religionis in habitu Deo serviens, apud S. Andream, Killideorum abbas effectus, annis quinque vixit; ibique moriens sepultus est." Scotichron., lib. iv., cap. 25 (vol. i., p. 204. ed. Goodall). Which Wynton briefly expresses in English :—

> " Kyng he sessyd for to be,
> And in Sanct Andrewys a Kylde."—*Cronykel*, vi. 10.

Hector Boece borrows the statement, substituting for *Keledei* the supposed Latin equivalent :—

Owing to the Saxon relations created in Scotland by Queen Margaret, an element was introduced into this society which paved the way for its extinction: " Anno ab incarnatione Domini MCVIII. ac tempore regis Malcolmi et sanctæ Margaretæ,* electus fuit Turgotus, Prior Dunelmensis, in Episcopum Sancti Andreæ, consecratusque est Eboraci tertio Kalendas Augusti, et stetit per annos septem. In diebus illis totum jus Keledeorum per totum regnum Scotiæ transivit in Episcopatum Sancti Andreæ."† .This is a loose and exaggerated statement; but there can be little doubt that Bishop Turgot checked the Culdees in their alienation of church property at St. Andrews; for, as the writer in the Great Register says, " nec potuit tantum auferri malum usque ad tempus felicis memoriæ regis Alexandri." This was Alexander I., whose accession to the throne preceded Turgot's to the see by one year. Eadmer, a monk of Canterbury, was sent for by the king, and was, at his instance, elected successor to Turgot, but did not receive consecration. Robert, an Englishman, and a canon of St. Oswald's in Yorkshire, was brought to Scotland, with five others, to promulgate the rule of St. Augustin, and made abbot of Scone, from which office he was promoted to the see of St. Andrews, in 1124, but was not consecrated until 1128. He carried out with great zeal the work which his predecessor had commenced; and finding in King David a prince whose views regarding monastic discipline were coincident with his own, he founded and endowed at St. Andrews a priory of regular canons, to which the hospital formerly belonging to the Culdees, together with their influence, was transferred, and in juxtaposition with which the elder community became enfeebled, and eventually sank into insignificance.

" Summo deposito magistratu in piorum cœtum, qui in divi Andreæ Apostoli tum ædibus erant (cultores Dei ea ætate) migrans, tonsus cœnobio se sacravit." Scotor. Hist., lib. xi., (p. 217 *b*). BUCHANAN, more explicitly: " Ejerato sponte magistratu, ad Culdeos, hoc est, Dei cultores (ita enim illius ætatis homines monachos vocabant) se velut in portum recepit." (Rer. Scoticar. Hist., vi. 17.) But RUDDIMAN, in a note on the passage, justly objects to this interpretation of the term, inasmuch as the word is written *Keledei* in ancient authorities. He is not more happy, however, in deriving it " a cellis." Opera BUCHANANI, vol. i., p. 173.

* Malcolm Cennmor and his queen Margaret died in 1093. Their son, Alexander I., succeeded in 1107.

† Chronicon Dunelmense, cited by SELDEN in his " ad Lectorem," of Sir R. TWYSDEN's Hist. Angl. Scriptores, X., p. vi. Also USSHER, Brit. Ec. Ant., cap. 15 (Works, vol. vi., p. 197).

Keeping up their old rules and observances, the representatives of the primitive establishment retained the title of Keledei ; and when they first present themselves, after the long night of silence in which their history slumbers, we find them giving way to the newly introduced order of regulars, who had taken in hand to reform the ecclesiastical discipline of the church, and awaken the dormant religion of the diocese. The priory of regular canons of St. Augustin was formally recognised at St. Andrews in 1144,* and, shortly after, one of the fraternity undertook to draw up a sketch of the history of its church, partly with a view to appropriate its past glory, and partly to justify the recent reform of its economy. The writer, probably bishop Robert, or the prior of the same name,† strongly condemns the degenerate condition of the Keledei; and though the picture is perhaps overdrawn, as by an unfriendly hand, and occasionally indistinct in its representations, it is still a record of great historical importance. Having adverted to the decay of religion at St. Andrews, consequent upon the death of St. Regulus and his followers, it proceeds to describe the more recent particulars of its ecclesiastical condition in the following manner:‡—" There were kept up, however, in the church of St. Andrew, such as it then was, by family succession, a society of thirteen, commonly called Keledei, whose manner of life was shaped more in accordance with their own fancy and human tradition, than with the precepts of the holy fathers. Nay, even to the present day their practice continues the same ; and though they have some things in common, these are such as are less in amount and value, while they individually enjoy the larger and better portion, just as each of them happens to receive gifts, either from friends who are united to them by some private tie, such as kindred or connexion, or from those whose *soul-friends*, that is, spiritual advisers, they are, or from any other source. After they are made Keledei, they are not allowed to keep their wives within their lodgings, nor any other women, who might give rise to injurious suspicions.

" Moreover, there were seven beneficiaries, who divided among themselves the offerings of the altar ; of which seven portions the bishop used to enjoy but

---

* EVIDENCES, M, No. 3

† There is a similarity in style between the foundation charter of 1144 and this record, especially in their use of the word *nichilominus*. EVIDENCES, M, Nos. 2, 3.

‡ EVIDENCES, M, No. 2.

one, and the hospital another ; the remaining five were apportioned to the other five members, who performed no duty whatever, either at altar or church, and whose only obligation was to provide, after their custom, lodging and entertainment for pilgrims and strangers, when more than six chanced to arrive, determining by lot whom and how many each of them was to receive. The hospital, it is to be observed, had continual accommodation for a number not exceeding six ; but from the time that, by God's goodness, it came into the possession of the canons till the present it is open to all comers.

" The above-mentioned beneficiaries were also possessed of their private revenues and property, which, upon their death, their wives, whom they openly lived with, and their sons or daughters, their relatives, or sons-in-law, used to divide among themselves : even the very offerings of the altar at which they did not serve,—a profanation which one would blush to speak of, if they had not chosen to practise. Nor could this monstrous abuse be corrected before the time of Alexander of happy memory, a sovereign of exemplary devotion to God's holy Church, who enriched the church of the blessed Apostle Andrew with possessions and revenues, loaded it with many and valuable gifts, and invested it with the liberties, customs, and royalties which appertained to his royal donation. The lands also called the Boar's Chase, which the above-named King Hungus had presented to God and to the holy Apostle St. Andrew at the time that the relics of St. Andrew arrived, but which were subsequently usurped, he restored to their possession, with the professed object and understanding that a religious society should be established in that church for the maintenance of divine worship. Because hitherto there had been no provision for the service at the altar of the blessed Apostle, nor used mass to be celebrated there, except upon the rare occasions that the king or bishop visited the place: for the Keledei were wont to say their office after their own fashion in a nook of a church which was very small. Of which royal donation there are many witnesses surviving to this day. And it was further confirmed by his brother Earl David, whom the king had constituted his heir and successor upon the throne which he now occupies."

From this laboured and ill-digested statement we learn that, at some period anterior to 1107, the ecclesiastical community of Cill-Righmonaigh had become parted into two sections, and that each carried with it a portion of the spiritu-

alities and temporalities, which we may reasonably conceive had been originally combined. One party was the Keledei, consisting of a prior and twelve
brethren, who numerically represented the old foundation, and as clerical
vicars performed divine service, having official residences, and enjoying certain
estates as well as the minor dues of the sacerdotal office. With them also, as
the clerical portion of the society, rested the election of the bishop, when a
vacancy occurred in the see. The other party included the bishop, the elee-
mosynary establishment, and the representatives of the abbot and other greater
officers now secularized, yet enjoying by prescription another portion of the
estates and the greater ecclesiastical dues. The chief censure is directed against
these; but it is to be taken with some limitation, because the bishop was one of
them, and the hospital represented another.

In 1144 the hospital, with its parsonage or impropriation, was transferred to
the regular canons, and they were confirmed in the possession of two more of
the parsonages which had already been assigned to them, the bishop retaining
his own seventh, thus leaving three of these sinecures in the former condition.*
And matters continued so till 1156, for in that year Pope Adrian IV. only confirmed to the canons regular the hospital and their two-sevenths.† But in that
or one of the two following years, the old impropriators having probably dropped
by death, resignation, or amotion, Bishop Robert granted to the canons all the
portions, reserving only his own.‡ Finally, in 1162–3, Bishop Arnold surrendered his seventh, and thus put them in possession of the whole.§ The seven
portions were then consolidated, and went into a common fund. Thus, in the
first instance, the regular canons seem to have been established on the reversion
of the secularized property of the old foundation.

There were now two rival ecclesiastical bodies in existence at St. Andrews—
one the old corporation of secular priests, who were completely thrown into
the shade, and shorn of many of their privileges and possessions ; and the other,
that of the regular canons, who virtually represented the secularized portion of
the old institution, and entered on the enjoyment of their estates. But this
rivalry or coexistence was very distasteful to the chief authorities both lay and
ecclesiastical, as soon became manifest. Immediately upon the foundation of

* EVIDENCES, M, No. 3.　　† Ibid., No. 3, note.　　‡ Ibid., No. 7.　　§ Ibid., No. 10.

the latter house, King David, as he also did in the case of Lochlevin, made an ordinance that the prior and canons of St. Andrews should receive into incorporation with them the Keledei of Kilrimont, who were to become canons, together with all their possessions and revenues; that is, provided they would consent to conform to canonical rule. But in case they should refuse, they were to have a life interest in their possessions; and, according as they dropped, their places were to be filled up on the new foundation by regular canons, whose number was to equal that of the existing Keledei; and that all the farms, lands, and offerings of the Keledei should be transferred to the use of the canons of St. Andrews in frank and quit almoigne.* In 1147, Pope Eugenius III. decreed that thenceforward the places of the Keledei, according as they became vacant, should be filled with regular canons.† But the Keledei were able to withstand the combined efforts of king, pope, and bishop; for we meet with a recurrence of this provision under successive pontiffs till 1248;‡ and yet we find the Keledei holding their ground. Nay, in 1160, King Malcolm actually confirmed them in a portion of their possessions.§ In 1199 we find them engaged in a controversy with the prior of the other society, which terminated in a compromise by which the tithes of their own lands were secured to them, they at the same time quitting claim to all parochial fees and oblations.‖ They were also vicars of the church of the Holy Trinity of Kilrimund, which was the parish church of St. Andrews.¶ And it was not till 1273 that they were debarred from the prescriptive right to take part in the election of a bishop.** They met with like treatment in 1279, and again in 1297, when William Comyn, the provost of the Keledei, went to Rome, and lodged a protest against the election then made, on the ground of their exclusion; but Boniface VIII. decided against him.†† He appealed again in 1328, but with no better success.‡‡ In 1309 the Keledei were still in possession of their lands in the Cursus Apri.§§ In 1332, when William Bell was chosen bishop, they were absolutely excluded

---

* EVIDENCES, M, No. 4.   † Ibid., No. 5.   ‡ Ibid., No. 5, note.
§ Ibid., No. 9.   ‖ Ibid., No. 12.   ¶ Ibid., No. 14.

** Pope Eugenius III., in 1147, had vested the election exclusively in the canons regular: " quem vos, communi consensu, vel fratrum ecclesie vestre pars consilii sanioris secundum Deum canonice provideritis eligendum." Regist. Priorat. S. Andree, p. 49. EVIDENCES, M, No. 18.

†† EVIDENCES, M, Nos. 19, 20.   ‡‡ Ibid., No. 22.   §§ Ibid., No. 21.

from taking any part in the election, and the claim does not appear to have been ever after revived.* Neither does the name Keledei occur again in existing records, although the corporation still continued in the enjoyment of their privileges and possessions. In the succeeding centuries frequent mention is made of the institution under the names of the "Præpositura ecclesiæ beatæ Mariæ civitatis Sancti Andreæ," the "Ecclesia beatæ Mariæ de Rupe," and "the Provostry of Kirkheugh;" and the society is said to have consisted of a provost and ten prebendaries. Their superior was variously styled "Præpositus Sancti Andreæ," "Præpositus capellæ Sanctæ Mariæ," "Præpositus capellæ regiæ:" and the common seal bears the legend—S. CAPITVLI ECCLESIE SANCTAE MARIAE CAPELLAE DOMINI REGIS SCOTORVM. After the Reformation the provostry became vested in the Crown ; and in 1616 was annexed, together with the appendant benefices, to the see of St. Andrews.†

SECTION III.—DUNKELD. VISIT

The church of Dun-caillenn, now called Dunkeld, was founded, it is said, about the year 820. The Annals of Ulster, at 864, record the death of Tuathal, son of Artgus, chief-bishop of Fortren, and abbot of Dun-caillen. Fortren‡ was another name for Pictland, and, according to the above authority, the principal ecclesiastic of this great territory had his seat at Dunkeld, where he was also abbot. This combination of office was quite in keeping with the usage in Ireland ; and it is only reasonable to suppose that the society to which this bishop belonged was that which in subsequent records is presented to notice under the name of Keledei. His successor in the abbacy does not appear to have enjoyed episcopal orders ; for his obit in the Annals of Ulster, at 872, simply styles him, "Flaithbertach, son of Muircertach, superior (*princeps*) of Dun-caillden." In 964, according to the same chronicle, "Donnchadh, abbot of Dun-caillenn, was slain in the battle of Moneitir ;" and again, in 1045, Cronan,

---

* EVIDENCES, M, No. 23.   † Martine, Reliquiæ Divi Andreæ, pp. 93, 209.

‡ Fortrenn is said to have been one of the seven sons of Cruithne. (Irish Nennius, pp. 126, 155.) In Irish Records the word is often used to denote Pictland. Poꞃcꞃen occurs in the Felire of Ængus (Jan. 31) in the sense of "powerful."

abbot of Dun-caillenn, lost his life in a domestic encounter.   This Cronan, who is called Crinan in the Pictish Chronicle, was married to Bethoc, daughter of king Malcolm II., and by her was father of the famous Donnchadh, or Duncan as he is called by the Scotch, who was slain by Macbeth. The abbacy had now become an appanage of the crown ; for Edmund, a younger son of Malcolm III., in a grant to the Keledei of Lochlevin, is styled " Abbot of Dunkeld, and moreover Earl of Fife."   Thus, too, at an earlier date, in Ireland, Cormac mac Cuillenain was bishop of Cashel and king of Munster; and when he fell at Ballaghmoon, in 908, Flaithbertach, son of Inmainen, who had been abbot of Scattery, and took part in the battle, succeeded him as king of Cashel.   But in Dunkeld, while the *abthein*, or abbacy, together with its lands, descended to the Earl of Fife, the inferior ministers retained their corporate and clerical condition as the officiating ministers of the church.

Dean Mylne, who was a canon of Dunkeld, about 1485, has left to us, in his History of the Bishops of Dunkeld, the following description of their ancient chapter :*—" In this monastery Constantine, king of the Picts, placed religious men, commonly called Kelledei, otherwise Colidei, that is, God-worshippers, who, however, after the usage of the Eastern Church, had wives, (from whom they lived apart when taking their turn in the sacred offices,) as afterwards grew to be the custom in the church of the blessed Regulus, now called St. Andrews.   But when it seemed good to the supreme controller of all Christian religion, and when devotion and piety had increased, St. David, the sovereign, who was the younger son of King Malcolm Canmor and the holy Queen Margaret, having changed the constitution of the monastery, erected it into a cathedral church; and, having superseded the Kelledei, created, about the year 1127, a bishop and canons, and ordained that there should in future be a secular college.   The first bishop on this foundation was for a time abbot of that monastery, and subsequently a counsellor of the king."

In the concluding passage the writer seems to imply that the Kelledei, who occupied the monastery which was attached to the mother church, were removed from this position, and constituted a college of secular clergy, while their former place was assigned to a society of regular canons, with the bishop,

---

* EVIDENCES, N, No. 2.

now made diocesan instead of abbot, at their head. These two corporations coexisted for nearly two centuries; and as at St. Andrews, so at Dunkeld, Silgrave's catalogue notices the collateral societies of *Canonici nigri* and *Keldei.*

SECTION IV.—BRECHIN. VISITED 9 4 97 ?

Brechin in Forfar was one of the churches where David I. revived the episcopal office, and secured its succession. Under him the bishop and Keledei had a common interest, for by a charter he granted certain rights to "the Bishops and Keledei of Brechin."[*] And they appear to have continued in this close relation with harmony during the reigns of his immediate successors; for various grants which were made by bishops of Brechin between 1180 and 1222 are attested by such witnesses as " Bricius, prior Keledeorum de Brechin;" " Gillefali, Kelde;" "Mathalan, Kelde;" "Mallebryd, prior Keledeorum nostrorum," or, " Prior de Brechyn."[†] About 1210, Malebryd, the prior, and the Keledei, and other clerks of the chapter of Brechin, ratify a donation made by the bishop to St. Thomas's of Arbroath.[‡] Meanwhile, however, the element which was destined to extinguish this old corporation was springing up among them. The prior of the Keledei, who formerly as a witness ranked next to the bishop, now gives place to the archdeacon; and a dean presently makes his appearance, to the exclusion of the prior, until, in 1248, the dean rises to capitular supremacy, the Keledei are ignored, and the cathedral style runs,—" Dean and Chapter of Brechin."[§] After this the Keledei of Brechin appear no more.

But long anterior to this date a large portion of their property had been alienated; for Leod, abbot of Brechin, and his grandson Dovenald, and Malisius, abbot of Brechin, and his son John, the abbot, and his son Murgund, made grants of church possessions; and when they appear as witnesses to royal charters, they rank next after the earls, who again come after the ecclesiastics, and, among them, the priors; so that, in the table of precedence, the ecclesiastical order which had been subordinate to the abbot is reversed with a long interval, and the abbot of Brechin becomes, in consequence of his secular condition, a second-rate layman, and a fourth-rate member of society.

[*] EVIDENCES, O, No. 2.   [†] Ibid., Nos. 3–8, 13–22.   [‡] Ibid., Nos. 10–12.   [§] Ibid., Nos. 24, 25.

BRECHIN Cathedral : Rev R K Mackenzie MA BD PhD.

Here then, in Brechin, we have a very compact Culdee case. There is a well-marked round tower, modernized, no doubt, at its apex, but bearing evidence in its general character that it belongs to about the period of Kenneth, son of Malcolm, that is, 970–992, to which the Pictish Chronicle justifies us in referring its erection, by its concluding sentence, " Hic est qui tribuit magnam civitatem Brechne Domino." Taking the tenth century, then, as the date of this building, we have an Irish ecclesiastical round tower of respectable antiquity which was, as it were, the gnomon of the original monastic group. The place totally disappears from history till St. David's reign, when it reappears, having an abbot, a layman, enjoying considerable possessions ; a bishop living in society with a college of Keledei ; the prior of the Keledei, a Celt, and ranking next to the bishop. Presently an archdeacon is introduced, who takes precedence of the prior; subsequently a dean appears on the stage, but in a subordinate position, and with him a chapter ; and at last, about the middle of the thirteenth century, the Keledei are absorbed, and the bishop, with his dean, and chapter of precentor, chancellor, treasurer, archdeacon, and six prebendaries, become the numerical representatives of the antecedent corporation, and so they continued till prelacy was overthrown in Scotland.

Section V.—Rosemarkie.

The origin of the church of Rosmarky, or Rosmarkin, as it is called in ancient records, is ascribed by tradition to St. Boniface, surnamed Queretinus,* a foreigner, who lived in the seventh century, and whose legend in the Breviary of Aberdeen identifies him with Boniface the Fourth, who died in 615.† . But this fiction sets the entire history of the pope at such flagrant defiance, that it

---

* Boece calls him *Bonifacius Queritinus.* He also represents him as associated with St. Molocus, now far advanced in years (Hist., lib. ix., p. 172 *b*). This was Moluoc of Lismore, who died in 592. The Acts of St. Boniface style him " Albanus Kiritinus cognomento Bonifacius." (Acta SS. Mart., tom. ii., p. 449.)

† Pars Hiemalis, Propr. Sanctor., fol. 69 *ba*–70 *ba*. Hector Boece wavers between Boniface III. and " ab hoc pontifice missus legatus, et ob id rudi populo papa creditus." He describes him as entering the frith of Tay—" *Taum* æstuarium," and proceeding up it to the mouth of the little

is unworthy of refutation or further notice. The name of St. Boniface, how-ever, has from an early date been associated with the church of Rosmarky, both on seals and in records ; and his day is set down in the Scotch calendars at the 16th of March.[*] The day of his festival, and his *alias* name Queretinus, instead of Italy, point to Ireland, as the quarter from which the founder of this church came, and we may with safety conclude either that Boniface was an assumed name,[†] or that the memory of some later ecclesiastic who was so called has been confounded with that of the Celtic founder. In the Irish calendars of Tamhlacht and Marian Gorman, under the above named day, the 16th of March, is found the commemoration Cuꞃιτανι epꞃcoιp ocuꞃ abb Ꞃuιꞃ mιc baιꞃenꝺ, that is, " of Curitan, bishop and abbot of Ros-mic-Bairenn,"[‡] who, beyond all reasonable doubt, is the *Queritinus de Rosmarkyn* of the Scotch.[§] We may therefore assume that the church of Rosmarky, which in course of time became the cathedral of the diocese of Ross, was an Irish foundation ; and if the conjecture of the calendar of Donegal, that this Curitanus was the bishop of that name who attended the synod of Birr under St. Adamnan,[||] be

river which divides Gourea or Gowrie from Angus (Hist., lib. ix., p. 172 *b*). The Utrecht MS. of the saint's Acts calls this river the "flumen Gobriat in Pictavia." (Acta SS. Mart., tom. ii., p. 449.) This gives us an early form of the name Gowrie. The Inver-Gowrie River nearly di-vides Gowrie in Perthshire from Angus or Forfar. Here, near the shore, in the parish of Liff, is the old church of St. Boniface. New Stat. Acct., vol. xi., p. 581 ; Old Stat. Acct., vol. xiii. p. 117.

[*] Alban Butler erroneously assigns his festival to the 14th.

[†] As Winfrid, the apostle of Germany, about 723, assumed the name Bonifacius instead of the " rugged northern one" that he received at his baptism.

[‡] This is the earliest form of the name Rosmarkin on record. Ꞃoꞃ mbaιꞃcιnn would more nearly agree with the Scotch form. The Calendar of Donegal has Ꞃoꞃ-meιn, and there is clearly some uncertainty as to the exact name. Dr. Kelly identifies it with the Irish Rosbercon, but this is mere guess work. (Martyrol. of Tallaght, p. 11.)

[§] The *k* sound, as in French, is sometimes represented in Latinized Gaelic names by *qu*. Thus Cummian, in his Paschal Epistle, 634, writes the name Ciaran in the form *Queranus.* (Ussher, Sylloge, Ep. xi., Works, vol. iv., p. 442.) The Roman Quirites were called from Cures. St. Bo-niface's Acts have *Kiritinus*, which sufficiently represents the Celtic Cuꞃιταn.

[||] Its Acts, known as the Cáin Ꞁꝺamnaιn, are preserved in a beautiful vellum MS. at the Bod-leian Library, Oxford (Rawlinson, 505, p. 305); and in a more modern copy among the O'Clery MSS. at Brussels. In this record the name of Cuꞃιταn epꞃcop " Bishop Cuiritan" appears in the list of the attending ecclesiastics, and also as one of six guarantees. It is doubtful, however,

correct, its origin·belongs to the latter half of the seventh century. Of its succeeding history we have not a particle of information till the former half of the twelfth century, when King David revived the see, and assigned to it a diocese. Silgrave's catalogue designates the society as Keledei, that is, the representatives of the old secular college. Early in the thirteenth century, however, the cathedral body was reconstituted, for at 1224 we find a dean of Rosmarkyn, and a chantor, chancellor, treasurer, archdeacon, sub-dean, succentor, and canons, at various dates in the course of the same century.*

Section VI.—Dunblane.

Blaan, the founder and patron saint, is commemorated in the Felire of Ængus and the other Irish calendars, as well as the Scotch, at the 10th of August. A Life of the saint, compiled by George Neuton, archdeacon of Dunblane, recognises his Irish extraction, and states that he came over to Scotland in company with his uncle Catan. He was of the Dalaradians of Ulster by his father's side, and his mother is said to have been the daughter of Aidan, king of the Scotch Dalriads, so that his date may be referred to the end of the sixth or the early portion of the seventh century. His church of Dunblane, like other kindred foundations, was probably the seat of a small monastic fraternity, among whom he exercised the functions of abbot and bishop ; but whether any of his successors were invested with episcopal orders is not related : and indeed, in the great interval which occurs between the periods when the Irish cease to speak and the Scottish records resume the story, we are entirely in the dark as to the condition of this church. When the diocese was defined, whether by King David, or, what is more likely, by Earl Gilbert, it was made conterminous with the earldom of Stratherne ; and the bishop was some-

---

whether he is the saint of March 16, or Cairitan of Druimlara, Mar. 7, or Curitan of Cillmordithruibh, of Aug. 9. It is worthy of remark that among the chiefs who attended this synod we find the name of bꞃuioe mac Oeꞃιlι ꞃι Cꞃuιchen τuαιch, " Bruide son of Derili, king of Pict-land." But S. Boniface's Acts state that "Nectanius rex Pictorum" was his contemporary and benefactor. The former died in 706, the latter in 621.

* Origines Parochiales Scotiæ, vol. ii., part ii., pp. 573–580.

times territorially styled "Episcopus Stradernensis," or " de Stratheren," and his archdeacon, "archidiaconus de Stradhern."* The church of Dunblane afforded both a name and a cathedral to the diocese, the latter being probably small, and recommended to notice rather by prescriptive sanctity than by any architectural pretensions. Its ministers thus raised in diocesan importance were the Keledei, who, according to Silgrave's catalogue, were the religious society of the church. Beyond this notice I have found no express mention of the existence of this order at Dunblane, although Scotch writers, even those who do not refer to this authority, assert, as in the case of Scone, (what *à priori* is very likely, but needs record evidence for the proof,) that its clergy were in the twelfth century, and continued in the next to be, of this special class.

To the alienation of church property by these, and the consequent gaps in the episcopal succession, it is probable that Bishop Clement had reference in 1238, when he complained to Rome that, whereas the church of Dunblane had in time of old been vacant for a hundred years and more, nearly all its possessions were usurped by secular persons; and although several bishops had subsequently been instituted. yet, through their simplicity and negligence, the former usurpations had not been recovered, but, on the contrary, the remainder, which had escaped the hands of the spoilers, was almost entirely alienated and wasted. On his appointment he found the church so dismantled, that he had not where to lay his head in his cathedral. There was no college there, only a country chaplain performed divine service in the church, which was stripped of its roof. His own revenues also were so slender and miserable, that they scarcely yielded him a suitable maintenance for one half of the year.† All this looks like Culdee appropriation. Yet before 1210, Gilbert, Earl of Stratherne, is said to have devoted a third of his earldom to the church and bishop of Dunblane.‡

The neighbouring church of Muthel seems to have grown on the decay of Dunblane; and its ecclesiastics, as we shall presently see, occupied the foremost position in the diocese.

---

* Regist. de Aberbrothoc, p. 155; Regist. Priorat. S. Andreæ, p. 319; Regist. de Aberbrothoc, p. 148.

† Regist. de Aberbrothoc, p. 176.

‡ Fordun, Scotichron., lib. viii., cap. 73 (vol. i. p. 529).

SECTION VII.—DORNOCH.

If the church of Durnach was not founded by St. Barr in the early part of the seventh century, it certainly owes its origin to a wave of Irish immigration, which, previously to the Norse occupation of the northern extremity of Scotland, brought over with it the veneration of the patron saint of Cork. In Ireland the epithet *Finn* (or Fair) is sometimes prefixed to his name, and his principal church is locally known as St. Finbar's. In Scotland also his name generally appears in this form, and " St. Fimber of Dornoch" is his designation in the Sutherland charters. In the calendars of both countries he is commemorated on the 25th of September.

The church of Dornoch may therefore be regarded as an Irish foundation, out of which grew, in course of time, that peculiar development of the ministerial office called Keledean. What the ecclesiastical process was through which it passed under Norse rule we are not informed, but King David accepted it as the most venerable church in the earldom when he defined the diocese of Caithness, and made this its cathedral centre. Andrew, bishop of Catanes, appears on record in 1146. And the period to which Silgrave's catalogue refers, when it represents the Keldei as the capitular society of Katenes, was probably that which filled up the interval between this prelate and Bishop Gilbert, who, on his elevation to the see about 1222, found the cathedral church mean, and its ministrations discharged by a single priest. Instead of which he built a new church, and established therein a chapter, consisting of the usual dignitaries and five canons. He became eventually the patron saint†

---

* The editor of the Origines Parochiales Scotiæ calls him " a native of Caithness and bishop of Cork, who flourished according to some authorities in the sixth century, and according to others in the eleventh." (Vol. ii., pt. ii., p. 597.) He had several commemorations in Scotland, though certainly not a native of it, and his name has been transferred to the map of that country in the island of Barra. The truth is, he was the son of Amergin, of the Hy-Briuin of Connacht, but was born in Olehan, a territory of the county of Cork, near Cloyne. Ancient copies of his Latin Life are preserved in Marsh's Library, and Trinity College, Dublin, and in the Bodleian at Oxford. Copies of his Irish Life exist among the O'Clery MSS. at Brussels, and in the library of the Royal Irish Academy.

† Origines Parochiales Scotiæ, vol. ii., pt. ii., p. 603.

Dornoch Cathedral
The Very Rev. Dr James Scrimpson

of the church, and with his name is to be associated the virtual extinction of the Keledei in this diocese.

SECTION VIII.—LISMORE.

The diocese of Argyle, or Argiul, as the name is written in Silgrave's catalogue, had as its cathedral the church of St. Moluoc, in the island of Lismore.

It was founded by St. Lughaidh, familiarly called Moluoc, an Irishman, who died in 592.[*] He is noticed in the principal Irish chronicles, and in all the Irish calendars at the 25th of June ; on which day he is commemorated in the Scottish calendars also, under the name of Molocus, and in the Breviary of Aberdeen is styled a bishop.[†] His bell and pastoral staff were long preserved in this church,[‡] and are still in existence.

The monastery founded by St. Moluoc no doubt continued to exist through successive ages,[§] until, in the course of time, its society, in conformity with

---

[*] *Obitus Lugide Lissmoir, i. e. Moluoc.*—Tighernach, 592. *Obitus Lugide Lismoer.*—An. Ulst., 591. The parallel entry in the Four Masters, who do not appear to have been aware that it referred to Scotland, is at 588. Their learned editor, Dr. O'DONOVAN errs in supposing it belonged to Lismore in the county of Waterford (vol. i., p. 213, note ʳ). The Irish monastery was not founded till 636. But the question is placed beyond all controversy by the Felire of Ængus :—

Lam Luoc ᵹlan ᵹelbaı
ᵹrıan Lirrmoir bealbaı.

With my Luoc the pure, resplendent,
The sun of Lismore the pleasing.

Where the ancient note adds,—Moluoc Lirrmoir ı nÁlbaın, "Moluoc of Lismor in Alba." The words Lam Luoc are incorrectly joined, and made the name *Lamluoc*, in the Obits and Martyrology of Christ Church (Introd., p. lxv.), where also there is an oversight in referring Kill-delga in Ardgall, St. Moluoc's Irish church, to Scotland. It is now Kildalkey, in Meath; and Ardgall is a district in the north-west of the county. Ardgall is very different from *Airer-Gaedhail.*

[†] Pars Æstivalis, Propr. Sanctor., fol. 5 *b.*

[‡] Origines Parochiales Scotiæ, vol. ii., pt. i., p. 163.

[§] The immediate successor of the founder does not appear to have been a bishop. *Naeman ab Lismoir* [*obiit*].—Tighernach, 611. The Four Masters, by borrowing this entry (An. 610) seem again to refer the subject of it to Ireland ; and their learned editor falls into a like error (vol. i., p. 236, note ᵖ). In 635, another head of the abbey died : *Eochoid ab Lismoir quievit.*—Tighernach. So the Annals of Ulster at 634. The Four Masters, in order the more conveniently to locate this

H

the progress of native monasticism, settled down into the condition which obtained for them the name of Keledei. During this long period the office of
bishop, if it was preserved in this church, was, in all probability, intermittent,
and at such times as it did exist, was of a conventual rather than of a diocesan
character. And after that, in the infancy of diocesan distribution, Dunkeld
obtained territorial jurisdiction, Lismore was included in it, and continued to
be a portion of that great diocese till about the year 1200, when it was severed
by pope Innocent III., and formed with the mainland of Argyle into a diocese,
sometimes named *Lismorensis*, but more generally *Ergadiensis.** Silgrave's
catalogue calls it *Argiul*, and styles its chapter *Keledei*. But this society did
not long retain their cathedral position, for there is charter evidence to show
that before 1251 a dean and chapter had been called into existence ;† and in
1249 pope Innocent IV. recognises the right of electing the bishop as vested in
the Canons of this church.‡

SECTION IX.—HY.   *ULISITED 9 · 6 · 97.*

Silgrave's catalogue styles the Monastery of Iona *Abbatia in Insula*, and
its society *Keledei*. Notwithstanding all that has been written concerning the
emanation of the Culdees from Iona, and their essentially Columbite character,
there is only one other record of their existence in Hy, and that of a compa-

abbot in the Irish Lismore, (which was not founded till 631 of their computation,) postpone Eochaidh's death till their 634, that is, three years *after*, whereas Tighernach and the Annals of Ulster
record it the year *before.* He died on the 17th of April, and his name is found at that day in the
Calendars of Tamhlacht, of Marian Gorman, and of Donegal, as Eochaiồh abb Liʀmoiʀ. Here
again the learned editor of the Four Masters errs in regarding this as the Irish Lismore (vol. i.,
page 253, note ᶥ).

* Even after the diocese became established there was an interval of some length between its
bishops. In 1249 we find Pope Innocent IV. describing the " Sedes episcopalis Ergadiensis in
quadam insula maris posita" as vacant for above seven years. Baluzii Miscell., tom. vii., p. 442.
This was the blank between bishop William, who was drowned in 1241, and Alan, who was
elected in 1250.

† The name of the first dean on record is *Gillemoluoc* (Orig. Paroch. Scot., vol. ii., pt. i., p. 161),
—a very appropriate one, Ɉilla-Moluoc, signifying "Servant of Moluoc," the founder.

‡ Baluzii Miscellanea, *ut supra*.

— Not enough detailed info. to find 'culdee' place
— need to go to Nat. Mans. Rec. Edin. !!

ratively recent date. The Annals of Ulster relate, at 1164, that a deputation of the chiefs of the family of Ia, consisting of Augustin the arch-priest, Dubsidhe the lecturer, MacGilladuff the recluse, MacForcellaigh head of the Ceili-ndé, and such as were of eminence in the island, waited on the abbot of Derry, and invited him to accept the abbacy of their church.* From this we learn that the Céli-dé of Hy were only a section of the community, whose superior was styled a "head" not "prior," and took a low rank among the notables of the place. He probably held a position similar to that of præcentor elsewhere, and his subordinates were most likely the clerical body who performed the ordinary services of the church.

Section X.—Lochlevin. VISITED 8 - 4 - 97.

A primitive monastery, founded on an island in Loch Levin, flourished during several centuries, and possessed a chartulary or donation book, written in Gaelic, an abstract of which, in Latin, is preserved in the register of the priory of St. Andrews.† The first memorandum in the collection states that Brude, son of Dergard, the last of the Pictish kings, bestowed the island of Lochlevin on God, St. Servan, and the Keledean hermits dwelling there in conventual devotion. Also, that the said Keledei made over the site of their cell to the bishop of St. Andrews, upon condition that he would provide them with food and raiment; that Ronan, monk and abbot, a man of exemplary holiness, on this occasion granted the place to Bishop Fothadh, son of Bren, who was in high repute all through Scotland. The bishop then pronounced a blessing on all who should uphold this covenant between him and the Keledei, and, *vice versâ*, his curse on all bishops who should violate or retract the same.‡ This is a very interesting record, not only as affording a glimpse of the Scottish Church, and the Céli-dé in particular, at a period where history is painfully silent, but as a striking example of undesigned coincidence between the independent memorials of Scotland and Ireland; the latter of which record

---

* Evidences, F, No. 11.   † Evidences, P, No. 1.   ‡ Evidences, P, No. 2.

H 2

Photos - Supposed 1000 yr old Culdee grave slab with snake symbol & motif (quatrefoil??) JaG Doubts authenticity on art-historical grounds

at the year 961 "the death of Fothadh mac Brain, scribe, and bishop of the islands of Alba."[*]

This is followed by a grant from the memorable Macbeth and his wife Gruoch to the Keledei of Lochlevin, of certain lands, one of the boundaries of which was the *Saxum Hiberniensium.* This grant was made between 1037 and 1054. There is another donation from the same to St. Servan of Lochlevin and the hermits serving God in that place.[†]

Malduin, Tuathal, and Modach son of Malmichel, successive bishops of St. Andrews, appear in their order as the donors of lands and privileges to the *Keledei heremitæ.*[‡]

In the early part of St. David's reign one Robertus Burgonensis made an attempt to deprive these Keledei of some of their possessions, and the matter was left to arbitration. Upon a solemn hearing of the case the seniors of Fife, among whom was Morrehat, of venerable age and an Irishman, were sworn in evidence, and sentence was pronounced by Dufgal filius Mocche, " pro monachis id est Keledeis."[§]

Their fate, however, was sealed about 1145, when king David, under the influence of feelings which I have already adverted to, declared that "he had given and granted to the canons of St. Andrews the island of Lochlevene, that they might establish canonical order there ; and the Keledei who shall be found there, if they consent to live as regulars, shall be permitted to remain in society with, and subject to, the others ; but should any of them be disposed to offer resistance, his will and pleasure was that such should be expelled from the island."[||] Robert, the English bishop of St. Andrews, who dictated this stern enactment, was not slow to carry its provisions into effect; for immediately after, he placed these Keledei in subjection to the canons regular of St. Andrews, and converted their old conventual possessions into an endowment for his newly erected priory. He even transferred the ecclesiastical vestments which these *Chelede* possessed, and their little library, consisting for the most part of ritual and patristic books, the titles of which are recited in the instrument.[¶]

---

[*] Annals of the Four Masters, A. C. 961. See REEVES's Adamnan's Life of St. Columba, p. 394.
[†] EVIDENCES, P, Nos. 3, 4.   [‡] Ibid., Nos. 10, 11, 12.   [§] Ibid., No. 13.
[||] Ibid., No. 15.   [¶] Ibid., No. 14.

Thus terminated the ·separate and independent existence of one of the earliest religious foundations in Scotland, which probably owed its origin to St. Serf, in the dawn of national christianization; and after a recorded occupation by Keledean hermits from the ninth century down, was, before the middle of the eleventh, brought into close connexion with the see of St. Andrews, through the influence of one of the earliest recorded bishops of the Scottish Church, who was probably a Céle-dé himself, and allowed to exercise a kind of episcopal superintendence over his own community of St. Andrews and the neighbouring monasteries, foreshadowing a function which afterwards developed itself in diocesan jurisdiction, and eventually became invested with metropolitan preeminence.

SECTION XI.—ABERNETHY. VISITED 8 - 4 - 97.

The Scottish tradition concerning this church, as expressed in the oldest historical monument of the country, the Chronicon Pictorum, is, that it was founded by St. Brigid in virtue of a grant made to her by Nechtan, a Pictish king, who, while an exile in Ireland, had visited her at Kildare, and sought her intercession for his restoration to the throne.* John of Fordun found a similar statement in the private records of the place; so that, whatever difficulty there may be in reconciling King Nechtan's date with that of St. Brigid, it is clear the ancient Scotch admitted the Irish origin of this church. It was probably an affiliated cell of Kildare; and though a nunnery in the first instance, subsequently was transformed, like Kildare itself, into a collegiate establishment of monks. Thus, Fordun states that to St. Brigid and her nine virgins were granted all the lands and tithes which the prior and canons enjoy from ancient times. In this church, he adds, three elections (that is of bishops, and at successive periods) took place, when as yet there was but one solitary bishop in Scotland, and that this was for some time the principal seat, both regal and episcopal, of the whole kingdom of the Picts.† There is every reason to suppose that its condition was similar to the larger Irish monasteries of the time, and that out of it grew, by the transmission of defects and the superaddition of abuses, that ecclesiastical state which characterized the Keledei of the twelfth century.

* EVIDENCES, Q, No. 2.   † EVIDENCES, Q, No. 3.

The register of the priory of St. Andrews fortunately enables us to catch one or two glimpses of its ancient economy, ere it was borne down by the irresistible progress of the regular system.

About the year 1100, a certain grant was made to St. Andrews in the presence of Nessa, and Cormac son of Macbeath, and Malnechta son of Beollan, priests of Abernethyn, and Mallebride, a priest, and Thuadhel, and Augustin, priest, Keledei, and Berbeadh, rector of the schools of Abyrnethin.*

At this time the Keledei of Abernethy were its ecclesiastical corporation ; but at the close of the twelfth century, the secularizing tendency of native monasticism had done much to impoverish them. Laurentius son of Orm, the abbot, was a layman, and as such gave precedence to the prior in witnessing a charter, yet he was in a position to grant away the advowson of the church and half the tithes, which he bestowed upon the newly founded abbey of Arbroath, while the Keledei of Abernethy were to enjoy the other half, besides the tithes of the abbot's own demesne, which the Keledei of that place had hitherto received.†

In 1214 a controversy arose between the Keledei of Abernethy and the convent of Arbroath regarding certain tithes ; and it was decided by the arbitrator, the bishop of Dunblane, against the Keledei, and so emphatically as to forbid a recurrence of the question.‡

Before the close of the thirteenth century they had entirely disappeared. The finishing blow was struck in 1272, when, as John of Fordun relates, the priory of Abernethy, which had previously consisted of Keledei, was converted into a society of canons regular.§

Another and more substantial record exists of the Irish character of this church in the ecclesiastical round tower, which constitutes Abernethy one of the two places in Scotland where structures of this class have been preserved.

SECTION XII.—MONYMUSK.

The founder of the church of Monymusk, in Aberdeenshire, is said to have been Malcolm Canmore, who, about the year 1080, when proceeding on a mili-

---

* EVIDENCES, P, No. 9.
‡ Ibid., No. 7.

† EVIDENCES, Q, No. 4.
§ Ibid., No. 9.

tary expedition, vowed* that if he returned in safety he would make a liberal offering to God and St. Andrew.† The probability, however, is that he was a restorer, not a founder, and that, as in the subsequent case of Deir, he revived a decayed monastery and enlarged its endowments. At all events, Monymusk was affiliated, at the above date, to the church of St. Andrews, and partook of its discipline as an institution of Keledei. Subsequently it received further augmentations from the Earls of Mar ; and in various charters from 1200 out, its clergy are styled " Canonici qui Keledei dicuntur," or " Keledei sive canonici ;"‡ while their church is called " ecclesia beatæ Mariæ de Munimusc."§

In 1211 a complaint was laid before the Pope, by William, bishop of St. Andrews, in which he stated that certain Keledei who professed to be canons, and certain others of the diocese of Aberdeen, in the town of Monymusc, which pertained to him, were endeavouring to establish a system of regular canons, contrary to right and his desire. Whereupon a commission was issued to the abbots of Melrose and Dryburg, and the archdeacon of Glasgow, empowering them to examine into the case and adjudicate thereon. Accordingly they held their court ; and their award was, that the Keledei in future should have one refectory and one dormitory in common, and one oratory without a cemetery ; and that the bodies of the Keledei,¶ and of clerks or laymen who might die when with them, should receive the rites of sepulture at the parish church of Monymusc ; that the Keledei should be twelve in number, and that Bricius the thirteenth, whom the Keledei were to present for confirmation to the bishop of St. Andrews, should be their master or prior ; that on his retirement or death, the Keledei were to choose three of their society, from among whom

* Athelstan made a similar vow in 936, when on his way against the Scots. See part iv. sect. 1, *infra.*

† Collections on the History of Aberdeen and Banff, vol. i., p. 169 (Spalding Club, 1843).

‡ Evidences, R, Nos. 4, 8, 9, 11, 17–21.

§ The church of the Keledei at St. Andrews was also called St. Mary's. The society had been vicars of the church of the Holy Trinity, which was the parish church of St. Andrews previously to the consolidation of the rectory and vicarage in 1258. Sir James Dalrymple on this fact founded his sweeping assertion, that " the common practice of the Culdees was to dedicate their principal churches to Holy Trinitie, and not to the Blessed Virgin or any Saint." Collections, p. 248.

¶ The composition at St. Andrews was more liberal to the Keledei, " exceptis corporibus Keledeorum, qui ubi voluerint sepelientur." Evidences, M, No. 12.

the bishop was to select the one he considered best suited to become prior or master ; that it should not be lawful for them at any future time to take vows of canonical or monastic life without the bishop's consent, nor exceed the limitation prescribed for the number of their body ; that when a Keledeus died or withdrew, those who remained were to fill up the vacant place ; and that the newly elected member was, upon his admission, to swear before the bishop or his deputy that he would observe the terms of this composition.*

This society, which consisted of secular priests, thirteen in number, was probably the representative of an ancient monastic foundation. Its early connexion, however, with St. Andrews, reduced it to a condition of secondary importance, and deprived it of the presence of a bishop, whose place was to some extent supplied by a prior or master. We observe them excluded from all parochial functions, and, as regarded the rights of the parish church, placed upon the footing of ordinary parishioners. Further, we perceive that they were bound by no vows, and that their peculiarity consisted in their collegiate character and the absence of spiritual cure. Nay, an effort on the part of some of the members to bind themselves by voluntary obligations, and assume the condition of Regulars, was resisted by the ordinary ; and they were compelled to adhere to their original discipline, which being lax and anomalous speedily led to their suppression, or their reconstitution under a new name. The change, indeed, seems to have originated in themselves, from a sense of their own defects. The same bishop whose remonstrance led to the foregoing decision, soon after, at the request of the prior and Keledei of Monymusk, forbade any person who had made a regular profession in this house to be received elsewhere without the prior's license.† This transition state of their discipline will account for the peculiar way in which they are spoken of in charters of this date, as when Duncan, Earl of Mar, styles them *Keledei sive Canonici.*‡ Presently the alternative is dropped, and in subsequent charters they are simply termed *Canonici,* till 1245, when they vanish from the page of history, and in their stead there appear the " Prior and Convent of Munimusc of the order of St. Augustin."§

---

* EVIDENCES, R, No. 14.   † Ibid., No. 15.
‡ Ibid., No. 16.   § Ibid., No. 22.

Section XIII.—Muthill.

[handwritten margin note: Dunblane declined / M. Grew. / R 47]

Intimately associated with the church of Dunblane was that of Muthel, which gives name to a large parish adjoining that of Dunblane on the north. Concerning its foundation and early condition history is silent. The veneration, indeed, entertained there in old times for St. Patrick's Well, and that of Struthill, with its adjacent chapel,* reminds us of St. Patrick's famous well at Struell,† near Downpatrick, and may indicate some faint traces of Irish influence at a remote period. We know that in the twelfth century there existed in this place a society of Keledei, who held a prominent place in the diocese of Dunblane. " Malpol, prior Keledeorum de Mothel," and " Sithach et Malcolm Keledei de Mothel," are witnesses to a charter of the bishop of Dunblane about the year 1178.‡ Another charter, of somewhat later date, is witnessed by " Malpol, prior Keledeorum," and " Michael, persona de Mothel, et ejus capellanus Mackbeth."§ " Malgegill, prior Moethill," and " Gillemichel, persona de Moethel," attest a similar instrument in the year 1200.∥ Malkirg, prior Kelledeorum de Mothle,"¶ is witness to a charter of confirmation, about 1214.** These Keledei have been generally referred by Scotch writers to Dunblane; but they do not appear to have had any further connexion with its church than as occupying an adjoining parish, and belonging to a community which grew into importance upon its decline.

---

* New Statistical Account, vol. x., pp. 313, 314.

† Struthill and Struell are corruptions of the Gaelic ꝛꝛuċaıꞃ " a stream." Reeves's Ecclesiastical Antiquities, p. 42.

‡ Evidences, S, No. 2.　　　§ Ibid., No. 3.　　　∥ Ibid., No. 4.

¶ The name occurs in charters in the forms—*Mothel, Modhel, Meothill, Meothel, Moethel,* and *Mothle.* The last of these is for *Mothla* the genitive of *Mothail,* and shows how frivolous is the supposed etymology of the name Mothel, quasi *Mote-hill.* New Stat. Acct., vol. x., p. 311. In Ireland there are three places so called, namely Maothail-Bhrogain, now Mothell, in the county of Waterford; Maothail Manchain, now Mohill, in the county of Leitrim; and Mothell, in the county of Kilkenny. *Maothail,* sometimes written *Maethail* and *Moethail,* makes in the genitive *Maothla* or *Moethla,* which very nearly approaches the Scotch form *Mothle.* It is derived from maoth " soft," and signifies " spongy ground."

** Evidences, S, No. 5.

I

SECTION XIV.—MONIFIETH.

In Forfarshire, adjoining Dundee on the north-east, is the parish of Moni-
fieth, which once possessed a house of Céli-dé.   This we learn from an accidental allusion in a solitary charter.   In 1242, Matilda, Countess of Angus,
granted to the church of Arbroath all the land on the south side of Monifodh,
which the Keledei held in the time of her father.*   This was the expiring rem-
nant of an ancient society, whose endowments were lost in part through the
vicious administration of their secular affairs, while the remainder was handed
over to a neighbouring monastery, whose practice was considered more ortho-
dox, and its recognition of Anglo-Norman law more express.   The evidence
that the early endowments of this church had been misappropriated lies in the
fact that at the above date there was an abbot of Monifodh, who was a layman,
and who as such, notwithstanding his possessions, took his place as a witness
to several charters at a considerable interval after the vicar of the same parish.†

PART IV.—THE CÉLI-DÉ OF ENGLAND AND WALES.

SECTION I.—YORK.

THAT the Scottish use of an ecclesiastical term should run parallel with its
employment in Ireland, might naturally be expected, considering the relation
of the two countries as regarded both their church and language.   But that
we should find in the heart of Saxon Northumbria such a term as *Colideus* lin-
gering ages after the Irish impress on the religion of that province had been
obliterated, is truly remarkable.   There existed in York, till the dissolution of
monasteries, an hospital called St. Leonard's, the chartulary of which, a beauti-
fully written volume, engrossed in the reign of Henry V., passed into the
Cotton collection, where it is now preserved in that section of the British Mu-

---

* EVIDENCES, T, No. 4.   † Ibid., Nos. 1, 2, 3, 5.

seum library. From this book DUGDALE has printed, in his Monasticon, an abstract, which furnishes us with the following particulars.*

When king Athelstan was on his march against the Scotch, in 936, he halted at York, and there besought of the ministers of St. Peter's church, who were then called *Colidei*, to offer up their prayers on behalf of himself and his expedition, promising them that, if he returned victorious, he would confer suitable honour upon the church and its ministers. Accordingly, after a successful campaign, he revisited this church, and publicly returned thanks for the favour which heaven had vouchsafed to him. And observing in the same church men of holy life and honest conversation, then styled *Colidei*, who maintained a number of poor people, and withal had but little whereon to live, he granted to them, and their successors for ever, for the better enabling them to support the poor who resorted thither, to exercise hospitality, and perform other works of piety, a thrave of corn from every ploughland in the diocese of York,—a donation which continued to be enjoyed until a late period, under the name of Petercorn. The record goes on to state that these Colidei continued to receive fresh accessions to their endowments, and especially from Thomas, whom William the Conqueror advanced to the see of York in 1069. This prelate rebuilt the cathedral church, and augmented the revenues of its clerics. The Colidei soon after erected or founded in the same city, on a site which had belonged to the crown, an hospital or halting place for the poor who flocked thither; to which were transferred the endowments which the said Colidei or clerics had hitherto received. William Rufus removed the hospital to another part of the city; and king Stephen, when further augmenting its resources, changed its name from St. Peter's to St. Leonard's hospital. It contained a master or warden, and 13 brethren, 4 secular priests, 8 sisters, 30 choristers, 2 schoolmasters, 206 beadsmen, and 6 servitors.†

It would appear that these Colidei were the officiating clergy of the cathedral church of St. Peter's at York in 936, and that they discharged the double function of divine service and eleemosinary entertainment; thus combining the two leading characteristics of the old conventual system, which was common to

---

* EVIDENCES, U.

† DUGDALE, Monasticon Anglicanum, vol. vi., pt. ii., p. 607 (Lond. 1846).

the Irish and Benedictine rules. But when things assumed a new complexion, and a Norman archbishop was appointed, and the foundation of a new cathedral laid, and a more magnificent scale established for the celebration of divine worship in this metropolitan church, the Colidei, or old order of officiating clergy, were superseded; and while they were excluded from their cathedral employment, they received an extension of their eleemosinary resources, and, in order to mark their severalty, they were removed to another quarter of the city, whither they took their endowments with them, and thus continued through several centuries, under an altered economy and title, till all memory of their origin had perished, save what was recorded in the preamble of their charter book.

The existence of the name *Colidei* at York in the beginning of the tenth century indicates some surviving traces of the Celtic school of ecclesiastical discipline. For the name is undoubtedly technical, and a form of Céli-dé suited to the ears of a people who were ignorant of Celtic, but were familiar with Latin; and as the etymology of Colideus was in such harmony with the profession of the Céli-dé, the adaptation which the ear suggested was sanctioned by an apparent fitness. When this transformation of the name took place it is hard to say; but the memoranda from which the chartulary derived this its earliest entry seem to indicate that before the year 936 the term had undergone the change. At all events it is a curious vestige of early Irish influence, discernible amidst long continued Saxon usage, which, as we learn from BEDE, was, in ecclesiastical polity, antagonistic to the Scotic system.

To this special mention of York may be added another authority, which has reference to the south of England. In the Cotton collection is preserved a Privilege which king Ethelred is alleged to have granted to the church of Canterbury. It is written in Saxon, with a counterpart in Latin. In the former there is a passage to this effect: " I observe and clearly perceive this discipline far and wide corrupted through the laxity and negligence of the *priests*,"[*] which the Latin counterpart represents in these words: " Dei servitium passim nostra in gente a *cultoribus clericis* defleo extinctum et tepefactum."[†] And Dr. LINGARD, who first drew attention to the passage, observes: " In the charters the

---

[*] WILKINS, Concilia, vol. i., p. 282 *a*.   [†] Ibid., p. 284 *a*.

prebendaries are termed *cultores* clerici, a singular expression, which seems to intimate that the collegiate clergy were even then styled *Culdees*—cultores Dei —in the south as well as the north of England."*

SECTION II.—BARDSEY.

In the year 1188, Gerald Barri, accompanying Archbishop Baldwin in his circuit of Wales, visited the priory of Nevyn, in the southern extremity of Carnarvon. Here he lodged one night; and we may suppose that in the hours of relaxation conversation ran upon the wonders of the little island, three miles in circuit, lying off to the south, called Ynys Ennli by the Welsh, and Bardsey by the Saxons, as it is known at this day. This spot, very difficult of approach, and water-walled by nature, was the seat of a famous abbey, founded about the year 516, to which were attracted such multitudes of holy men, whose remains were interred there, that it became in the middle ages the most famous place of pilgrimage in Wales, and was called the *Roma Britanniæ.*† Here the ancient monastic discipline of the country, akin to that of Ireland and Scotland, lingered to a later date than on the mainland, where facilities of access rendered reconstruction more easy. It was, probably, the circumstance that the religious order of the place was not referrible to any of the prevailing systems which drew from the pen of Gerald Barri the following curious notice: "Iacet autem extra Lhyn insula modica quam monachi inhabitant religiosissimi, quos Cælibes vel Colideos vocant. Hæc autem insula ab aeris salubritate quam ex Hiberniæ confinio sortitur, vel potius aliquo ex miraculo ex Sanctorum meritis, hoc mirandum habet, quod in ea seniores præmoriuntur, quia morbi in ea rarissimi: & raro vel nunquam hic nusquam moritur, nisi longa senectute confectus."‡ There is something remarkable in Giraldus' association of the terms *cœlibes* and *colidei,* between which there is no etymological connexion whatsoever ; and the more so, as his previous experience of Ireland had, in the case of Inis-na-mbeo, suggested a similar expression, " pauci Cælibes, quos cælicolas vel Colideos vo-

---

* History and Antiquities of the Anglo-Saxon Church, chap. xiii. (vol. ii., p. 294, ed. 1845).

† USSHER, Brit. Eccl. Antiq., cap. xiv. (Works, vol. vi., p. 44).

‡ GIRALDUS CAMBRENSIS, Itinerarium Cambriæ, ii., 6 (p. 865, ed. Camden).

cant."* The Welsh island, too, was remarkable for exemption from disease, while the Irish one afforded security from death. In both cases the salubrity of situation, coupled with long accumulating reverence, gave rise to the popular belief, which might have been dissipated had any innovation taken place in the religious constitution of their societies within the traditional memory of man.

When Bardsey again appears in history, it is in a record of Carnarvon of 1252, where the ecclesiastics of it are styled *Canonici*, most probably regular; for, as contrasted with them, the occupants of the neighbouring house of Aberdaron were styled *Canonici Seculares*. The latter was subject to Bardsey, which probably adopted about this period the regular discipline called after St. Augustin.

Here then, in the only Welsh institution where the existence of Colidei is recorded, we find regular canons as the representatives of the ancient order. Now, as the order of canons represented a class of ecclesiastics who occupied an intermediate place between the monks and secular clergy, so we may regard these Colidei, out of whom the British canons grew, to have been of a somewhat similar nature—at first all secular, that is, not bound by vows, and differing only from secular clergy in that they lived aggregately, having a common house, table, and oratory. But when, in the middle of the eleventh century, a separation took place between those who adopted the stricter observance introduced by Ivo of Chartres, and those who adhered to the old system, then the distinctive terms of *regular* and *secular* canons were introduced; and the same variety which existed in practice between these two sections seems to have prevailed among the Keledei or Colidei, until the stricter portion abandoned the name for that of regular canons of St. Augustin; and the laxer portion, which retained it longer, held on till they were either summarily extinguished by suppression, or gradually merged in the absorbing mass of the better organized and more effective system.

In one place in Ireland, the island of Devenish, they held their ground to the Reformation collaterally with regular canons; and in another, Armagh, they discharged an office which, with the name, survived the Reformation; but

---

* Part II., Section vi., *supra.*

in Scotland, where Celtic usage, when brought into competition with Saxon institutions, gave way at a much earlier date, the name and office of Keledei disappear from the page of history in the year 1332, and the only vestige of them which survived till later times was the provostry of Kirkheugh at St. Andrews; while in York it was reserved for Norman policy to put the Colidei in a subordinate position, and to divorce them from that venerable church on whose ruins rose the gorgeous cathedral, with the sumptuous appointments of which the traditional poverty and simplicity of Athelstan's Colidei would hardly have been in keeping.

EVIDENCES.

A.—Servus Dei, &c.

" Ob singularem vitæ sanctitatem monachos etiam Servos Dei dictos notandum est." Altaserra, Asceticon. pp. 139, 143 (Par. 1674). The early use of the epithet in this limited sense is shown by the following examples :—

S. Hieronymus, *qui clar.* 378. (Opp. ed. Vallarsii, Veronæ, 1734.)

" Crebra virginum monasteria, monachorum innumerabilis multitudo; ut pro frequentia servientium Deo, quod prius ignominiæ fuerat, esset postea gloriæ." Epist. xcvi. ad Principiam Virginem (tom. i., col. 950).

S. Augustinus, *qui clar.* 396. (Opp., Venet. 1729.)

" Regula ad Servos Dei." (tom. i., col. 789). " Dicet aliquis, Quid ergo prodest servo Dei, quod prioribus actibus quos in sæculo habebat relictis, ad hanc spiritalem vitam militiamque convertitur, si eum adhuc oportet, tamquam opificis, exercere negotia ?" De opere Monachorum, cap. 25, sec. 32 (tom. vi., col. 495). See also cap. 3, sec. 4 (col. 477); cap. 16, sec. 17 (col. 487, 488); cap. 16, sec. 19 (col. 489); cap. 17, sec. 20 (col. 489); cap. 19, sec. 22 (col. 491); cap. 23, sec. 28 (col. 494); cap. 27, sec. 35 (col. 498). " Servitus Dei." Ibid., cap. 22, sec. 25 (col. 492). " Vident plerumque, ut fit, transire servos Dei, cognoscunt ipso habitu vel vestis, vel capitis, vel fronte notos habent." Enarratio in Psalmum cxlvii. (tom. iv., col. 1656). " Redeant ad feliciorem consuetudinem suam, quæ famulas Dei tanto amplius decet, quanto minus indigent." Epist. 211 (tom. ii. col. 784). " Denique si latens est dolor in corpore famulæ Dei." Ibid. (col. 786).

Possidius, *qui clar.* 430. (Opp. S. Augustini, Venet. 1729.)

" Sub sancto et cum sancto Augustino in monasterio Deo servientes, Ecclesiæ Hipponensi clerici ordinari cœperunt." Vita S. Augustini, cap. 11 (tom. x., App. col. 264). " Feminarum intra domum ejus nulla umquam conversata est, nulla mansit, ne quidem germana soror, quæ vidua Deo serviens multo tempore usque in diem obitus sui præposita ancillarum Dei vixit." Ibid., cap. 26 (col. 275). " Ob hoc ergo dicebat, numquam debere feminas cum servis Dei, etiam castissimis, una manere domo." Ibid., cap. 26 (col. 275). See also cap. 2 (col. 259); cap. 3 (col. 259); cap. 10 (col. 264); cap. 23 (col. 273).

Salvianus Massiliensis, *qui clar.* 440. (Ap. Gallandium, Biblioth. Vett. Patr., tom. x., p. 50 *b*.)

" Et si quando aliquis Dei servus, aut de Ægyptiorum cœnobiis, aut de sacris Hierusalem locis, aut de sanctis eremi venerandisque secretis ad urbem illam officio divini operis accessit." De Gubernat. Dei, viii. 4.

S. Gregorius Magnus, *qui clar.* 590. (Opp. Paris., 1705.)

" Dei servus," "servus Dei." Dialog., lib. i., cap. 2 (tom. ii., col. 157). Equitius abbas " Dei famulus." Ib. cap. 4 (col. 165). " Dei famula," in the Greek version rendered μοναστρία. Ib., cap. 4 (col. 166). "De transitu Romulæ ancillæ Dei," rendered Περὶ τῆς τελευώσεως Ρωμύλλης μοναστρίας. Lib. iv., cap. 15 (col. 395). S. Benedictus, "Dei famulus." Lib. ii., cap. 1 (col. 212); cap. 6 (col. 224); cap. 13 (col. 236); cap. 15 (col. 240); cap. 19 (col. 245); cap. 22 (col. 249); cap. 23 (col. 253).

"Maurus Dei famulus," also called "Maurus monachus." Lib. ii., cap. 4 (col. 221). "De Isaac servo Dei—sub ejus magisterio in omnipotentis se Domini servitutem dederunt." Lib. iii., cap. 14 (col. 301, 304). "De Eutychio et Florentio servis Dei." Lib. iii., cap. 15 (col. 308). "Martinus monachus" is styled, "Dei famulus." Lib. iii., 16 (col. 313). "De Eleutherio servo Dei," who was "pater monasterii beati Evangelistæ Marci," lib. iii., cap. 33 (col. 349). "Cujusdam servi Dei qui in Samnio fuerat inclusus;" called also, "Dei famulus," lib iv., cap. 9 (col. 385). See lib. iv., cap. 47 (col. 456). "In quo etiam oratorio servorum Dei congregationem esse constituit." Epist., lib. iii., 37 (tom. ii., col. 650). See Epist., lib. iii., 53 (col. 662); lib. vi. 30 (col. 816); cap. 48 (col. 827), cap. 56 (col. 833); lib. vii., 10 (col. 856). "Gregorius Secundino servo Dei incluso." Epist. ix., 52 (col. 964). "Quia servorum Dei pater—defunctus est : visum mihi est latorem præsentium Barbatianum monachum pro eorundem monachorum gubernatione transmittere." Epist. ix., 91 (col. 997). See Epist., lib. xiii., 2 (col. 1215); 3 (col. 1216); 9 (col. 1224). "Multos de Ecclesiastica, seu sæculari familia novimus ad omnipotentis Dei servitium festinare, ut ab humana servitute liberi, in divino servitio valeant familiariùs in monasteriis conversari." Decreta, v., 6 (col. 1290). "Si quis monacham, quam Dei ancillam appellant, in conjugium duxerit, anathema esto." Decreta vi., 3 (col. 1293). Labbé, Concilia, tom. vi., col. 1312 (Venet. 1729); renewed in same words in Concilio Romano, 721. (Labbé, Concilia, tom. viii., col. 187.)

ZACHARIAS PAPA, An. 744.

"De monachis, id est ancillis Dei." Epist. (ib., col. 244).

CONCILIUM GERMANICUM, An. 742.

"Servis Dei per omnia armaturam portare—omnino prohibuimus." Can. 2 (ibid., col. 270).

"Quisquis servorum Dei vel ancillarum Christi." Can. 6 (ibid., col. 271). See Concil. Liptinense, can. 2 (ibid., col. 275); Concil. Suessionense, cap. 3 (ibid., col. 291).

B.—THE TERM *CÉLE.*

Céle, socius, maritus. Zeuss, Gram. Celt., i., pp. 22, 243, 245, 371. Sometimes written *céele*, *céile.* Ib., p. 23. *Céle ingine* (maritus filiæ) gener. Ib., p. 371. Paradigm of declension, ib., p. 244. With the termination *sine* (*saine*) is formed the abstract noun *cocéilsine*, societas. Ib., 23, 371, ii., 739. See Stokes, Irish Glosses, p. 105, No. 882. In the pronominal use it signifies *alius.* Zeuss, pp. 370, 371 : *dobarcélib*, i. e. aliis ; *friarceiliu*, i. e. contra alios. Ib., p. 248. In this sense is used the cognate Cambrian *cilid*, ib., p. 408 ; and the Cornish and Armorican *y gele*, *egile.* Ib., pp. 407, 409. ⁊ céile, "each other," is the modern form for apoile, alailiu. O'Donovan, Ir. Gram., p. 136. "*Ceile*,

K

each other." Lhuyd, Archæologia. Hence also the adverbial use, ó céile, asunder; ꝺα céile, together; cpé n-α céile, to and fro. O'Donovan, Ir. Gr., p. 268.

In a secondary sense céile is glossed cαpᴅιc, "a friend," in the Leabhar Breac, where it occurs in the epilogue to the Felire of Ængus:

<table>
<tr><td>huαpαl αchpαιꝝ pαιche</td><td>" Patriarchs, prophets,</td></tr>
<tr><td>ꝺo Cpιpc cιαpcαp céli.</td><td>To Christ though they are friends."</td></tr>
</table>

O'Davoren also explains it by cαpα, "a friend." Stokes, Three Irish Glossaries, pp. 65, 139. From it is formed the verb celιóιm, "I visit," of which we have an old inflexion *celide*, "to visit," in Zeuss, vol. ii., p. 1050, gl. 6.

In the sense of *servus*, we find the compound *sóirchele*, that is, free-servant, synonymous with *sóirmug*, as the gloss on *libertus*. Zeuss, i., pp. 40, 371; and the derivative verb, in the inflexion *fochelfatar*, they will serve. Ib., p. 1057, gl. 15. O'Davoren explains ceile by ꝝιllα, *a servant*, in the passage ceile cαιch αcomαιp αchomhꝺeꝺh, "the servant of every wish of his Lord." Stokes, Three Ir. Gloss., p. 63. "*Ceile, Oglach,* a servant." Lhuyd, Archæologia. "Ceile, a servant; hence Céile Ꝺe, *Colideus,* or *Coli-Dei,* an order of religious formerly subsisting in Ireland, England, and Wales, so called from being the servants of God: they were called Culdees in Great Britain." O'Brien, Irish Dict. in voc. Ceile, a servant; Ceιllpιne, "homage, submission." O'Reilly, Irish Dict., in voc. *Ceile,* "A spouse; a husband; a wife; a servant." Armstrong, Gaelic Dict., in voc.

C.—Céle and its Compounds, as Proper Names.

1. CELE, son of Anrothan, lord of Ui Crimthannain. Four Mast. 921. Cele, son of Suibhne, abbot of Slane. Ib., 1001. Cele, bishop of Ardachadh. Ib., 1048. Cele, son of Donnagan, bishop of Leinster. Ib. 1076.

2. CELECLAMH, anchorite of Ardmacha. Ib., 950. That is, "servant of the lepers."

3. CELECLERECH, bishop. Calendars, July 8. That is, "servant of the clergy."

4. CELECRIST, saint. Four Mast. 721. *Dormitacio Cheili-crist.* An. Ult. 726. His festival was the 3rd of March, at which day Colgan notices him, under the Latinized name *Christicola,* as if céle and *colo* were kindred words. Actt. SS., p. 454. See Lanigan. Eccles. Hist., vol. iii., p. 162. O'Donovan renders the name "Servant," or "Vassal of Christ." Four Mast., vol. i., p. 320, note ᵏ.

5. CELEDABHAILL, son of Scannall, successor of Comhgall of Bennchar. Four Mast. 917, 926, 927. The Annals of Ulster give the name in the simple form *Cele,* at 927, 928.

6. CELEDULAISI, of Devenish. An. Ult. 750; Four Mast. 746.

7. CELEIESU, abbot of Cillmoinne. An. Ult. 814; Four Mast. 810. That is, "Servant of Jesus."

8. CELEPEDAIR, abbot of Ardmacha. Four Mast. 757. O'Donovan renders the name " Servant of Peter." Four Mast., vol. i., p. 360, note ⁵.

9. CELETIGHERNAIGH, abbot of Cluain-eois. Four Mast. 714. O'Donovan renders it "Servant of St. Tighernach." Four Mast., vol. i., p. 313. St. Tighernach was the founder and patron saint of this church, now called Clones.

10. MAC CELE. Four Mast. 1257, 1331.

11. UA CELE. Four Mast. 1026, 1050, 1053.

D.—THE CULDEE CONTROVERSY.

When Alexander Milne, canon of Dunkeld, drew up his memoir of the bishops of that see, he was led to take notice of the old religious body, " quos nominavit vulgus Kelledeos aliter Colideos, hoc est colentes Deum." (Vitæ Dunkeldensis Ecclesiæ Episcoporum, p. 4: Edinb., 1831). This was the form of the name and the interpretation in Scotland at the close of the fifteenth century.

Hector Boece, in 1526, by the publication of his "Scotorum Historiæ," gave to his countrymen a gratifying but vicious statement of their ancient history, both civil and ecclesiastical, and he is the earliest writer that I have been able to discover who uses the term *culdeus* or culdee. Not satisfied with any date later than St. Tertullian or St. Cyprian, he represents a coeval body of Christian teachers in North Britain, whose practice he thus describes :—" Cœpere et nostri eo tempore, Christi dogma accuratissimè amplexari : monachorum quorundam ductu et adhortatione, qui quòd sedulo prædicationi vacarent, essentque frequentes in oratione, ab incolis cultores Dei sunt appellati. Invaluit id nomen apud vulgus intantum, ut sacerdotes omnes ad nostra pené tempora, vulgo Culdei, .i. cultores Dei sine discrimine vocitarentur. Pontificem inter se communi suffragio deligebant, penes quem divinarum rerum esset potestas." (Lib. vi., fol. 92 *b.*) Descending in the reign of the alleged Crathlintus, 273–322, he introduces to notice as distinguished fellow-labourers, " Amphibalus antistes. Modocus priscus, Calanus, Ferranus, Ambianus, et Carnocus Dei cultores (Culdei prisca nostra vulgari lingua dicti) Christi servatoris doctrinam, omnes per Scotorum regiones concionando multis piisque sudoribus seminando." (Fol. 99 *a.*) Surely these Culdees were a remarkable group ; for Amphibalus was the mantle of St. Alban, who was put to death in 303 ; Modocus, our Moedoc of Ferns, died in 624 ; Calanus, Ferranus, and Ambianus, were no men if they were not Caelan, Forannan, and Abban, Irish saints of the sixth century ; while Carnoc, the South Briton, adopted Ireland as his home. Our author, when he comes to treat of St. Andrews, describes the original clergy of that church as having been " in eo a primæva ejus conditione, primum sacerdotes Dei cultores vulgo appellati." (Fol. 105 *b.*) And when he arrives at the period of the Roman mission, he observes : " Erat Palladius primus omnium, qui sacrum inter Scotos egere magistratum, a summo pontifice episcopus creatus : quum antea populi suffragiis ex monachis et Culdeis pontifices assumerentur." (Fol. 128 *b.*)

K 2

Bishop Lesley, in 1578, repeats the words of Boece, " Dei cultores (Culdei nostra vulgari lingua dicti.") (De Origine, &c., Scotorum, lib. iii., cap. 34, p. 115, ed. 1675.)

Four years after, the same sentiments derived additional plausibility from the elegant scholarship of George Buchanan, when repeated with little alteration in his great work. (Rerum Scoticarum Historia, lib. iv., cap. 46; and lib. vi., cap. 17.)

Archdeacon Monro, who made a tour of the Western Isles in 1594, commences his narrative with Man, " whilks sometime, as auld historiograpers sayes, was wont to be the seat first ordynit by Fynan king of Scottis to the priest and the philosophers called in Latine Druides, in English Culdeis and Kildeis, that is worshippers of God, in Erish Leid Draiche, quhilks were the first teachers of religion in Albion." (Miscellanea Scotica, vol. ii., p. 113.)

Next came Thomas Dempster, the notorious hagioclept, who published in 1622 his " Apparatus ad Historiam Scotticam," in which he told the world that the Culdees were the Σεμνοθέοι of the Greeks; and, as to their order, were identical with the regular canons of Lateran as reformed by St. Austin. (Lib. i., cap. 13, pp. 54, 146.) To this exposition he added, in his masterpiece of 1627, the opinion that they were the *Therapeutæ* of Greek ecclesiastical writers.—" Culdei, seu Keldei, sacerdotes erant, qui ab assiduis in fide laboribus, sic dicti, id est *Deum timentes.* Floruerunt ab initio fidei a Scotis receptæ anno cciii. nomen usque ad patrum nostrorum memoriam pervenit." (Historia Ecclesiastica Gentis Scotorum, lib. i., num. 45, 313, pp. 33, 180.)

Meanwhile Sir Henry Spelman was preparing to break down the Scotch monopoly of the Culdees, and to dissipate a portion of the error which was current concerning them. His information on the subject was principally derived from a communication by bishop Ussher, who generously forestalled the publication of his own great history, in this portion of its contents. His Glossary, which was published in 1626, under the article *Culdei*, starts with Boece's description, and then, on Ussher's telling, subjoins that the term obtained also in *Enhli* sive *Berdseya* insula ubi *monachis,* et in Hibernia ubi *presbyteris secularibus* est attributum."

The matter of Spelman's article was more fully set out, in 1639, by Ussher, then Archbishop of Armagh, in his Britannicarum Ecclesiarum Antiquitates (pp. 636–639, 659; or Works, vol. vi., pp. 173–177, 197); but he left the etymology of the name uncorrected, and drew too largely from Boece and Dempster.

A very remarkable specimen of etymology, certainly the most original which has been proposed for the word Culdee, is found in a communication, made about the year 1635, by bishop Bramhall, wherein, referring to the see of Armagh, he writes : " The rectories of Donoughmore, Mullabracke, Crogan, Derrinous, Tynan, Mounter-Henry, Clonfeecle, with the vicarage of Leywalliglees, and the tithes of ten villages in the parish of Killsleue, and seven townes and many other parcells of lands, though much of them was actually in the possession of Churchmen, yet indeed they were appertinent to the Pryory of the Colideans, or, as the Irish call them, Gallideans or God's Cockes, in Armagh ; and were so found by inquisition, and begged by Mr. Murry, and passed in a patent to one Chase." (MS., Lambeth Library, No. 943, p. 535.) The Armagh Culdees might have replied in the words of the Bangor people,—" Scoti sumus non galli."

The Archbishop of St. Andrews appeared in 1639 as the historian of the Church of Scotland, and, as a matter of course, adverted to the Culdees of Boetius, and had the courage to reject the old derivation of Cultores Dei, substituting one, however, which was more objectionable: "It is more like this title was given them from their living in these Cells, where people assembled to hear service. Somewhat it maketh for this, that in certain old Bulls and Rescripts of Popes I find them termed *Keledei,* and not *Culdei.*" (Spotswood's History of the Church of Scotland, pp. 4, 51: Edinb., 1668.)

So far the question had been handled on its literary merits; but, in 1646, a Frenchman gave a new turn to the investigation, when David Blondel employed the statements of the Scotch writers for polemical purposes, and, throwing in the Chronicle of Durham, framed from them an argument in support of his theory of church government. (Apologia pro Sententia Hieronymi de Episcopis et Presbyteris, sect. iii., p. 315: Amst., 1646.)

He was followed by the learned John Selden, whose services in the compilation of Sir Roger Twysden's "Historiæ Anglicanæ Scriptores Decem" are acknowledged by the editor, and speak for themselves in his able introduction. Availing himself of the opportunity offered by the mention of Keledei in a chronicle of Durham, he enters largely into the discussion of their peculiarities, and, after the example of Blondel, views them in accordance with his own ecclesiastical sentiments. His communication bears the date of 1652. (Ad Lectorem, pp. vi.-xxi., reprinted in his Works, vol. ii., cols. 1130-1146.)

Controversy on the subject slumbered a little; and Sir James Ware, in 1658, published his Antiquitates Hibernicæ. In cap. xvii., sec. 4, of that work, he briefly treats of the "Colidei sive Culdei, i. e. Cultores Dei appellati," of Ireland, but adds nothing to what was already made known by Ussher, beyond a reference to the Colidei of York. This section was subsequently enlarged by Harris, the editor of his works (vol. ii., p. 236).

Another Frenchman, in every way qualified for the investigation, undertook to treat of the Culdees; and the invaluable Glossary of Du Cange, which appeared in 1678, embodied in a scholar-like form all the information on the subject which had been published down to that date. (Glossarium Mediæ et Infimæ Latinitatis, voce *Colidei.*)

In 1681, controversy was renewed in Richard Baxter's "Treatise of Episcopacy," where the writer briefly adverts to the history of the Scotch Culdees as a testimony in favour of his views, but throws no new light upon the matter. (Part ii., cap. 25, p. 224.)

George Martine, who wrote a history of St. Andrews, in 1683, under the title "Reliquiæ Divi Andreæ," was led by his subject to notice the Culdees, but he retains the old interpretation of "Cultores Dei, Colidei." The parochial name Kirkaldy he proposes should be Kirkculdie, as if Cella Culdeorum; and he adduces, from the old register of St. Andrews, the Baronia Caledaiorum, which was a portion of the Culdee estates (pp. 22, 23: St. Andrews, 1797).

While the polemical discussion about the Culdees was righting itself, the literary investigation of the subject was making no progress, but rather retrograding in the hands of incompetent etymologists. This appears in Bishop Lloyd's "Historical Account of Church Government," which was published in 1684. The seventh chapter of this work is devoted to the Culdees; but the learned author is utterly at fault when he writes: "What they were, their Name sufficiently sheweth. For they were called *Kelledei,* or in the old Scotch, *Kyldees,* (as I suppose) from *Cylle,* which signifies a Cell, as well in the *Welsh* or old *British* Tongue, as in the *Scotish* or *Irish.* From hence by addition of *Tee* (or *Dee* in composition), which signifies a House, the word *Kyldee* signifies a House of such Cells." (Sec. 3, p. 138.)

Next year Dean Stillingfleet, afterwards Bishop of Worcester, published his Origines Britannicæ, in which he accepts Bishop Lloyd's derivation. " Kil, as appears by the Scottish historians, was a place of devotion. . . . . And from hence the clergy of this church [Kilremont] were called Killedees (from which title the fiction of the ancient Culdees came, as the Bishop of St. Asaph hath truly observed.") (Preface, p. lvi.)

Tanner, in the first edition of his Notitia (1695), calls the Colidei of York *Culdees* (p. 249), and subsequently added " or secular canons," cxxix. 23 (ed. Nasmith, 1787). " Not to make any mention here of the old *Scottish* Monks or *Culdees*, of whom we had none in *England*, except at *St. Peter's* in *York*, because they were the same with the Monks of the *Irish* Rules." (*Ib.*, Preface.)

Sir James Dalrymple, in 1705, published his " Collections concerning the Scottish History," in which he drew pretty freely from the old chartularies of Scotland, and thus brought to light a new and valuable mass of evidence; but his book was written for a controversial end, and therefore history or antiquities did not get fair play. He treats largely of the Scotch Culdees, as regards their mediæval condition (pp. 122, 123, 129, 137, chap. ix., pp. 225–285).

Jeremy Collier, in 1708, took a brief and dispassionate view of the Culdee question, but made no addition to the existing store of knowledge. (Ecclesiastical History of Great Britain, vol. i., pp. 180 *a*, 497 *a*.)

Sir Robert Sibbald's " History of Fife," published in 1710, brought to light some fresh matter relative to the mediæval condition of the Culdees in Scotland, but, like Dalrymple's collections, there is an absence of literary freedom in the discussion of the question.

An anonymous pamphlet, of 162 pages, appeared at Edinburgh in 1714, entitled, " Some Remarks upon Sir James Dalrymple's Historical Collections. With an Answer to the Vindication of the Ecclesiastical Part of them." The author was John Gillan, Bishop of Dunblane. In the ninth chapter, pp. 114–148, he discusses the record history of the Scotch Culdees, with special reference to Sir James Dalrymple's arguments, and makes a valuable contribution to the published evidences by printing the Lochlevin charters, from the Register of St. Andrews (pp. 160–163).

A real step in advance was taken in 1718, by the publication of John Toland's Nazarenus. The writer, who was a native of Inishowen, and, as Shane O'Tuholan, spoke Irish as his mother tongue, was able to apply a branch of knowledge to the subject which hitherto had been unemployed. Justly censuring the etymological surmises of Lloyd and Stillingfleet, he declares that the Culdees were " constantly called Keledei, from the original Irish or ancient Scottish word *Ceile-de*, signifying *separated or espoused to God :* these having been likewise very numerous in Ireland, and in all the Irish writers invariably known by this name. From *Ceile-de* many of the Latin writers make *Colidei* in the plural number; and others, who did not understand this word, did from the mere sound (like our two great bishops' derivations) interpret it *Cultores Dei*, whence the modern word *Culdees*, though it be *Keldees* and *Kelledei* in all the ancient Scottish writings. *Ceile de*, both name and thing, cannot be deny'd by any man who's tolerably versed in the language of the Irish and their books." What he adds is more open to exception, " The Keldees were commonly laymen, and marry'd, as I noted before [in note 66]; but, like *bishop* and *monk*, the word remained the same, after the ideas were changed with the condition of the men. But it seems no change could prevent the extinction of the Keldees." (Letter ii., pp. 49–57.)

The remarks of Toland drew down upon him, in 1723, the criticism of a very inferior genius, and who, as a Cumbrian, was totally unfit to meddle with Irish etymology. Bishop Nicolson, justly dissatisfied with Toland's conclusions, took exception also to his Irish scholarship, and, rejecting the derivation *Ceile-de*, hit upon the Benedictine habit, and thus developed his discovery: "The short story of these Monks is, That they were of the Irish Rule; carried into Scotland by St. Columb, and thence dispers'd into the Northern parts of England. They were so named from the black Habit which they wore: for *Culdee* signifies as plainly *a black monk* (from the colour of his Hood or *Coul*), as *Culwen* signifies a *White* one." (The Irish Historical Library, Preface, p. xxx.) This is as much as to say that Culdee is derived from cochaḷḷ ƀubh, or, to adopt his Anglo-Irish compound, *coul*-ƀubh! Unfortunately the Columbites wore white.

The views of Dalrymple and Sibbald found, in 1726, an able opponent in their countryman, George Crawford, who was the more formidable because he drew from record sources, and employed his materials in the true spirit of an antiquary. (Lives, &c., of the Officers of the Crown and of the State in Scotland, vol. i., pp. 6, 428–432.)

A period had now arrived when the literature of Scotland was to be "reformed from Hector Boethius," and this revolution was due to Thomas Innes, whose Critical Essay, in 1729, broke down the fictions of the old belief. He was not able, however, to shake off the Columbite error, as appears from his ingenious application of the expressions, "Deo serviendi non sæculo," and "Dei famulus," as employed by Venerable Bede in reference to the Scotic missionaries of Northumbria (Hist. Eccl. iii., 26). "All this made so deep an impression on the people that not only they thronged in to hear them, and to receive their blessing and instructions, when any of them came into their neighbourhood, says Bede, but it obtained to them among the vulgar, the peculiar name of Servants of God, expressed in former times by the word Ceiledee or Keledee, so famous in our country in following ages, but whether originally Pictish or Gaelic is not easy to determine at this distance of time. However though the word Keledee be now become obsolete, it is still expressed in Gaelic by the word Gildee or Guildhee, which hath the same signification, and almost the same sound." And again, concerning Dunkeld, "Milne tells us that the religious persons placed in it for performing Divine Service were called Killdees, which, as we observed elsewhere, was the vulgar name given in those days to churchmen in our country, especially to those that lived together in communities. They were originally the same with the Columbites, formerly so called, because they followed the rule of S. Columba." (The Civil and Ecclesiastical History of Scotland, pp. 191, 331.)

The office which Selden performed in prefacing Twysden's collection was to some extent repeated, though in a different tone, by Walter Goodall, in 1755, who furnished Bishop Keith with a Preliminary Dissertation to his "Large New Catalogue of the Scottish Bishops." This essay, which was pronounced by Pinkerton, in 1789 and 1814, to be "the best account of them [the Culdees] yet given," introduces the subject with these remarks: "As to the Culdees, it is very certain, that there was a sort of monks, and secular priests too, who went under that appellation, not only among the Scots, but also among the Britons and Irish, and even among the northern English, who were first converted by the Scots, particularly in the cathedral of York" (pp. viii.-xix., ed. 1755; pp. lii.-lxvii., ed. Russell, Edinb. 1824).

The same writer, in 1759, again takes notice of the Culdæi: "Quales? non nisi presbyteri seculares quos vocant et monachi, eadem omnia cum reliqua ecclesia professi, si tonsuræ formam, et paschatis observandi regulam ante A. D. DCCXV. exceperis: quorum collegia ab ipsis episcopis plerumque et instituta et dotata sunt . . . . Keledeorum nominis etymologiam quod attinet, haud ferenda videtur ea quam Boethius et Buchananus tradunt, quasi cultores Dei sic dicti fuissent; nam in scriptis antiquioribus, non ut vulgo hodie Culdei, sed semper Keledei dicuntur: atque hæc ipsa observatio contra Nicolsonum Carliolensem episcopum facit, qui Culdeum nigrum monachum, a cuculli colore denotare contendit. *Culla* quidem prisca nostratium lingua cucullus interpretatur; sed quid hoc ad Keledeos? Alii nomen a Græcis mutuatum volunt, perinde ac alios ecclesiastico-rum titulos, quales sunt episcopus, presbyter, diaconus, monachus: Κελλιωται enim apud illos dicuntur monachi cellulis inclusi. Sed cum in tota occidentis ecclesia raro, si unquam fiat Kelede-orum mentio, nisi apud Brittones Scotosque, et horum discipulos Hibernos Anglosque boreales, vocabulum Scotici potius originis esse exinde colligi videtur, idque priscæ nostræ linguæ peritiores, sensu ad rem accommodatissimo, servum Dei denotare, et ex vocabulis *Keile*, servus; et *Dia*, Deus, componi asserunt; quæ sententia magis arridet." (Johannis de Fordun Scotichronicon, Introductio, p. 68.)

In the same year Marianus Brockie, a Scotchman, and prior of the Scotch monastery of St. James at Ratisbon, reproduced, in an elegant form, with additions, Holstenius' Codex Regularum. Among the *Additamenta* in the second volume is an "Ordo Monasticus," which was taken from a Dunfermlin manuscript, and brought to Ratisbon by Servanus Thomson in 1526. It purports to be the Rule of St. Servan of Culros, but, as I have elsewhere shown, is nothing more or less than an appropriation from Ricemarch's Life of St David. (Adamnan's Life of St. Columba, p. 338.) The editor in his Observatio Critica repeats many of the old fictions concerning the Culdees and their antiquity, and associating St. Servanus with them, he turns Culros into Kil-Ros, "ita quod Kil-Ros extiterit verum *Kilideorum Promontorium ;*" and of the occupants he says, "Cum igitur longe ante adventum Sancti Palladii, in hodierna Scotia extiterint Monasteria, quorum inquilini nomina-bantur *Kiledei* vel *Kildei* ab ipsis cellis quas inhabitabant, non a cultu quem ibi exercebant, sic appellati" (pp. 62, 63).

The correct derivation is given for the word Culdee, but otherwise there is nothing worth notice on the subject, in the "History of the Province of Moray," which the Rev. Lachlan Shaw published in 1775.

Sir David Dalrymple (Lord Hailes) despatches the order, in 1776, with the summary sentence, "I imagine the Culdees either were or wished to be *independents.*" (Annals of Scotland, 1153, p. 95.)

In 1788, Bishop Skinner published his Ecclesiastical History of Scotland, in which he treats of the Culdees (vol. i., p. 161-8), rather with a view to correct existing misapprehensions than to throw any new light on the question.

Nationality and prejudice were generously sacrificed by the candid John Pinkerton, in 1789, when he asserted—"The Culdees were surely only Irish clergy. At first they seem to have been regular monks, who followed the rule of St. Columba; and generally their societies consisted of twelve and a chief, in imitation either of Christ and the apostles, or of Columba and the twelve monks who came with him from Ireland. In the gradual corruption of the monastic order, they married; and left their Culdeeship to their children : and, after the havoc introduced by the Danes, usurped the rank of secular clergy. In short, they were merely corrupted monks, such as abounded in all the countries of Europe, till the eleventh century, when the popes were forced to institute canons regular, whom the princes gradually introduced into the chief monasteries, instead of the old depraved monks. . . . The Culdees thus united in themselves, the distinctions of monks and of secular clergy; being apparently, from Columba's time to the eleventh century, the only monks and clergy in Scotland; and all Irish, as formerly shown." ("An Enquiry into the History of Scotland," vol. ii., p. 272, ed. 1814.)

Some of the contributors to Sir John Sinclair's "Statistical Account," who were Gaelic-speaking clergymen, unfortunately helped to obscure the subject by their etymological fancies. The Rev. James M'Lagan, in 1792, thus accounts for the name: " *Cuil* and *Ceal*, signifying a sequestered corner, cave, &c. Those who retired to such a place were called *cuildeach*, plural *cuildich ;* which they who spoke, or wrote Latin turned into *culdeus* and *culdei*, altering only the termination" (vol. ii., pp. 461, 462). Thus also the Rev. Dugal Campbell, in 1795: " Culdee is a Gaelic word, signifying a monk, or hermit, or any sequestered person. Cuildeach is common to this day, and given to persons not fond of society. The word is from *cuil*, a retired corner. . . . One place in I is still called the Culdee's Cell. Cathan, or Cothan Cuildich, signifies the Culdee's cell or couch" (vol. xiv., p. 200). These writers were evidently disciples of James Macpherson, whose " Fingal," published in 1762, had indoctrined a large portion of the literary public. His theory of the founders of Christianity in Scotland was : " These missionaries, either through choice, or to give more weight to the doctrine they advanced, took possession of the cells and groves of the Druids; and it was from this retired life they had the name of *Culdees*, which in the language of the country signifies *sequestered persons.*" (Dissertation, &c., p. vii.)

The " Life of St. Columba," which appeared in 1798 from the pen of Dr. John Smith, continues the Scotch notion of the Culdee succession from the founder of Hi, but rectifies the error of his brethren in the Statistical Account : " They themselves seem to have assumed no other name than that of *Famuli Dei*, or servants of God; or, in their own language, *Gille-De*, which was Latinized into Keledeus (as Comganus Kele-De, or Keledeus; Ængusinus Keledeus, &c., *ap. Colgan.*), whence the English name of *Culdees*" (pp. 118, 162).

Ireland produced the next expositor of the Culdee history in the person of Dr. Edward Ledwich, who, like some of his Scotic predecessors, derives the order from St. Columba, and assumes as a portion of their history all that Bede and Cummian say concerning the Scotch monks, including in it the Lindisfarn succession. Borrowing, with reservation as regarded his own order, the polemical views of a Scotch writer, he has strung together a narrative which is only interesting for the description and drawings which he gives of the abbey of Monaincha (pp. 102–120, Dublin, 1803).

George Chalmers, a very painstaking Scotch antiquary, published, in 1807, the first volume of his " Caledonia." In this work he devotes a chapter to the Culdees, and exhibits the conclusions from an extended examination of Scotch records and Irish writers, in a methodical and interesting form. But he leans to the etymology *cél,* the Welsh for a " shelter" or " hiding," and thus impairs his credit as a critic (pp. 434–439).

The year 1811 produced the first monograph upon the Culdees, when Dr. John Jamieson of Edinburgh published his " Historical Account of the Ancient Culdees of Iona," a quarto volume of 417 pages. The title of this work indicates the erroneous assumption on which it is founded, and which pervades the early part of it, while the author allows his sentiments on church polity to tincture the whole. The Appendix, which consists of charters and other early records, was of considerable value till superseded by the publications of the Bannatyne Club.

Everything which had hitherto been written on the Culdees was distanced, in 1822, by Dr. John Lanigan's discussion of their history and constitution, in the fourth volume of his " Ecclesiastical History of Ireland" (pp. 290–316). He reviews all the evidences on the subject, and with much ability, though occasionally with some asperity and coarseness, disposes of the reasoning and statements of those who differed from him. In the etymology of the name, however, he disregards record authority, and judging with Colgan that the title *Ceile-De,* as applied to Ængus, was an epithet of special application, felt reluctant to extend it to an order. " Accordingly," he writes, " it appears to me, that the original name was *Ceile-Dae,* that is, a man living in community ; for *Ceile* in Irish signifies *together,* and *Dae* a man" (p. 301).

The third volume of the " Rerum Hibernicarum Scriptores" bears the date 1824. Dr. Charles O'Conor, the learned editor, was tempted by the curious entry concerning the Céle-de in the Four Masters, at 806, to append the following note : " Ordo erat Religiosa, antiquitus, ni fallor, Druidica, quæ abjecto Ethnicismo, et Christi fide amplexa, nonnulla tamen veterum instituta servasse videtur. Colideorum austeritate, et aliquando etiam fictis miraculis, vulgi simplicitas decepta est" (p. 315). It would seem that, notwithstanding his emphatic condemnation of Macpherson's Ossianic imposture (Rer. Hib. SS., vol. i., proleg., pt. ii., p. xii.), he had accepted that writer's Culdee theory.

A new edition of Keith's " Scottish Bishops" having been called for, Bishop Russell undertook the office of editor, and, in 1824, annexed a Supplement to Goodall's Preliminary Dissertation, which he intended as a reply to the polemical part of Dr. Jamieson's " Historical Account." Being of a controversial character, there is, as might be expected, little in it of literary interest.

In 1829, a very wholesome and successful corrective to the Ossianic epidemic was administered in our "Transactions," by Edward O'Reilly, who, in a paper read before the Academy on the 25th of May in that year, proved that the name Culdee was derived from the Irish words *Ceile De,* " signifying literally, *the spouse of God,* or a person totally renouncing the service of the world, and devoting himself entirely to the service of the Almighty," and concluded " from his etymology of the name *Culdees,* that he [Macpherson] was so little skilled in the Gaelic language, as to be incapable of translating the genuine poems of Ossian, if he had them before him." (Transactions R. I. A., vol. xvi., Antiqq., pp. 175, 209.)

Francis Barham, Esq., edited the octavo edition of Collier's " Church History," which was published by Strahan in 1840. He introduces a long editorial note taken from Chalmers' " Caledonia," to which he prefixes the startling announcement, " The history of the Culdees has ever been a mystery, and ever will be so." (Vol. ii., p. 618.)

This production received a very practical refutation in the following year by the appearance of the "Liber Chartarum Prioratus S. Andreæ," edited with all imaginable skill and elegance by the accurate Thomas Thomson. The preface is from the pen of the accomplished Cosmo Innes, who makes the following judicious observations on "the parts of our Record which remove the obscurity that has surrounded the history of the Culdees. Their transactions are abundant. We become familiar with them, and, but for their antiquity, their unintelligible name, and unknown founder, we should seek in vain for the grounds of the hot controversy which it has been their singular fate of late to excite. It is probable they most nearly resembled in their constitution the order of Canons Regular of St. Austin, who may be considered as the 'reformed' Culdees of Scotland : since we find the Culdees sometimes styled Canons ; the two orders first living together under the same rule of discipline ; and latterly the Austin Canons everywhere taking the place of the Culdees. What is certain, at least, we find the Culdees, like the other religious orders, acquiring lands and churches for their communities from kings and nobles, which Bishops and Popes confirmed in their favour. Indeed, generally they were intimately connected with the Bishop, and formed the chapter for Episcopal election in several dioceses, till their laxity in monastic observances, along with the introduction and increasing strictness of other monastic orders, led to their decay and downfall" (p. xv.).

In 1843 the old Columbite story of the Culdees was reproduced in reference to Iona, by the writer of the parochial memoir of Kilfinichen and Kilvicuen in the "New Statistical Account" (vol. vii., pt. 2, p. 323). But there had been an antecedent service in the publication of some original Culdee documents in the "Registrum de Dunfermelyn" by the Bannatyne Club, under the editorship of Cosmo Innes. This year also gave to the public "The History of St. Andrews," by the Rev. C. J. Lyon, the third chapter of which work treats of the Culdees, but misrepresents them as "acknowledging as their head, for several centuries, the celebrated abbot of Iona" (vol. i., p. 26).

But 1844 is the *annus mirabilis* in the literature of Culdee history. In it the Hon. Algernon Herbert made a series of communications to the "British Magazine," on the "Peculiarities of Culdeism," which were characterized by a strange combination of originality and learning with wild theory and sweeping assertion. He discusses the origin of the name with much ability, but is presently borne away in the development of his theory, that "under the shell of orthodoxy Culdeism contained an heterodox kernel." This he conceives to have consisted in their secret mysteries, and the practice of human sacrifice. He holds that Scotch freemasonry originated in Iona, and uses the term Culdeeism to denote what he calls the Oceanic churches, namely the Patrician church of Ireland and the Columban church of North Britain (vol. xxvi., pp. 1–13, 248–259).

These papers were answered in the same year and volume by the Rev. William Gowan Todd, under the signature W. G. T., who with much soberness and judgment exposed the weakness of his correspondent's hypothesis, and the fallacies in his arguments (pp. 149–155, 292–297). The Welsh portion of Mr. Herbert's communications were also met by Mr. John Griffith, in three articles under the same title (pp. 631–637 ; vol. xxvii., pp. 25–31, 141–152).

The following year produced a valuable contribution to the Culdee history in the Rev. William G. Todd's "History of the Ancient Church in Ireland," which was entirely new in its nature, and, as the writer states, was chiefly derived from information supplied by the great Irish scholar, Mr.

Eugene Curry. The chief interest in this dissertation arises from its being the first notice which was taken in print of the Irish Rule of the Celi-de, as preserved in the Leabhar Breac. The name Cele-de is interpreted *the spouse of God*, adopting Toland's acceptation of the word *céle ;* and a summary of the Rule is given (pp. 65–69).

The year 1847 produced the " Carte Monialium de Northberwic," edited for the Bannatyne Club by Cosmo Innes, in which are some notices of the Keledei of Muthel.

This book was followed, in 1848, by a still more important one, the " Liber S. Thome de Aberbrothoc," published by the same Society, under the able superintendence of the same editor. In the preface he informs us that " the chartulary is peculiarly rich in notices of the Culdees. At Abernethy a convent of them existed, though, perhaps, in little more but in name, to the end of the reign of William the Lion, when they seem to have expired, and there is no trace of their rights or claims having been transferred to St. Andrews. The chapter of Brechin at first consisted entirely of these Columbites. The successive bishops speak of them with affection as ' Keledei nostri.' Towards the end of William's reign we find an infusion of other clerks in the chapter ; the Prior of the convent of Culdees being still the President. In 1248, the last year of the reign of Alexander II., the Culdees have disappeared altogether, and the affairs of the Cathedral are managed in the ordinary modern form, by the Dean and Chapter" (p. xxvii.).

The Bollandists next take up the subject ; and Joseph Van Hecke, under the signature J. V. H. when dealing with St. Regulus, in 1853, treats largely of the Culdees, and even transfers to his pages a considerable portion of Dr. Jameson's history. ("Acta Sanctorum," Octob., tom. viii., pp. 163–180.) In the derivation of the name, he wavers, as a foreigner naturally might, between the conflicting theories of natives : "Hiberni enim a *Ceile* vel *Kele-De*, id est, *Servus Dei*, Deicola deducunt appellationem, alii vero a *Ceile, simul,* et *Dea, homo,* ita ut vox composita *homines in communi viventes* significet" (p. 165 *a*).

A second monograph on the Culdees appeared at Edinburgh in 1855, bearing this title : " The History of the Culdees, the Ancient Clergy of the British Isles," by the Rev. Duncan M'Callum. Its chronological range is from A. D. 177 to 1300, and within those limits embodies nearly every error and misapprehension concerning the class, which has been put forward from the days of Boece to its own publication.

Cosmo Innes again appears, in 1856, as the editor of the "Registrum Episcopatus Brechinensis." It is another valuable contribution to the charter history of the Scotch Culdees. " Among the few architectural relics of that early church, the Culdees of Brechin, like the Culdees of Abernethy, have left us one of those remarkable ' round towers' which serve to perpetuate the memory of the Irish origin of the church which gave them birth. We have charter evidence of a college of Culdees at Brechin existing before, and remaining for some time after, the erection of the Episcopal see. There is proof, indeed, that, upon its erection, the old Culdee convent and its Prior (submitting, it may be, to stricter rule of discipline), became, as perhaps in other cases, the electoral Chapter of the new Bishoprick. But the head of this Culdee convent, the Abbot of Brechin, had already become secularised, and had appropriated to himself, and transmitted to his family, the territories which his predecessors had administered for the church." (Preface, p. iv.)

Possessed of every scrap of information which Scottish records could furnish, the same indefatigable scholar sums up the evidence, in 1860, in these emphatic words : "Whatever may have been their original institution and discipline, the Culdees, in the time of David I., lived in a manner that must have been inconsistent with any monastic or collegiate discipline. They were generally married, which brought about the appropriation of the common property by the individual members of the house; and not less certainly led to a hereditary succession in the office of the priesthood, than which no greater mischief can befall a church and country. We are not to be surprised, then, that David, the friend of religion and civilization, endeavoured first to reform these irregular monks, and afterwards, finding them irreclaimable, everywhere superseded them, by the introduction of the strict orders brought from France and England." (" Scotland in the Middle Ages," p. 111; see also pp. 108–114.)

"The Culdees," a paper read, in Edinburgh, by the Rev. W. L. Alexander, D. D., on the 15th of August, 1860, proves that neither record evidence nor sober reasoning is sufficient to break down popular prejudice. The writer declines " to sketch the history of the Culdees," and contents himself with stating, "that, founded by Columba in the latter half of the sixth century, they spread themselves over the southern parts of Scotland, and established colleges on the model of the parent institution at Iona in many places, from which as centres they diffused the blessings of education, social culture, and religion, among the surrounding population, and despatched missionaries to carry the same to more distant regions." And it is well that he has avoided the dangerous field of history, when a chance approach to it results in the discovery that " It was avowedly to make room for men who would live according to *ordinem canoniculum*, that these men, whose offence was that they refused to live *regulantur* according to monastic rule, were expelled from the dwellings they had held for centuries, and from possessions they had done so much to render fruitful and of value." (" Ter-centenary of the Scottish Reformation, August, 1860." Edinb., 1860, pp. 13, 17.)

E.—EXTRACTS FROM ANCIENT IRISH TALES.

No. 1.—*Legend of St. Moling, from the Book of Leinster, a Manuscript of the early half of the twelfth Century.*

Ρechτaρ óóρum oc eρnaιзchι ιnna eclaιρ. Conacca ιn noclach cucι ιρa τech. Ετach coρcaρóa ιmbι ocuρ óelb óeρρcaιзche leιρ. Maιch ριn a chleριз aρρe. Ɑmιn aρ Molιnз. Cιó na bennachaι ρeo óampa aρ ιn τ-óclach. Cιa aται ρeo, aρ Mollιnз. Meρρe, oρ ρe, Cριρτ mac Óe. Nιeτaρ ón aρ Molιnз. Inταn óo τheιзe Cριρτ óo acallam na céle

One time, as he was praying in his church, he saw the youth *coming* to him into the house. A purple garment *was* about him, and he had a distinguished countenance. That is good, O cleric, said he. Amen, said Moling. Why dost thou not salute me? said the youth. Who art thou? said Moling. I, said he, am Christ, the Son of God. This is not possible, said Moling: when

nϽé nıpo chopcapϽa na . . . . . Ϸo cheıȝeϽ,
achc ıppechcaıϷ na cpóȝ .ı. na loϷop ocup
na clam.—Fol. 204 *b.*

Christ approaches to converse with the Céli-dé,
it is not in purple . . . . . he comes, but in forms
of the miserable, i. e. of the sick and lepers.

No. 2.—*The same Legend, from the Book of Lismore, a Manuscript of the fifteenth century.*

Molınȝ Luachpa Ϸalca Ϸo MaeϷoc Pepna.
Ip o Moeϸoc po ȝaϷpom cech Molınȝ : Ϸe
Uıϸ Ϸeaȝaϸ mopa Laıȝen Ϸo pom. Peachc
Ϸo Molınȝ oc epnaıȝchı ına eclaıp conn-
Ϸaca ınϷ oclach cuıce ıp ın ceach : ecach
copcapϷa uıme ocup ϷealϷ Ϸıppcaıϸéı laıp.
Maıc pın, a cleıpıȝ op pe. Amın, ap Molınȝ.
Mıpı Cpıopc mac Ϸe, op pe. Nı Ϸecap on,
ap Molınȝ. In can no céıȝeaϷ Cpıopc
Ϸ'acallam na ceıle-nϽe nı ba copcapϷa
pıȝϷa a eϷaé, acc ıp a peaécaıϷ na cpoȝ
ocup na loϷap ocup na clam, no céıȝeaϷ.—
Fol. 87 *aa.*

Moling of Luachair, foster-son of Maedoc of
Ferns. It was from Maedoc he received Tech-
Moling: of the Uí Deagad Mora of Leinster was
he. Once, as Moling was praying in his church,
he saw a youth *coming* to him into the house ;
garments of purple were about him, and he had
a distinguished countenance. That is good, O
cleric, said he. Amen, said Moling. I am
Christ, the Son of God, said he. It is not possible,
indeed, said Moling. When Christ comes to converse with the Celi-nDe, not royal purple *are* his
clothes ; but it is in the forms of the wretched,
and of the sick, and of the lepers that he comes.

No. 3.—The following story, copied by Mr. Eugene Curry from an ancient romance, in which is
related the capture of king Guaire Aidhne by Dermot son of Aodh Slaine, and his subsequent
removal to Tara, though it does not throw much light on the name Céle-dé, supposes it to have
been understood as a common designation before the year 645.

Maıé op Ϸıapmaıc, cıϷ apa nϷeıne Ȝuaıpe
ın po ϷeıϷ ucuc ? Inn ap Ϸıa pa ın ap
Ϸuıne ? MaϷ ap Ϸıa Ϸo Ϸepa nı ınnoppa.
MaϷ ap Ϸuıne nı cıϷpe ol acá co peıpȝ
ocup luınne. Ϸo éaeé éucu. Nı Ϸampa a
Ȝuaıpe ol ın Ϸpuch. Cınȝée peéaı. Nı
Ϸampa a Ȝuaıpe, ol ın clam. RocϷıa, op
Ȝuaıpe. Poéeıpc a ȝao Ϸó. Nı Ϸampa op
a céılı. Pocheıpc ın pcıach, ın Ϸelȝ, ın
mϷpacc, ın cpıpȝ. Nıc aın, op Ϸıapmaıc.
Cap pon claıϷeb a Ȝuaıpe ol Ϸıapmaıc.
Nı Ϸam a Ȝuaıpe, op ın Céıle Ϸé. An bıc
a Ϸıapmaıc, op Ȝuaıpe, ço call mo lénı Ϸım
Ϸon Ceılıu Ϸe. Maıch, op Ϸıapmaıc, po
ȝıallaıpıu Ϸo pıȝ aıle .ı. Ϸo mac Ϸé ; apo mo
ȝıallpa Ϸuıcpeo ımoppo, ol Ϸıapmaıc.

Well, said Diarmait, what does Guaire display
this great munificence for ? Is it for God ? is
it for man ? If it is for God, he will give something now ; if for man, he will not, because he
is angry and furious. Give me something, O
Guaire, said a buffoon. He let him pass. Something for me, O Guaire, said a leper. You shall
have it said Guaire, *and* he threw him his spear.
Something for me said his comrade, *and* he threw
him the shield, the brooch, the cloak, the girdle.
It will not save thee, said Diarmait. Come under the sword, O Guaire, said Diarmait. Something for me O Guaire, said a Céile-dé. Stay a
little, O Diarmait, said Guaire, till I take off my
shirt for the Ceïle-dé. Good said Diarmait, thou
hast submitted to another king, i. e. to the Son
of God : here is my submission to thee now, said
Diarmait.

Ατραραċτ ιαραm οcυρ nορ ταρbιρ αρρ α οιb ιαmαιb, οcυρ αρbeρατροm ba ιeċ ροτα α ιάm οno υαιρ ρικ οc ροċταικ κα Céιι κóé.

He arose then and bestowed from his two hands: and he said himself that one of his arms was longer than the other from that time out, that which was stretched to the Céli-dé.

No. 4.—*Extract from the Book of Fenagh.*

εοικ ιmορρο mac οcυρ ceιeoeι comαρba κα ηόζι ικ οαρα ηαρρτοι béc ρο τηόζ Ιρα.— Fol. 1 *a*, line 10.

John, also, son and céle-dei, comharb of the Virgin, was the twelfth Apostle whom Jesus chose.

s/he aes célide 'visitig four G'Dwyer 81 p 17.

F.—Extracts from the Irish Annals.

No. 1. A. D. 806 [*recte* 811].—Ιρ ικ mbιια-oαικρι τάικιc an Céιe Oé ooκ ραιρcce a κoeρ coραιbh τιορmαιb cen eτhαρ ιοιρ, αcυρ oo beρτeα ρoυαζ ρcριοbτα oo κικί bó τριαρ α κoéκαo ρροιceρτ oa ζηαοιoeιαιb, αcυρ oo beιρτί ρυαρ oορβōιρι í an τακ ταιρcceo an ρροιceρτ. No τeιζηeo an mac eccαιιρι cech ιαοι oαρρ an ραιρρζe ρooeρ ιαρ ττაιρcαιρικ an ρροιceρτა.—*Four Masters. Chronicon Scotorum*, 811.

In this year the Céle-dé came over the sea with dry feet, without a vessel; and a written roll was given him from heaven, out of which he preached to the Irish; and it was carried up again when the sermon was finished. This ec-clesiastic used to go every day southwards across the sea, after finishing his sermon.

No. 2. A. D. 919 [*recte* 921].—Ωαοκαch Céιe Oé oo τιαchταικ ooκ ραιρρζe ακιαρ oo oeκαm ρeċτα ερeακκ.—*Four Masters. Chronicon Scotorum*, 921.

Maonach, a Céle-dé, came across the sea west-wards, to establish laws in Ireland.

No. 3. *Eodem anno.*—ζορραιch Ua hιοmαιρ oo ζαbáιι ροραb ι καċċιιαιċ, αcυρ αρo Ωαċα oορccαικ ιαιρ ιαραί, αcυρ ια α ριόζ ιρικ Sαċαρκ ρια ρéι Ωαρταικ, αcυρ κα ταιζe eρκαιζe oo anacaι ιαιρ co κα ιυċτ oo Chéιιb Oé αcυρ oo ιοbραιb.—*Four Masters.*

Godfrey, grandson of Ivar, took up his residence at Ath-cliath; and Ardmacha was after-wards plundered by him and his army, on the Saturday before St. Martin's festival; but he spared the houses of prayer, with the Céli-dé, and the sick.

No. 4. An. 920 [*recte* 921].—Inoɼeд Aɼ-
macha hɪ .ɪu. Iд. Nouembɼɪɼ o Ʒallaɪb
Achachach .ɪ. o Ʒochbɼɪch oa Imhaɪɼ cum
ɼuo eχeɼcɪcu .ɪ. ɪɼɪn cɼachuɼn ɼɪa ɼeɪl
Maɼcaɪn, acaɼ na caɪʒɪ a aeɼnaɪʒhɪ дo-
anacal laɪɼ con a luchc Дe celɪbh Дe acaɼ
дɪ lobɼaɪbh, acaɼ ɪn ceall olchena, nɪɼɪ
ɼaucɪɼ ɪn ea cecɪɼ eχuɼcɪɼ ɼeɼ ɪncuɼɪam.—
Annals of Ulster.

The spoiling of Ardmacha on the 10th of November by the foreigners of Dublin, i. e. by
Godfrith, grandson of Ivar, with his army, on
the Saturday of St. Martin's feast; who saved
the houses of prayer, with their people of God,
the Céli-dé and the sick, and the whole church-
town, except some houses which were burned
through neglect.

No. 5. A. D. 947.—Annuɼ mɪɼabɪlɪum, ɪд
eɼc, accaɼla an дuɪllen дo nɪm, acaɼ accuд-
caɪд an Cele Дe дon ɼaɪɼɼʒe a nдeɼ дo
ɼɼoɼcec дo Ʒaeɪдealaɪb.—*Chronicon Scotorum.*

A year of wonders, that is, *in which* the leaf
came from heaven, and in which the Céle-dé
used to come off the sea from the south, to preach
to the Gaeidhel.[*]

No. 6. A. D. 1031 [*recte* 1032].—Conд na
nbochc, cenд Celeд nДe acaɼ ancoɪɼɪ
Cluana mɪc Nóɪɼ, дo cеɪд cɪonól aɪɼʒe дo
дoccaɪд Cluana ɪ nIɼeal Chɪaɼáɪn, acaɼ ɼo
eдhbaɪɼ ɼɪche bó uaɪд ɼeɪn ɪnncí. Aɼ дó дo
ɼáɪдeaд—

    A Chuɪnn Chluana,
    Accloɼ cú a hEɼɪnд ɪ nAlbaɪn :
    A chɪnд oɼдaɪn.
    Nochan uɼa дo chɪll дaɼʒaɪn.
          —Four Masters.

Conn-na-nBocht, head of the Céli-dé, and anchorite, of Cluain-mic-Nois, the first that invited a party of the poor of Cluain to Iseal-
Chiarain, and who presented twenty cows of his
own to it. Of this it was said :—

    " O Conn of Cluain,
    Thou wast heard from Erin in Alba :
    O head of dignity,
    It will not be easy to plunder thy church."

No. 7. A. D. 1072 [*recte* 1073].— Cɼén
coɪnnɼeд la Muɼchaд mac Conchoдaɪɼ ɪ
nIɼɪoll Chɪaɼáɪn, acaɼ ɼoɼɼ na Célɪд дe, ʒo
ɼo maɼдaд ɼechcaɪɼe na mbochc ann, conɪд
дe cuccaд Maʒ Núɼa дo na дoccaɪд.—*Four
Masters.*

A forcible refection was taken by Murchadh,
son of Conchobhar, at Iseal-Chiarain, and from
the Céli-dé, so that the superintendent of the
poor was killed there : for which Magh-Nura
was given to the poor.

---

[*] There is no entry corresponding to this, at the parallel year, in the Annals of Ulster (946), or the Four Masters
(945); but the Annals of Inisfallen, at 931, have Дuɪlenn дo nɪmh ɼoɼ alcoɪɼ nImblecha Ibaɪɼ, acaɼ ɪn cén
дo labɼoo ɼɪɼ na дoenɪb, acaɼ ɪɼʒanca ɪle aɼchena ɪɼ ɪn bluaдaɪn ɼe, " A leaf from heaven on the altar
of Imlech-Ibhair, and the bird spoke to the people, and numerous wonders besides in this year." Dr. O'Conor
incorrectly renders дuɪlenn by *pluvia:* In the romantic tale called " The Sea-wanderings of Snedgus and Mac
Riagáil" (MS., T. C. D., H. 2. 16, p. 391), mention is made of a дuɪllen or " leaf," which was given to the wan-
derers, and which was afterwards preserved on Columcille's altar at Kells. See Reeves's Adamnan's Life of St.
Columba, p. 323; O'Curry's Lectures, p. 332.

No. 8.—The preceding entry has no counterpart in the Annals of Ulster, but is borrowed from the Annals of Clonmacnois, of which the following is Conall Mageoghegan's rendering:—A. D. 1069 [*recte* 1073], "Murrogh O'Melaghlyn, prince of Meath, did so oversette the family of Moylekyeran mac Con-ne-Moght in Isill-kyeran, and the poor of that house, that the steward of that family was slain by them: for which cause Moyvoura was granted to the poor."

No. 9. A. D. 1076 [*recte* 1077].—Slóiʒheaḋ la cléipchiḃ Leiċe Moʒa im mac Maoilḃalua ʒo Cluain Dolcáin ḃionnapḃaḋ 1 Rónáin a Cluain Dolcáin ap nʒabail aḃoaine ḋó ḃap papuʒhaḃh mic Maoilḃalua. Conaḋ annpin ḃo paḃaḋ peʒlep co na ḟepann i cCluain Dolcáin ḃo Celiḃ Dé ʒo bpaċ maille pe ḃa piċiċ ḃécc ḃo cuʒaḋ in eneclann ḃo mac Maoilḃalua.—*Four Masters.*

An army was led by the clergy of Leth-Mogha, with the son of Maeldalua. to Cluain-Dolcain, to expel Ua Ronain from Cluain-Dolcain, after he had assumed the abbacy, in violation of the son of Maeldalua. It was on this occasion that a church, with its land, at Cluain-Dolcain, was granted to Céli-dé for ever, together with twelve score cows, which were given as a mulct to the son of Maeldalua.

No. 10. A. D. 1132.—Uaipeipʒe Ua Neachcain, cenḃ Céleḃ nDé Cluana mic Noip, acup a ppuiċ ḟenóip ḃéʒ.—*Four Masters.*

Uareirghe Ua Neachtain, head of the Céli-dé of Cluain-mic-Nois, and its venerable senior, died.

No. 11. A. 1164.—Maiċi muincepi la .1. in pacapc mop Auʒupcin, acap in ḟep leiʒinn .1. Dubpiḃe, acap in ḃipeptach .1. Mac Ʒillaḃuiḃ, acap cenn na Ceile nDé .1. Mac Ḟopcellaiʒ, acap maiċi muinncepi la apcena, ḃo ċiaċċain ap cenn comapba Coluim cille .1. Laiċbeptaċ hui bpolcain ḃo ʒabail aḃoaine la a comaipli Somaipliḃ acap ḟep Aepep Ʒaiḃel acap Innpi Ʒall, cono apcaei comapba Pacpaic acap pi Epenn .1. Ua Lochlainn acap maiċi cenel Eoʒain e.—*Annals of Ulster.*

The chiefs of the family of Ia, viz., Augustin the great priest, and Dubsidhe the lector, and Mac Gilladuff the hermit, and Mac Fairchellaigh the head of the Céli-nDé, and the chiefs of the family of Ia in general, came to meet the coarb of Columcille, namely Flaithbertach Ua Brolchain, *to invite him* to accept the abbacy of Ia, by the advice of Somhairle and the men of Argyle and Innse Gall. But the coarb of Patrick, the king of Ireland, namely, Ua Lochlainn, and the chiefs of the Cinel-Eoghain, prevented it.

No. 12. A. D. 1170.—Maolmópḃa mac Uaipeipʒe, ppuiċ penóip ḃéḟeapcaċ, ponup acup paiḃḃpep Cluana mic Noip, cenḃ a Chéleḃ Dé, ḃo écc i mi Nouember.—*Four Masters.*

Maelmordha, son of Uaireirghe, a learned charitable senior, the prosperity and affluence of Cluain-mic-Nois, and head of its Céli-dé, died in the month of November.

No. 13. A. D. 1200.—Uaipéipʒe mac Maoilmópḃa mic Uaipéipʒe Ui Neachcain uapal ppuiċ ḃo ppuiċiḃ Cluana mic Noip,

Uaireirghe, son of Maelmordha, son of Uaireirghe O'Neachtain, one of the noble sages of Cluain-mic-nois, a man full of the love of God.

M

pep lán vo veḟepc, acuṗ vá ʒach poalċıó
apċena, acuṗ ceann Céle nᴅé Cluana vécc
an veaċmaó lá vo ṁapċa.—*Four Masters.*

No. 14. A. D. 1479.—Pıapuṗ mac Nıoclaıṗ
hUı Plannaccaın váı ına ċananaċ copaıó hı
cCloċaṗ, ına ṗeappún acuṗ ına ṗpıóıp Céıle
nᴅé ına phacpıpca ı nᴅaıṁınıp, acuṗ ına
oıpıcel ap Loċ Eıpne, paoı véṗeapcaċ ċpaıó-
veaċ veıʒeınıʒ vaonnaċcaċ vecc ıap mbpeıċ
buaóa ó veaṁan acuṗ ó óoṁan.—*Four Masters.*

No. 15. A. D. 1595.—ᴅala an ʒobepnopa
no lıon pıóe vpeıpcc, acuṗ vo lonnaṗ ıap
mapvaó a ḃpacaṗ, acuṗ po popconʒaıp pop
a ṗlóʒ aıóme coʒla an caıpceoıl vo óénaṁ
leó vuṗ an ccaéṁpaıccíp a epʒaḃaıl pop
ṁuıncıp Uı ᴅoṁnaıll bácaṗ ann. ᴅo pónaó
leó poṁ ınᴅpın vo ċpanncaınʒel, acuṗ vo
ċuḃaċlaıḃ na cCéıleó nᴅé, acuṗ vá ʒaċ
aıóme panʒacaṗ a leṗ baı ıpın maınípcıṗ.—
Four Masters.

and of every virtue, and head of the Céli-ndé of
Clon[macnois], died on the tenth of March.

Piarus, son of Nicholas O'Flanagan, who had
been a canon chorister at Clogher, a parson, and
prior of Céli-dé, a sacristan at Devenish, an official on Loch-Erne, a charitable, pious, truly
hospitable, and humane man, died, after having
gained the victory over the devil and the world.

As for the governor [of Connacht], he was
filled with anger and fury after the killing of his
kinsman; and he ordered his army to construct
engines for demolishing the castle [of Sligo], to
see whether they could take it from O'Donnell's
people, who were in it. These they constructed
of the rood-screen, and of the cubicles of Céli-
dé, and of other furniture which they found be-
fitting for the purpose in the monastery.

G.—METRICAL RULE OF THE CÉLI DÉ.

ᴅo Chelıu ᴅe ınpo pıp.

ᴅıa mbem po mam ċleıpċeċca,
    Iṗ uapal ın beṗṗ;
Uıchıʒem ın noebh eclaıp
    In cach cpach vo ʒpeṗṗ.
Ancan po chlomap clocán,
    Nı pupaıl ıncípp,
Cocbam cpıohe polam puaṗ,
    Ceılʒem ʒnuıppı pípp.
Canam pacep ocuṗ ʒlóıp,
    Nachaṗ caıplı cpıpc,
Sénam bpuınne ocuṗ ʒnuıp
    Aṗóe cpuıchı Cpıpc.

OF THE CÉLI DÉ DOWN HERE.

If we be under the yoke of clergyhood,
    Noble is the calling:
We frequent the holy church
    At every canonical hour perpetually.
When we hear the little bell,
    The tribute is indispensable;
We lift up a ready heart,
    We cast down our faces.
We sing a Pater and a Gloria,
    That no curse fall *upon us;*
We consecrate the breast and face
    With the sign of Christ's cross.

Map po hippam in neclaip
Slechtam co bo chpi;
Ni pillem ᵹluíne nama
In vomnach Veuí.
Ceilebpam ip cuinpiᵹem,
Cen lobpa cen lén;
Spuich in pep aoᵹlávamap,
Coimviu nime nél.
Piᵹlem leᵹam aipnaiᵹchem,
Cach immet a nipt:
Peibh na pée peᵹha lat,
Ria ᵹloipi co teipt.
Caet cač ᵹpav pia čomavap
Peib vo beba coip,
Amail ainmniᵹčip vo cač,
Ochá teipt co noin.
In taep ᵹpaiv von naipniᵹchi,
Vonv aipppiunv co cept;
Aep leiᵹinn vo popcetul,
Peibh ata a nept.
In vocbav vonv umalloit,
Peib počá atli:
Ap ip vilep vo viabul
Copp no vémeni.
Lubap vonv anecnaiv,
Vo peip cleipech caiv:
Saechap ecnava na ᵹhin,
Saechap buipb na laim.
Ceilebpav cač oen tpacha
La cač nopv vo ᵹniam:
Cpi plečtain pia ceilebpav,
A tpi inna nviaivh.
Cuae ocup vichpato,
Raichínchi cen chlóen
Cen povopv cen imchompopib.
Vleᵹap vo cač oen.

As we enter the church,
We kneel thrice;
We bend not the knee only
On the Sundays* of the living God.
We celebrate, and we instruct,
Without weakness, without sorrow:
Noble is the person we invoke,
The Lord of the heaven of clouds.
We watch, we read, we pray,
Each according to his strength:
According to the time, you contemplate,
At gloria until tierce.
Each order proceeds according to its duty.
According to the proper manner,
As is appointed to each,
From tierce to none.
The people in orders (priests), for prayer,
For the mass rightly:
The readers for teaching
According as is their strength.
The youth for humility,
As is in the law:
For the property of the devil
Is a body that hath pride.
Labour for the illiterate,
After the will of pious clerics:
The wise man's work *is* in his mouth,
The ignorant man's work *is* in his hand.
Celebration each canonical hour
With each order we perform:
Three genuflexions before celebration,
Three more after it.
Silence and fervour,
Tranquillity without guile,
Without murmur, without contention,
Is due of every one.

—*MS. Trin. Coll. Dubl.* H. 2. 16. cols. 224, 225.

* Domnach may signify " church;" but possibly there is reference here to the practice of standing which was anciently enjoined on the Lord's Day. See Bingham, Antiqq., lib. xiii., cap. 8, § 3 (Works, vol. iv., p. 325, ed. 1840).

H.—Prose Rule of the Céli Dé.

Incipiṫ Riaġail na Celeḋ nḊe.
O Moelṗuain cecinit.

biaiṫ pṗointiġe acaṗ maġniṗicaṫ ṗaiṗ eṫ
eġo ueṗo acaṗ aṗaile: hi ṗeṗṗam chanaṗ.

Ṗoġni aṗṗ ṫiuġ ḋo meṗcaḋ acaṗ mil ṗaiṗ
ciṗṁe na pṗimṗollamun .i. hi noṫlaic acaṗ
in ḋi chaiṗc.

Ni ḋleġaiṗ ṗleḋuġaḋ no ol coṗma in hiṗ
noctiḃuṗ, ḋaiġ ḋula ḋo laim aṗ a baṗach.

Loimm naiṗṗ in ḋominiciṗ in choṗġaiṗ
maiṗ ḋo aeṗ ḋuṗṗenḋi. Ciḋ n-ochṫ ṗelainḋ
imoṗṗo i nḋomnaiġiḃ in choṗġaiṗṗ maiṗ, ni
cuṗċaill, ni caiṫeḋ imoṗṗo ṗiam na iaṗam,
niṗi in ṗeṗia Ṗaṫṗici, acaṗ ciḋ in ṫan ḋin
ḋoṗcuiṗiṫeṗ ṗi ṗoṗ ain no ceṫain, iṗ loimm
naiṗṗ ḋoġniṫeṗ inḋe hinḋoin no alliḋ.
O ḋo cuiṗiṫeṗ ṗeċṫaṗ aine, iṗ anḋ ḋoġniṫeṗ ṗelainḋ (.i. leaṫ).

Aṗan ḋin, ni ḃi imṫhoṗmach ḋe laṗ na
Celiuḋa Ḋé, ciḋ iṗ na ṗollamnaiḃ, aċṫ ḋo
ḋiġ acaṗ anḋlanḋ acaṗ aliṗ ṗeḃuṗ. Ḃṗaiṗ-
ṗeċ ḋin ni ḃiġbanḋ in aṗan, cia ṫecma ni ḋi,

Here beginneth the Rule of the Céli Dé.
From [what] Moelruain composed.

The Beatus of the refectory, and Magnificat in addition to it, and Ego vero,* &c.: it is sung standing.

Thick milk and honey are mixed, on the eve of the chief festivals, i. e. at Christmas,† and the two Easters.‡

Feasting or the drinking of beer is not lawful on these nights, because of going under the hand§ to-morrow.

Skimmed milk *is allowed* on the sundays of the great Lent‖ to people of severe penance. Though eight selanns¶ are not prohibited on the sundays of the great Lent, they do not consume them before or after,** unless on the festival of Patrick; and when, however, this falls on friday or wednesday, skimmed milk is what is used on it, at noon or allid. When it goes beyond friday, the selanns are then used (i. e. half).††

Of bread the Célidé do not get an increase, even on the solemn festivals, but they do of drink and condiment, and other things. But kale, though they should have some of it, does not

---

* Psalm lxviii. 14, or lxix. 6 (Vulg.). The *Beatus* was probably the benediction or grace said in the refectory before meat; the *Magnificat*, S. Luke, i. 46.

† The Irish noṫlaic, and the Welsh *nadolig*, are forms of *natalicium*, as the French *noël* is of *natalis*.

‡ From *pascha* comes, by the accustomed conversion of *p* into *c*, the Irish chaiṗc. The "Great Easter" was Easter-day; the "little Easter," was the Sunday after, or Clausum Paschæ.

§ That is, confession. The priest raises his hand in the absolution, whence the modern expression, ḋul ṗa láim ṗaġaiṗc, "going under the hand of the priest," denotes going to confession.

‖ The "great Lent" was the forty days before Easter; the "little Lent" was the period preceding Christmas, or Advent. The Irish choṗġaiṗ, the Welsh *grawys*, the Breton *chuarais*, are loan words from the Latin *quadragesima*.

¶ A *selann* was a ration of honey consisting of four eggfuls.

** That is, on the intervening week days.

†† That is, half a selann, or two eggfuls, each.

baiʒ anblannꞃibe leoꞃam .ı. aꞃꞃ ꞃuıꞃꞃı acaꞃ
nı hımm.

Oꞃou eıꞃc bın, no nı bo ṁoeċaıl no bo
ċaıꞃꞃe, no oʒ ćıꞃımm, no ublaı. Ní bíʒaıb ní
be aꞃán ınbꞃın ulı, mab bec be nach ae.
Non hec omnıa ꞃımul. Ublaı, ımoꞃꞃo, ma-
bac moꞃa, ıꞃ loꞃ a cúıc, no ꞃé laꞃın aꞃan.
Cıb ac beca bın, ıꞃ loꞃ bó béc bıb.

Cꞃı buınbe no ceċeoꞃa be luꞃꞃ. Mıllꞃen
bın no bꞃuċcan ní caıceꞃ leoꞃom, aċc ꞃıc
ċaıꞃꞃe be.

Doʒnıcheꞃ ımoꞃꞃo ʒꞃuċꞃach boıb aċc nı
ċeıc bınıc ınb acaꞃ nı auꞃċuıll ıaꞃam. buʒ
aıꞃe bın nı auꞃċuıll ꞃobıch ıꞃ aꞃan ꞃom.

Meaoʒ mıllꞃen bın nı hebaꞃ a oenuꞃ, aċc
cumaıꞃcċheꞃ ꞃoꞃ ʒꞃucın beoꞃ.

Iꞃe ın cuaꞃlocub aꞃ ċaıꞃc .ı. oʒa acaꞃ
blonoca acaꞃ ꞃeoıl oꞃꞃ n-allaıb acaꞃ mucc
n-allaıb.

Foʒnı bın ꞃoꞃcꞃaıb ꞃıach ꞃoꞃ coıce acaꞃ
blıʒꞃe acaꞃ cuċcꞃoꞃı ꞃo bıchın boꞃca ın
coꞃaıb ecıꞃ aꞃꞃ acaꞃ aꞃbaꞃ.

bıclıb na ꞃeola hı coꞃʒaꞃ maꞃ ın can bıꞃ
ı ceꞃcı aaꞃılle, aċc bın mınabe ʒell be an-
mannaıb ıꞃ ꞃeꞃꞃ a benum.

Felı ꞃꞃuchı bocuıꞃıcheꞃ ꞃoꞃ baꞃbaın no
maıꞃc ꞃꞃıa coꞃʒuꞃa bıa neċcaıꞃ leċh ꞃelaınb
ınncıb acaꞃ boċcan be ċoꞃmaım no mebʒuꞃce; mına be bın loım mebʒuꞃce no cınʒıc
ċoꞃmma.

subtract from the bread, because it is deemed
only condiment by them, i. e. *they get* milk in
addition to it, but not butter.

A slice of fish, or some maethail,[*] or cheese, or
a dry egg, or apples; all these do not diminish the
bread, if *there be* only a little of each. All these
things are not *used* at the same time. In case of
apples, if they be large, five or six of them, with
the bread, are sufficient; but if they be small,
twelve of them are sufficient.

Three or four sprigs of leeks. No millsen[†]
then nor druchtan[‡] is consumed with them, but
cheese is made of it.

Curds also are made for them, but no rennet
goes into it; and then it is not forbidden, and
the reason that it is not prohibited is, because it
is *considered* bread.

Millsen whey then is not drunk alone, but it
is mixed with grutin.[§]

The relaxation at Easter, i. e. eggs, and lard,
and the flesh of wild deer, and wild hogs.

Additional fines are imposed upon the cook, and
the milker, and the kitchener, in consequence of
spilling the produce, both milk and corn.

Fleshmeats may be used by you in the great
Lent, when other things are in scarcity: but
then, unless lives are in danger, it is better to
observe it.[‖]

On the noble festivals which fall on thursday
or tuesday, half selanns *are allowed,* and a
bochtan[¶] of beer or of diluted whey. If there be
not skimmed-milk, then diluted whey, or a goblet of beer *instead.*

---

* The word *maethail* is found in the sense of biestings. Here it probably signifies a kind of curds.
† *Millsen* may signify " cheese-curds." See O'Reilly, voc. Mılꞃean.
‡ *Druchtan,* "cheese-whey." O'Reilly.
§ *Grutin* is the name for the small curds which remain mixed with the whey, after the removal of the thicker
substance.
‖ Literally " to make it," that is, to perform the Lent fast.
¶ A *bochtan* was a measure equal to twelve eggfuls.

Pıꞅ ꞅollaċ bec ꝺo ṁenaꝺaıᵹ anꝺ, .ı. ceꞇꞃuıme. Cınᵹıꞇ coꞃma ꝺın, ın ꞇan ꝺo necmaıc nı heꝺaꞃ ꝺeoᵹ ꝺı, cıa noꞃ beꞇh hıꞇꞇu, aċꞇ lommanꝺ, uaıꞃ eꞃᵹaꞃıꝺ ꞃıꝺe hıꞇꞇaıꝺ acaꞃ nı luᵹa ꞃıanꞃ ꞃaılꞇe ꝺıꝺ aꞃ ꝺo ꝺıᵹ.

Nı ꝺenꞇaꞃ ımoꞃꞃo ꞃelaınꝺ ımbe loımmeꝺᵹuꞃce ınnꞇıb oıꝺċe maıꞃꞇe no ꝺaꞃꝺaın, no ꞃaꞇhaꞃn, no ꝺomnaıᵹ cıꝺ ꞃeċꞇaꞃchoꞃᵹuꞃ, cıꝺ ꞃeıl ꞃꞃuꞇhı, aċꞇ ın ꞃeıl bıꞃ ꞃoꞃ luan ꞃoceꞃꞇaꞃ ꞃoꞃ maıꞃꞇ, a mbı ꞃoꞃ ceꞇaın ꞃoceꞃꞇaꞃ ꞃoꞃ ꝺaꞃꝺaın, ambı ꞃoꞃ aınꝺıꝺen ꞃoceꞃꞇaꞃ ꞃoꞃ maıꞃꞇ ıaꞃ nꝺomnach.

Loım lemnaıċꞇ mına be naċ naıꞃ naıll, ꞅeꞇhꞃuıme ꞃaıꞃ ꝺı aqua.

Nı nech buꝺeꞃꞃın ꝺın ꝺaꞃbeıꞃ ꞃıach naılme laꞃ na Celıuꝺa Ꝺé, ꞃeꝺ alıuꞃ, acaꞃ ꝺo beꞃaꞃ o noꞇlaıc ꞃꞇeıll, acaꞃ o ṁınchaıꞃc cu noꞇlaıc moꞃ ıꞇeꞃum.

Inꞇı ꞇeꞇı ꞃꞃıuꞃ ꝺo mıꝺnoċꞇ ꝺo ꞃacaꞃꝺaıcc nama ċeıꞇ, acaꞃ nı ċeıꞇ ꝺo ċaılech, acaꞃ nı ċeıꞇ ıꞇeꞃum uꞃque aꝺ ꞃınem annı.

Ceıꞇ ıaꞃam ꝺo mıꝺnoċꞇ ꝺıblıaꝺna acaꞃ ꝺo

There is a small collation of gruel,* i. e. one fourth *of a meal.* When the goblet of beer happens, no draught of it is taken, though there should be thirst, but a lommand,† for it provokes thirst, and ye are not the less sensible of pleasure for your drink.

No selanns, in which may be skimmed milk whey, are made on the eves *of festivals which fall* on tuesdays or thursdays, or saturdays, or sundays, whether outside the Lent, or a noble festival, but the festival which falls on monday is put on tuesday; that which falls on wednesday is put on thursday, and that which falls on friday is put on tuesday after sunday.

New milk skimmed *is allowed* if there be no other kind of milk, and one fourth *part* of water mixed with it.

It is not a person himself that gives fiach nailme‡ among the Célidé, but another; and it is given from Epiphany§ and from little Easter‖ to the great Christmas following.

He who goes first to midnight,¶ it is to the sacrifice only he goes, and not to the chalice, and he goes not again until the end of the year.

He goes afterwards to midnight, the second

---

* Menaꝺach is explained by ᵹaꞃbán, "bran" or "whole-meal," in the MS. Glossary, Trin. Coll. Dubl. H. 3. 18.

† The word *lomman* is proved to mean "a sup" or "mouthful," by its being placed here in opposition to ꝺeoᵹ "a draught," or "drink." In the Glossary cited in last note we find the word thus explained: Loman .ı. ıꞃ connꞇan .ı. cꞃoꞃꞇa beꞇ ꞃꞃıꞃ na lomanaıb .ı. ꞃꞃıꞃ na bulᵹemaıb, "Loman, It is prohibited to practise the lomans, i. e., the sups." See O'Reilly, voc. bolᵹam.

‡ Pıach signifies "value," "price," "debt," and (n)aılmeaꝺ, "a prayer." It probably denotes some religious exercise. The term ꞃıachaıbne ꝺccurs lower down in the sense of "debt."

§ Epiphany, or Twelfth-day, is here styled Noꞇlaıc ꞃꞇeıll, "Christmas of the fragment," possibly from the old custom of breaking Twelfth cake on that day. In Archbishop Daniel's Irish version of the Book of Common Prayer (1608), the Circumcision is called La Noꝺloᵹ beaᵹ, "Little Christmas-day." So in the edition of 1702, Cımċıoll-ᵹeaꞃꞃaꝺ Chꞃıoꞃꝺ ꝺa nᵹoıꞃꞇıoꞃ ᵹo coıꞇċmn lá Noꝺlac beaᵹ, "The Circumcision of Christ, commonly called Little Christmas-day."

‖ That is, the Sunday after Easter, variously called, Quasimodo, Clausum Paschæ, Dominica in Albis, Low Sunday. See O'Donovan, Annals of the Four Masters, vol. i., p. 373.

¶ This seems to denote either a canonical hour, or some particular solemnity, possibly the *Nox Sacrata,* or Easter-eve, as distinguished from the cuꞃꞃ na caꞃc, or full service of Easter.

ċupp na caṙc apa baṙach. Ċepċia uice ḋi miḋnoċċ acaṙ ḋi ċupp na caṙc acaṙ noċlac. Ċepċia uice aṙ noċlaic acaṙ ḋi ċaiṙc acaṙ cinȝceḋiṙ. Ǫuinċo anno aṙ ṙollamnu acaṙ cinḋ .xl. oiḋche beoṙ. Sexċo anno cinḋ ceċ miṙ. Sepċimo anno cinḋ cec coecċiȝiṙ. Ṗoṙċ .uii. anno iṙ anḋ ċeiċ ceċ ḋomnaiȝ. Ṗaċeṙ ṙaiṙ ṙṙiuṙ acaṙ Ḋeuṙ in aḋiuċoṙium uṙque ṙeṙċina acaṙ ḋa ḋí láim ṙuaṙ ṙṙia nem acaṙ aiṙṅḋe na cṙoiċe coċ laim nḋeiṙṙ iaṗam ṙimiliċeṙ in ceċ aiṙḋ ṙic ✝ ṙiṙ acaṙ ṙuaṙṙ.

Iṙ hi ċṙa comṗaiṙ chṙáḃuiḋ leoṙaiḋe, aċċ iṙ cṙoṙṙiȝell ṙṙiuṙ, luiṙech léiṙe ḋin a ainmṙiḋe.

In ċan na ċiaȝaṙ ḋo láim ḋia ḋomnaiȝ ċiaȝaṙ ḋia ḋaṙḋain ina ḋeȝaiḋ, aṙ iṙ ṙo ṗaċa anaḋ cu ḋomnach aile ḋon ċí ċeiċ ḋo láim ḋo ȝṙeṙ ceċ ḋomnaiȝ; uaiṙ iṙ auṙ- ḋalċa leoṙom ḋo ȝṙéṙ in ḋí lá ṙin ṙṙi hoiṙṙenḋ.

Ṅi hécen ḋin na minchoiḃṙena ḋo miimṙaċiḃ acaṙ coṙaiḃ eṙṙai acaṙ écnach acaṙ ṙeṙȝ acaṙ aṙaile ḋo ṗuiṙeċ cu ḋomnach, aċċ a ṗaiṙiċiu amail ḋo ṙaȝḃaiċheṙ ṙoceċoiṙ.

year, and to corpus Paschæ on the morrow. The third time, to midnight, and to corpus Paschæ, and Christmas. The fourth time, at Christmas, and the two Easters, and Whitsunday.* In the fifth year, on the solemn festivals, and at the end of forty nights also. In the sixth year, at the end of every month. In the seventh year†, at the end of every fortnight. After the seventh year, they go every sunday : Pater sair‡ first, and Deus in adjutorium down to Festina,§ and thy two hands up towards heaven, and *making* the sign of the cross afterwards with the right hand in like manner in every direction, thus ✝ down and up.

It is the shrine of devotion with them, but the crossfigel‖ previously. The Armour of devotion is therefore its name.

When they do not go to hand¶ on sunday, they go on the thursday after it, for it would be too long to wait till the sunday following, for the person who habitually goes to hand every sunday, because these two days are always special with them at mass.

It is not compulsory to delay minute confessions of evil thoughts, and faults of idleness and peevishness and anger, &c., till sunday, but they may be confessed as they occur at once.

---

* From *Quinquagesima*, the Latin equivalent of Pentecost, comes the Irish loan word cinȝceḋiṙ.

† Seven years appears to have been a probationary term, as the religious duties increase annually to the seventh year. See Adamnan's Life of St. Columba (Irish Archæol. and Celt. Soc.), pp. 157-162.

‡ This may be a hymn beginning *Pater excelsus*, or it may be intended for *Pater Noster*.

§ That is,—V. " Deus in adjutorium meum intende." R. " Domine ad adjuvandum me festina."

‖ From *vigilia* comes ṗel, " a festival," and ṗiȝil, which O'Clery explains by uṙnaiȝċe ḋo ní ḋuine aṙ a ȝluiniḃ maṙ aċa ṙleaċċain, no meḋiċaċio, " a prayer which a person makes on his knees, such as genuflexion, or meditation." Again, he explains Cṙoiṙṗiȝill .i. uṙnaiȝċe, no ṙaiṙe, ḋo ȝní ḋuine aṙ a ȝlúiniḃh, aȝaṙ a lama ṙinċe a ȝcṙoiṙ, " A prayer or watching, which a person performs on his knees, with his hands extended cross-wise."—*Glossary in voc.* From this O'Reilly borrows " Cṙoiṙṗiȝil, praying with hands across."—*Dict.* But the exact meaning is determined by the following passage from the second Vision of St. Adamnan, compared with Exodus, xvii. 11,—uaiṙ in ċan conócḃaḋ Moiṙ a lamu h-i ċnoṙṙiȝill ṙṙi Ḋia no muiḋeḋ ṙoṙṙ na ȝenċiḃ. " for whenever Moses raised his hands *in* crossfigil to God, the heathen were defeated." Hence it appears that the gesture was that of the arms extended laterally, not crossed on the breast.

¶ That is, to confession. See note §, p. 84, *supra.*

In ci dorbeir a coibrena do anamchararc
mad pendi ina per ni hecen do a cabairc dó
anmcararc aile, acc in dorazba porc. Ni
carba din in coibrenuzud minic o bir in
brirrid minic beor.

Cenla ni dencar relaind and acc loimm
nairr, no cinzic dorma, acar mad cecma
leiz mela, ar ir znachride i pollamnaib acar
aprpelib cen pizill na cen piachaibne ind.
Meadzurce acar aran ann, priccaicher
an proind iaram iar noin.

In porraic din biaic do cecul cen bechaid
con porraic, procepc na poraice cra iaram.

Celebrad errarcain incan zaibcher ec-
nairce neich a ainnm bairce irred rozni
prirr. Sailm cra in can zabar. Cec la
zabail dib i perrom, aranle irruide, uair
incan bicher irruide do puirrim coclad. Dia
mbecher din ni bur hiriu ir perram ir emilc.
Di biaic dec arra na .lll. cenimmachca.

Pollach menadchi ar na peli, acar ar na
domnaizib do oerrpendi, acar ní bi raire
pizle doib acc in oen noin cec peli rruchi
ecir caire acar cinzcedir, mairc acar dar-
dain ecir di noclaic.

He who makes his confessions to a soul-
friend,[*] if he has done penance according to him,
need not make them again to another soul-friend,
except what he may have committed afterwards.
Frequent confession is of no profit, when the
violation is frequent also.

The selanns are not made on the cenla,[†] but
skimmed milk, or a goblet of beer, and if there
happen to be any honeycombs, for this is usual
in solemnities and high festivals, without vigils
or debt for it. Whey and bread *for dinner*, and
the dinner is taken after nona.

Now at the ablution, the Beatus is to be sung,
while they are in ablution. The preaching of
the ablution afterwards.

At the singing of the vespers,[‡] when intercession[§] is sung for a person, his baptismal name
is to be mentioned in it. When a psalm is sung,
it is to be sung by them successively, standing
and sitting, for when they sit *only* it induces
sleep, and if they stand too long it is tiresome.

Twelve Beatuses *are recited* during the Psalms.

A collation of gruel on festivals and sundays
to penitents, and there is no freedom from vigils
allowed to them, but on one evening, every high
festival between Easter and Whitsuntide; on
tuesday and thursday between the two Christ-
mases.‖

---

* Anamchara is a compound loan word from *animæ carus*, and is that which is commonly used to denote a
"confessor." In old Latin lives of the Irish saints it is generally rendered "pater confessionis," or "pater confessa-
rius." Colgan explains it by *synedrus*.

† This word is as yet unexplained. Possibly it may be derived from cen, "a feast."

‡ Errarcain is a loan word representing the Latin *vespertinus*.

§ The word ecnairc signifies "litany," "intercession," for the absent, and is more general than *requiem*, as it
extended to the living as well as the dead. See p. 94, *infra*. In the MS. Glossary, H. 3. 18., Trin. Coll. Dubl., ar
ecnairc is explained by ar imride, "at the intercession" (pp. 617, 626). It also occurs as a gloss on the word arnra
.i. ecnairc nad, "saying for the absent," (ibid., p. 1616). In the Tripartite Life of St. Patrick, it is used in reference
to the dead: roadnacht la Pacricc iarom ocur rozabad a eccnairce, "she was buried by Patrick afterwards, and her requiem was sung." (Brit. Mus., Egerton, 93, fol. 16, *a b*.) We find ecndairc as an ancient
gloss on *absens* in Zeuss, Gram. Celt., vol. ii., p. 853.

‖ See note, §, p. 86, *supra*.

Inti cpa nac caich peoil do ʒnep bopʒni papp mbic ip chaipc ppi poimcin cepci no ʒopcai do cecmaic ip in bliadain, uaip inci na cuaplaic ap caipc nipca ap a ndeni cup in caipc aile icepum.

In pacapc do ella a ʒpad, cia bech ap a pendi, nip. oippe iapam, pobich ni hupupa oippend do pip cen ʒpada.

In can cpa dopcuipichep peil ppuich pop pachupn, mad peccap copʒup dolluiochep in piʒell nona. Mad cecain imoppo no aindiden no luan pocepcap a paipe pop maipc, no dapdain, no pachupn.

Ip amnup cpa cainʒen in anmcaipoine pobic ma do bepap a ppepaid coip, ip mincaci a bpippio na a comallud. mina chaiobpe in canmchapa imoppo, dop ceic a chin paip, pobich ip lop la poipne andpom cabaipc a coibpen cen a pendaic. Ip pepp cpa poccpa alleppa doibpium cen ni ppecmai na coibpena.

Ip and ciaʒap co hanmcapaic aile, mad écen, iap cecuʒud don anmchapaic coípiʒ.

Ni popʒni cpa lap na Celiuda Dé coclad in dauppéiʒ. Ippeb din popʒni leopom .i. diap did ip in daupréiʒ co hiapmepʒi, acap na .lll. do checul doib, acap in noin ppainnic, acap codlaic co hoioche, acap concuilec o iapmépʒi co macain.

Diap eli din ó iapmepʒi co macain acap cecul na .lll. beop doib, acap coclaid iapam cu ceipc acap celebpac in ceipc hi comain ppi cac.

Ip eb popʒni lap na Celiuda Dé .i. pep oc

He who never eats fleshmeat takes a small portion at Easter, to prevent the occurrence of scarcity or famine in the year : for he who does not relax at Easter, he cannot do so till the next Easter following.

The priest who defiles his grade, even though he does penance, shall not offer the sacrifice afterwards, because it is not easy for a man without the grades to offer the sacrifice.

When a high festival falls on saturday outside Lent, the vigil at none is taken off. But if on wednesday, or friday, or monday, its freedom is transferred to tuesday, or thursday, or saturday.

Difficult indeed is the duty of the soul-friend, because if he gives the proper remedy, it is oftener violated than observed : but if the soul-friend does not give it, its liability falls upon himself; because several deem it enough to make the confession without doing the penance; but it is better to proclaim their welfare to them, though they do not respond to the penance enjoined by the confessor.

Another soul-friend may be gone to, if necessary, after the permission of the first soul-friend.

The Célidé shall not sleep in their oratory; and therefore what they do is this: two of them remain in the oratory till nocturn,* and the Psalter is sung by them, and at none they dine, and sleep till night; and they sleep from nocturn till morn.

Two others then *officiate* from nocturn till matins, and the Psalter is sung by them also, and they afterwards sleep till tierce, and they celebrate the tierce in common with all.

This is what is done by the Célidé : one of

---

* The meaning of iapmepʒi is determined by the following passage: Medon aidci, ... luid Ailill do'n cill; ip é cpacpon do deodaid in caillec do beim cluʒ do iapmepʒi, " At midnight, . . . Ailill went to the church, and this was the time when the nun came to ring the bell for nocturns." (Leabhar na hUidhre, fol. 31 *bb.*) It occurs in nearly the same words in another MS. cited by Dr. Petrie, in his Essay on the Round Towers. (Transactions R. I. A., vol. xx., p. 378.)

aipplezenð τρορcela acar piazla acar pept-
ai noem cen bit oc ppainð, ðáiჳ na bech a
menma ipin ppainð, aċt hin Ðomino, acar
ppainoιð o noin in pep ppitchar anð, acar in
ðιe pinჳuli et poჳantup ðe quo ppeðicatum
ept. Ðup manð bíp a menma in nocte an
cñ.

In cí na bui oc taipipim oppponð ðia ðom-
naჳ .l. ðo chetul ðo ina ḟeppam hi tiჳ
ninta, acar a ḟuile penta : ip e a luaჳ in
oιpnoinð ippeð ðelece .i. cét pleċtain acar
-pioʈpიჳ̈m ppi ðiait.

Cìð mop in ḟttu pop neoch nípp ib ðiჳ iap
n-iapmepჳι ðin piam, acar celebpað ðul
illιჳe popt.

Mað notpepჳaιchep ppia ჳilla, acar nipbi
τpipt no aιchip, ip ecen cét ðemenð popt
lamu ppiup, acar beċ pop bapჳin acar upci
in oιðċe pin.

Ni ðleჳap ðin ðo Ċele Ðé ol neich iap
tabaipt a ḟuail.

Τpopcað ceċa míp la muintip Moelpuain
uli .i. lechpit ðe apan, acar lechpit ðe
meðჳupce.

Ip coip ðin obbað na coìbpean in ti nað
penni ðo peip anmchaput, mina ċecma ðo
neoch anmchapait ðup lop laip i ḟocup .i.
ðup eolach piazla a nimċeċta in pcpiptuip,
acar ppi piazla na noem, acar conoċap am-
bepenð on anmchapait eolach ppip i cetna
comapnic bech nech imoppo ðia taιððpe a
ċoìbpena pop cech nae, acar penðichep iapam ippeip na piazla minchoìbpena. Ni aup-
ċuill pιcιpe ðia tabapathap cιð mac leჳinð
cιð mac clepech.

Cechapða na pennichep hi tip nEpenn
.i. coìbliჳe maipb (ιð ept muliep), ðial ppi
coìbðelaიჳ (.i. piaip no mჳein) toιcim po

them reads the Gospel and the Rules, and the
miracles of saints, while they *the rest* are dining,
in order that their mind may not be in the dinner, but in God ; and the man who preaches dines
after none, and during the day they are individually questioned about what was read ; that
their minds may be pure at night.

He who does not attend mass on sunday shall
recite fifty *psalms*, standing in a closed house,
with his eyes shut : it is the price of the mass,
and he shall perform one hundred genuflexions
and crossfigil, with Beatus.

Though great be the thirst of one, he shall
not take drink after nocturn, at any time, and
he shall say farewell going to bed afterwards.

If thou art angered by a servant, and thou
curse or abuse him, thou shalt receive an hundred
blows on the hands first, and be *put* on bread
and water that night.

It is not lawful for a Céledé to drink aught
after passing his urine.

There is a fast every month among the congregation of Moelruain,* i. e. half a meal of
bread, and half a meal of diluted whey.

It is right to refuse the confession of a person
who does not perform penance according to the
soul-friend, unless there happens to be a soul-
friend near whom he considers more learned in
Rules, in the ways of the Scripture, and in the
rules of the saints. Let him heed what he re-
ceives from the learned soul-friend whom he first
met, to whomsoever he may reveal his confession
each time, and let him afterwards be enjoined
penance according to the rules of frequent confession. It is not prohibited him to commit his
conscience to any one, whether he be a student
or a young cleric.

Four things are not received to penance in the
land of Erin, i. e. coition with the dead (i. e. a
woman) ; coition with a kinswoman (i. e. a sis-

---

* That is, the society of Tamhlacht-Moelruain, or Tallaght, where his chief monastery was. See p. 125 *supra.*

uaʀal ʒnaḃ (.ı. epʀcop no ʀacaṗc) ṗonneıʀ ċoıḃʀen uc ḃıcac .ı. ıʀʀeḃ ʀo ḃo ṗoıne ın ʀeṗ ʀo.

Acḃeʀac ʀonenḃ conıḃ ınılle acaʀ conıḃ ʀeṗʀ ḃo anmaın ın phıc ḃeac mın quam ın phıc moʀ anmın.

Ƿelı na n-aʀʀol acaʀ ın lıcha ʀnuchı acaʀ ın ḃomnaıʒ nı copmach pıce ıʀ coıʀ ınncıḃ, aċc mocacıo .ı. nı ḃuʀ ṁınıu aʀaıle.

hıccu ḃın ın can ḃıʀ ʀoʀʀaʒuḃaʀ ḃoċcan ḃo ṁeḃʒ no ḃlaċaıʒ, acaʀ uʀcı ʀaıʀ. ıc lomanḃ eḃaʀ ḃe.

Nech loınʒeʀ ʀe na cʀaċ no ċaıcheʀʀ ın maʀ naċ ʒnach ḃo ṫʀoʀcaḃ ınḃ ḃí oıḃche ʀoʀ uʀce acaʀ aʀan ḃo.

Ƿıalcıʒe ḃın acaʀ ʀualcıʒe ıc aḃḃaı ḃo ḃemnaıḃ ınḃʀın. Sénaḃ ḃo neoch na cıʒeḃ ʀın acaʀ a ṫénaḃ ʀen ın can cıaʀʀaıʀ ınncıḃ; ocuʀ nı ḃleʒaıʀ ıʀnaıʒche ınncıḃ ʀın, ʀeḃ Deuʀ ın aḃıucoʀıum uʀque ʀeʀcına.

ḃıaḃ ḃıʀ ın ḃomu quanḃo moʀıcuʀ alıquıʀ ın ea conʀecʀaʀe acaʀ ʀauʀeʀıḃuʀ ḃıuıḃeʀe ḃeḃec; quıa cıḃuʀ ın una ḃomu cum ınʀıʀmo cuʀcoḃıʀe uel cum moʀcuo quamuıʀ ʀanccuʀ ʀıc manḃucaʀe non ḃeḃec.

Iʀeaḃ ʀoʀcualaı Moelʀuaın la ʀʀuchı ḃı ḃeʀʒu ın cʀe, ıʀ ḃıulcaḃach Ƿacʀaıc hı nım acaʀ na hıʀʀı cuc ın nEʀınn, nach oen ḃeʀaıʒ a ċíʀ, acc aʀʀ a hoıʀcheʀ ına hıaʀchaʀ, acaʀ aʀ a cuaıʀceʀc ına ḃeʀceʀc.

Nıcon ʀıl ní ḃoʀʒnı ḃuıne caʀ cenḃ anma ınḃı acḃaıll nac coḃaıʀ ḃo ecıʀ ʀıʒıll acaʀ aʀʀcanaıc acaʀ ʒaḃaıl necnaıʀce acaʀ benḃaċcu mencı. Ƿılıı ʀʀo moʀcuıʀ ʀaʀencıḃuʀ ḃeḃenc penıceʀe.

ter, or a daughter); falling under a noble grade (i. e. bishop or priest); disclosing the confession, so as to say, This is what the man did.

Some say that it is fitter and better for the soul to take the small meal often than the large meal seldom.

On the feasts of the Apostles, and the high festivals, and sundays, it is not increase of the meal that is proper, but change, i. e. *to eat* more frequently than on other days.

When there is thirst, let him get a bochtan of whey, or of buttermilk, and water mixed with it. It is a lomand of it that is drunk.

A person who eats before his time, or who consumes more than usual, shall fast for it, two nights, on water and bread.

Now the privy-houses and the urine-houses they are the abodes of demons. Let these houses be blessed by any one going thither, and let him bless himself when he enters them, and it is not lawful to say any prayers in them, except "Deus in adjutorium" to "festina."

The food which is in the house, when any one dies in it, should be divided and distributed to the poor; because food ought not to be kept or eaten in the same house with a sick person or a corpse, though he be holy.

What Moelruain heard from learned men concerning the desertion of the land was, That Patrick, and the faithful whom he brought into Erin, will be repulsive in heaven to any man who deserts his land, except *so far as* to remove from the east of it to the west, and from the north to the south.*

There is nothing which a person does for a soul that has departed that does not help it, both vigil and abstinence, and singing the intercession and frequent blessings. Filii pro mortuis parentibus debent pœnitere.

---

* There seems to be a reference here to the great religious migrations from Ireland to the Continent which prevailed in the eighth and following centuries.

bliabain lan oin oo Moeoocc Pepna con a
ꞇuinꞇip uile pop upce acap bap̃in iap ꞇuap-
lucuo cnma bpanouib mic Echach o ipiupn.

Ouine oin oiambao ail apꞃꞇanaiꞇ acup
. . . oepna pꞇ oo ꞇixail aipe, ꞇicpaꞇ oⲥꞇmao
. . oeno pé mꞁp a mbeꞃeno iapam in ouine
. . oeno pé mꞁp oia apꞃꞇanaiꞇ, no oie ꞇhixail
. . . ᷒ aipe oo ⲥoolao poꞇlil co a éc.

. . ao ail oo ꞇuilleo apꞃꞇanaiꞇ beop ꞇixao
. . ꞇmao aꞇe aipe oia ṗiꞇ po in allꞇ ceꞇna
. . po a aꞇpi no a ceaⲥaip no a cuic. Rucpa
. . pꞁ uli, aⲥꞇ ba min oopona, ni ba han-
. . llain oo oin a ꞇixeba aipe oia ⲥoꞇlao pep
. . aoup. Pep oin na caⲥꞇa cu mop acap oo
. . maipꜩ lubpa no ꜩalap ꞇpia apꞃꞇaniꞇ becan
. . epail paip beop amail noeoin. Oia
. . ꞁnꜩe pep pex menpep bepaio cu bap a
. . ail paip beop.

Poꞇhpucao hinnimpiꞇin ip aupⲥaill, acap
. . copbao oon ⲥach oo beip ꞇap a ceno in
. . o pin. Ip paiⲥciu oon oep ꜩpaio ꞇapp
a ꞇeiꞇ ceno a copmao acap a coipecpao
iapam. Leꞇhpiꞇ oo oia acap alleⲥh eli oo
. . mailꞇ oeiꞇꞇ pein ap ꞇeiꞇ ꞇpopcao innpin.

. . npeal alaⲥꞇ oia ꞇic ꜩalap com bi poⲥ-
paib oe bap, aipplegꞇhep in mbaꞇhip pop
upce, acap popepeꜩap in banopeal ꞇapceno
na ꜩeni, acap oo bepap Plano no Cellach oo
aimmm paip, ap ip coiⲥⲥeno oo ṗip acap oo
mnai ceⲥꞇapoe, acap hibeo in maꞇhaip in

A whole year therefore was Moedoc of Ferns,
with all his people, *living* on water and biscuit
after ransoming the soul of Brandubh, son of
Eochaidh, from hell.[*]

A person who wishes abstinence, and his meal
has not been lessened for him, he may lessen one
eighth to the end of six months. What the person obtains afterwards to the end of six months
of his abstinence, or what is taken from his sleep,
it follows him till death.

If he desires more abstinence, let him abate
another eighth of his meal after the same manner till he reaches three or four of five *months.*
He has brought all then, but it was frequency
he practised. What he has lessened then of his
sleep is not unhealthy for him per gradus. But
a man who is much oppressed and weighed down
by sickness or disease, by abstinence, little is
enjoined upon him, *but* like an infant. If he
bears it for six months, he affords reason for im-
posing it upon him still *further.*

To bathe in imsitin[†] is prohibited, and it is
pollution to every one who puts this liquid upon
his head. It is defilement to those in orders on
whose head it is put; they are to be anointed and
consecrated after it. Thou shalt give half thy
meal to God, and consume the other half of it
thyself, for fasting is required for this.

A woman who is pregnant, on whom disease
comes, so that she is on the brink of death; let
the baptism be read upon water, and let the
woman put it on the head of the fœtus, and let
Flann or Cellach be given it as a name, for either
is common to man and woman,[‡] and let the mo-

---

[*] The legend of king Brandubh and the demons is preserved in the Book of Lecan, fol. 183 *a*, and a portion of
it is translated in the Life of St. Columba (Ir. Archæol. and Celtic Soc.), p. 205, note ᵃ. In the Life of St. Moedoc,
who is said to have been Brandubh's half-brother, the torments of the king are related to have been experienced in
a vision. Cap. 28 (Colgan, Actt. SS., p. 211 *a*). See O'Donovan's note on the Four Masters, An. 601, vol. i.,
p. 229.

[†] It is unknown what fluid is intended by this word.

[‡] These names most frequently belong to men, but we find some instances of their being borne by the other sex.

upce ʀin cu ceic caʀʀin nʒein, acaʀ iʀ bacͪiʀ
ᴅo.

Ჾalaʀ miʀcai biʀ ʀoʀ inʒenaib eclaʀa
ʀaiʀe a ʀiʒle ᴅoib oiʀec biʀ ʀoʀaib maicen
acaʀ ʀeʀcoʀ, acaʀ bʀochan ᴅo ᴅenam ᴅoib
am cͪeiʀc, ʀeciʀ aimʀiʀ ʀobicͪ ᴅleʒaʀ
aiʀmiciu in ʒalaiʀ ʀin. Niʀ ciaʒac ᴅin ᴅo
laim inᴅ aʀ omanᴅe ʀunc in illo cempoʀe.

Cuaʀa imchuiʀcͪeʀ ᴅo chein in ᴅomnach in
eᴅʀeʀc ᴅo neoch ni ᴅleʒaʀ ᴅo a ċaiċem, acͪc
a ʀoᴅail ᴅo boċcaib. ᴅobeʀaiʀ ᴅia ʀaċaiʀn
imnoin ʀiaċ aibne na hoiᴅċe luain.

Oʀᴅ beʀʀċa ᴅia miʀ ᴅoʀʒnicͪeʀ .i. ᴅia
ᴅaʀᴅain.

Iʀ amlaiᴅ ᴅin ʒabcͪaʀ ᴅechmaᴅa .i. ceċ
anma ceċcaʀ ᴅuine ᴅo lecuᴅ caʀ beʀnai,
acaʀ ceċ ᴅechmaᴅ mil ᴅib ᴅo ᴅia aċc ᴅoim
nama, ʀobicͪ ʒabaʀ ᴅia ʀaeċaʀ ceċ ᴅeċmaᴅ
caʀʀ.

Cʀi coʀba in ᴅie .i. eʀnaiʒċe acaʀ lubaiʀ
acaʀ leʒenᴅ. Roᴅbu ʀoʀcecail, no ʀcʀibenᴅ,
no uaimm necaiʒ, no cʀaill buʀ coʀba ᴅo
neoch ᴅoʀona aʀ na becͪaʀ in eʀʀa anᴅ, uc
ᴅominuʀ ᴅiᴢic, Non apaʀebiʀ uacuʀ in con-
ʀʀeccu meo.

Ni auʀbeʀca bicͪ comac ʒuiʀc : niʀ co-
culcai combaᴅ eim lacc : niʀ aculca nech
comba ᴅeicͪbiʀ.

Soeʀaᴅ eclaiʀi ᴅé : combacͪiʀ acaʀ comna acaʀ ʒabail necnaiʀce, co macaib ᴅo
leʒenᴅ, co n-ioʀaiʀc chuiʀʀ Cʀiʀc ʀoʀ ceċ
ni alcoiʀ.

Ni ᴅliʒiᴅ ᴅechͫaᴅu, na bo ċenᴅaich, na
cʀian annoci, na ᴅiʀe ʀeoic ᴅo ͫaimb mina

ther drink that water that it may go over the
fœtus, and it is *as* baptism to it.

During the monthly disease which is upon
virgins of the church, they are free from their
vigils while it is on them morning and evening:
and let gruel be made for them at tierce. Whatever time it happens, that disease is to be attended to. They shall not go to hand then, because they are unclean during that time.

A meal which is transferred from a distance
to sunday, a person is not entitled to consume,
but he shall divide it among the poor. On saturday, at the ninth hour, the debt of monday's
enjoyment is to be paid *by fasting.*

The order of tonsure: it is done every month,
i. e. on thursday.

Now the way in which the tithes are taken is
this: every animal which a man possesses is let
through a gap; and every tenth animal of them
is given to God, except the poor one; and also
the work of every tenth cart is given to God.

Three works every day: prayer, and labour,
and reading: there should be instruction, or writing, or sewing of clothes, or other work which is
profitable for one to do, in order that there
should be no idleness, as the Lord hath said,
Non apparebis vacuus in conspectu meo.

Keep not thy meal till it sours. Sleep not till
sleep oppresses thee. Accost not any one till it
is lawful.

The freeing of God's church: Baptism and
communion, and singing the intercession; with
the students at reading; with the offering of the
body of Christ upon every altar.

She is not entitled to tithes, nor to the heriot
cow, nor to the third of annoit,* nor to the dire

Flann, *daughter* of Dunghal, whose *son* was Flann Finna, died in 886; and Flann, *daughter* of Donnchadh, in 938.
Cellach, *daughter* of Dunchadh, died in 726; and the holy virgin Cellach ("Sancta Virgo Cellach"—Chron. Scot.
987,) died in 986.—*Four Masters.*
* Noit and annoit are explained by Lhuyd, O'Brien, and O'Reilly, "a church," "a congregation." In the

bet a ꝼꞃitḟpolaiꝺ ꞇecḣꞇa na ḣeclaiꞃi inꞇe
ꝺo baꞇḣiꞃ acaꞃ ċomnai, acaꞃ ᵹaḃail necnaiꞃce a manacḣ eꞇiꞃ ḃiu acaꞃ maꞃḃu, acaꞃ
coꞃꞃoiḃ oiꞃꝼenꝺ ꝼoꞃ alꞇoꞃ i nꝺomnaiᵹiḃ
acaꞃ ꝼollamnaiḃ, acaꞃ coꞃꞃaḃuꞇ aiḃme oᵹa
ceċ alꞇoꞃ ꝺiḃ. Nacḣ eclaiꞃ oc na ḃia a
ꞇecḣꞇa ni ḃliᵹ lan ꝺiꞃe eclaiꞃe Ꝺé, aċꞇ iꞃ
uaim ċaᵹuꞇ acaꞃ laꞇꞃanꝺ a ḣainm la Cꞃiꞃꞇ.

Ceċ eclaiꞃ ꞇꞃa i mḃi ꝼeꞃ ᵹꞃaiꝺ ꝺoṁie-
claiꞃiḃ ꞇuaiċe ni ḃliᵹ ꞇuaꞃaꞃꞇul a uiꞃꝺ.i. ꞇecḣ
acaꞃ aiꞃliꞃꞃe acaꞃ ḃeꞃᵹuꝺ. acaꞃ ḃecelꞇꞇ ceċa
ḃliaꝺna amuil ḃiaꞃ hi cumanᵹ na ḣeclaiꞃi.
Ṁacḣ cona inꝺuꝺ, bo ḃliċꞇ in ceċ ꞃaiċe
acaꞃ aiꞃeiꞃ imm ceċ coiꞃ aꞃ ċena. ḃaꞇḣiꞃ
ꝺin uaꝺeꞃium acaꞃ comna.i. ꞃacaꞃḃaic, acaꞃ
ᵹaḃail necnaiꞃce beo acaꞃ maꞃḃ, acaꞃ oiꞃ-
ꞃenꝺ cecḣ ꝺomnaiᵹ acaꞃ ceċ ꞃꞃimꝼollaman
acaꞃ ceċ ꞃꞃimꝼeli. Celeḃꞃaꝺ caċ ꞇꞃacḣa;
na .lll. ꝺo cheꝺul ceċ ꝺie aċꞇ mina ꞇoiꞃ-
meꞃci ꞃoꞃceꞇul no anmcḣaiꞃꝺiuꞃ. Nacḣ ꝼeꞃ
ᵹꞃaiꝺ ꝺin laꞃ na ḃi ḃliᵹeꝺ na eolucḣ no eoluꞃ
a ᵹꞃaꝺ ꝺo ꞇimꞇiꞃecḣꞇ cona ḃi ꞇualainᵹ celeḃꞃaꝺ acaꞃ oiꞃꞃiunꝺ ꝼoꞃ ḃelaiḃ ꞃiᵹ acaꞃ
eꞃꞃcop, niꞃ ḃliᵹ ꞃaiꞃe ꝼiꞃ ᵹꞃaiꝺ hi ꞇuaicḣ
no i n-eclaiꞃ.

Nacḣ eꞃꞃoc ꝺin ꝺoꞃḃeꞃ uaꞃal ᵹꞃaꝺ ꝼoꞃ
neocḣ na be ꞇualainᵹ naiꞃḃeꞃꞇa i cꞃaḃuꝺ
acaꞃ leᵹenꝺ acaꞃ anmcaiꞃꝺeꞃꞃa, acaꞃ eolaꞃ

---

seoit do mainibh,* unless she has the reciprocal
duties of the church *done* in her, as to baptism,
and communion, and singing the intercession
for her subjects both living and dead,† and has
offering upon every altar on sundays and solemnities, and unless every altar has its proper furniture. No church that has not its lawful things
is entitled to the full tribute of the church of
God, but its name among Christians is, A den of
thieves and robbers.

Any church, also, in which there is a priest
of the order of the laity,‡ he is not entitled to the
emoluments of his order, viz., a house and enclosure, a bed, and clothing every year, as good
as it is in the power of the church *to give.* A
sack *of wheat* with its indudh,§ a milch cow
every quarter, and every his just demand in like
manner. Of him is required then baptism and
communion, i. e. the sacrament, and singing the
intercession for the living and the dead, and the
offering every sunday, and every chief solemnity,
and every chief festival. Celebration every day;
to sing the 150 *psalms* every day, unless prevented by teaching or soul-friendship. Any man
in orders, then, who has not the law, or the
knowledge to perform the duties of his order,
and who is not able to celebrate and offer the
sacrifice before kings and bishops, is not entitled
to the freedom of a man of orders, in state or
church.

Any bishop, likewise, who confers noble orders upon any one who is not able to instruct
in religion, and reading, and soul-friendship, and

Brehon Laws, annaiꞇ signifies the church in which the patron saint was educated. The third part of the dues
accruing in such a church was probably reserved for the mother church or principal monastery.

* This signifies some species of ecclesiastical tribute or revenue.

† This proves that the ecnaiꞃc was something in the nature of a litany.

‡ Literally, " man in orders of the class of the laity." From what follows it seems to denote one whose deficiency
in education or other qualifications, notwithstanding his being in holy orders, disqualified him for discharging the
full offices of his calling, and for taking his place among the clergy.

§ Meaning of this word unknown.

peċċa acar piaʒla, acar ppepuiɔe cuibɔe ɔi ceċ peccaċ ap ċena ir bioba ɔo Ɔia acar ɔuine in cerpoc rin, uair ir immɔepʒaɔ ɔo Cpirc acar ɔia eclair an ɔo poine, ec iɔeo rex annor penicepec, acar cabpaɔ reċc cumala oir ppia henech in Ɔuileman beor.

Ir ɔe aca anmunna per nEpenn i cimna Pacpic, copaibe ppim erpoc ceċa ppim cɔaiċi i nEpinɔ, ppia hoipɔneaɔ oerpa ʒpaiɔ acar ppi coirecpaɔ eclairi, ppi hanmchaipɔine ɔo plachib acar oirċinnib acar ɔoep ʒpaiɔ, ppi noemaɔ acar bennachaɔ a clanɔ iap mbachir, ppia popconʒpaɔ lubpai ceċa eclairi, acar mac acar inʒean ppia leʒenɔ acar cpabuɔ; ap minap leʒac na mic in ceċ aimrip, icbela in uile eclair, acar ni bia cpecim, aċc ɔuibʒenncliʒeċc hi cir nEpenn.

Nach oen ɔin acbepa ɔechmaɔ a chuipp ɔo Ɔia pa leiʒenɔ biɔ cuma ɔo acar noaċnuiʒeɔ eclapa Epenn, acar ɔopbepeɔ cpecem innce iap na eloɔ. Naċ oen imoppa beperp a mac por cula o leʒenɔ iap na iopaipc ɔo Ɔia acar Pacpaic ir cuma ɔo acar nor bepeaɔ auɔpepca in becha uli por cula acar conpcapaɔ eclair nime acar calmain. Naċ oen cpa lap a leʒaic na meic auɔpapchap anɔ ɔo Ɔia acar Pacpic ɔleʒaicpiɔe pochpaic acar ɔulchinɔe i n-aimpepaib copib .i. loilʒech i pochpaicc na .lll. co na nimnaib acar cancacib acar liachcanaib acar combachir acar comna, acar ʒabail n-ecnapci acar co neolar a n-opɔaiʒche olchena com ba cualainʒ aipicen ʒpaɔ: aʒ acar mucc acar cpi meich bpacha, acar miach apba biɔ ina ɔuilchinɔe cecha bliaɔna cenmoċa ʒaipe acar ailʒine ɔo éciuɔ acar biaċaɔ illoʒ

who has not a knowledge of laws and rules, and of the proper remedy for all sins in general, is an enemy to God and man—that bishop is ; for he has offered an insult to Christ and his church, et ideo sex annos poeniteret, and he shall pay seven cumhals* in gold, also, as a penalty to God.

From this it comes that the names of the men of Erin are in the Testament of Patrick, that there should be a chief bishop in each chief territory in Erin, for ordaining men to holy orders, and for consecrating churches, for the soul-friendship of princes, and of herenachs, and of people in orders ; for sanctifying and blessing their children after baptism, for ordering works in every church, and training boys and girls to reading and piety ; for if the boys do not read at all times, every church will die, and there will be no religion, but black heathenism in the land of Erin.

Every one, therefore, who will give the tithes of *the fruit of* his body to God for learning shall be, as it were, a restorer of the church of Erin, and as bringing religion into it after it had vanished. But every person who recalls his son, after having offered him to God and Patrick, is as if he would bring all the offerings of the world back, and separate the churches of heaven and earth. And every one with whom the boys read who have been thus offered to God and Patrick is entitled to reward and salary at proper periods, i. e., a milch cow as a reward for *having taught* the Psalter, with their hymns and canticles, and lections, and baptism, and communion, and singing of intercession, and with the knowledge of the order in general, until they are capable of receiving orders. A calf, and a hog, and three sacks of malt, and a sack of corn shall be his recompense each year, besides a be-

---

* A cumhal was a bondmaid, and her value was three cows. See O'Donovan, in Book of Rights, p. 139.

mbenḋaccan. Ɑ́ċc ιaρ caιρρenaḃ na ρalm
acaρ na nιmonḃ ρo ċecóιρ ḃoρenaρ ιn loιl-
ᵹeċa, ιaρ caιρρenaḃ ḃιn ιn oρḃuρa ḃleᵹaρ ιn
ḃuιlċιnḃe acaρ ιn ḃecelc. Ọlιᵹιḃ ιmoρρo ιn
cṗuι no ιn ceρρoc ḃιa caιρρencaρ na ρaιlm
ρρoιnḃ cuιcιρ ḃe choρmaιmm acaρ buιḃ ιn
oιḃche ριn.

Iρ he cρa ḃo ρoιρce ḃo ṗaeċρaιḃ ιn ρao-
ċaρ ρa.ι. ρaeċaρ hι cρabuḃ, aιρ ḃo beρaρ
ρlaɩċ nιme ḃoncí laρ a leᵹċaρ acaρ noc-
leᵹa acaρ ḃoccoρριᵹ ιnnech bíρ ι conleᵹanḃ.

Naċ ṗeρ ᵹρaιḃ laρ a leᵹuc na meιcρι ιρ
ḃo ḃleᵹaρ a cuιnḃρech acaρ a coρc, acaρ
a cιmoρcun ṗρι huρḃu eclaιρι ρo cécóιρ aρ ιρ
ḃon eclaιρ acaρ ḃo Ọιa aιlceρ ṗρι haιριcen
ᵹρaḃ.

Naċ ṗeρ ᵹρaιḃ ᵹaιbeρ eclaιρ ρoρ a chubaρ
ιρ ḃo ḃleᵹaρ anmchaιρḃιne manach na he-
claιρe ριn, ṗιρu, macu, mna, ρceo ιnᵹena.

Nac oen ḃιn naċ aιριm maam nanmchaρuc
ρaιρ, co na bι ḃo ρeιρ Ọé no ḃuιne, nι ḃlιᵹ
comna ḃo cabaιρc ḃo, no ᵹabaιl necnaιρce,
no a aḃnocul ι neclaιρ Ọé, aρ ιρ uaḃ ρo ṗémḃeḃ
bιch ḃo ρeρ Ọé ιρ na heclaιριb ι cιρ n-Ɵρehn,
uaιρ ιρ amlaιḃ ιρ coιρ aιρmιce ιn aeρa
ᵹρaιḃ, acaρ comallaḃ a cιmnaι, amaιl becιρ
aιnᵹιl Ọé ecιρ ḃoιnιb, ρo bιch ιρ cρeoċu aca
coρnaιᵹche ρlacha nιme, ecιρ baċhιρ aoaρ
comna acaρ ᵹabal necnaρcι, acaρ auḃραιρc
ċuιρρ Cριρc acaρ a ṗolaι, acaρ ρρoceρc ρoρ-
cela, acaρ cumcach eclaιρι Ọé, acaρ aenca
ρeċhca acaρ ριaᵹlaι, acaρ ιρρeḃ on colaιᵹ-
ċheρ ḃo Ọιa hι calum.

Naċ oen ḃιn conρcaρa eclaιρ Ọé .ι. nocρen
acaρ noc cρean aρ ρaιnc acaρ ρoρmac noc

---

coming supply of raiment and victuals, as a
reward for blessing. Now it is immediately
after showing the psalms and the hymns,
the milch cow is paid, and after showing the
order, the salary and the raiment are due. The
doctor or the bishop to whom the psalms are repeated is entitled to a meal, for five persons, of
beer and food that night.

This is the labour which excels all labours,
i. e. the labour of religion; for the kingdom of
heaven is given to the person with whom reading is done, and who listens to the person that
reads.

Every man in orders, with whom these boys
read, is entitled to chastise, and check, and re-
strain them to the orders of the church at once,
because it is for the church and for God they are
fostered for the receiving of orders.

Every man in orders who takes *the charge of*
a church on his conscience, to him should be con-
fided the soul-friendship of the subjects of that
church, men, boys, women, and girls.

Any person, therefore, who does not reverence the rule of the soul-friend, so as that
he is not according to God or man, it is not
lawful to give him the communion, or to sing
his intercession, or to bury him in the church of
God; because he has refused to be according
to God in the churches of the land of Erin; for
it is right to reverence the men of *holy* orders,
and to do their bidding, they being as angels
of God among men, for it is through them the
kingdom of heaven is acquired, both by baptism, and singing of intercession, and offering
of the body of Christ and of his blood, and
preaching of the gospel, and sustaining the
church of God, and agreement of law and
rule, and whatever else is pleasing to God on
earth.

Any person, therefore, who separates from
the church of God *any of her property*, i. e. who

pippioe poppao a anma in nim mao co-
cipao, ap ippeo cunopao ip meppa oogni
ouine ip in bich .1. peicc a puioe in eclaip
nime, acap peicc a anma ppi oiabul, acap
peicc a cuipp a nilap mainche oo cuillem oo
na hib eclaipib, cu comail log a colla pepiu
bup mapb, ip aipe na bi ni oo oilepp laip oo
cupp na o'anmain no calum, acc ip le oiabul
uile; op in ci bip oc copcpao eclaipi Oé ipe
oin cocapcapa acap co capni inci nácbi inac
i innaib in ucht eclaipi Oé. Ip cpic acba-
tacap cumacta ceca placa acap a clano
acap a placemnap ina n-oegaio. Ip cpic oin
acbach cpecium in Choimoeo i cuacaib acap
cenelaib. Ip cpic ouincep oopppi nime, acap
epoplaiccep oopppi hipipnn, acap anaic an-
gil Oé oo coppuma in calman, acc can
cecaic oo cabaipc oigla popp an cinel oai-
nepia .1. opochoipcinoig oiumpaca acap
opochpig panncacha capmciachuc na cim-
napa Pacpaic ecip copcpao eclaipi acap
appeicc acap a cpeice, acap cumoach uaille
acap oiumpa; conio an ipiupn aca anouil-
chine popcea.

In ci oin conaing eclaip Oé con umloic
acap auplata acap comallao popp na cim-
napa Pacpaic pon be cec oiabla ipin bic
ppecnaipce acap placa nime cen popceno.

Roipam uile in plachep pin, pop aippillem,
pop aiccpebam in pecula peculopum. Amen.
Pinic.

---

buys or sells for covetousness or envy, sells the
resting place of his soul in heaven if he reaches
it; for this is the worst contract one can make
in the world, i. e. to sell his seat in the church
of heaven, and to sell his soul to the devil, and
to sell his body, for earning much wages, to the
churches, so that he eats the price of his body before he dies. And this is the reason he has nothing
peculiarly his own, of body or of soul, or of
earth, but all belongs to the devil; for he who
strips the church of God shall fall, and he who
is not in the bosom of the church of God, in
his will, shall melt away. It was through this
the powers of princes died, and their sons and
sovereignties died after them. It was through
this the religion of the Lord perished among
countries and peoples. It is through it the
doors of heaven are closed, and the doors of
hell are opened wide, and the angels of God
cease to watch the earth, except when they come
to wreak vengeance on the human race: that is,
the proud bad herenachs, and the covetous bad
kings, who transgress these testaments, both
in stripping the church, and selling and buy-
ing *her property,* and in supporting haughti-
ness and pride, shall have their reward in hell
hereafter.

But he who obeys the church of God with humility and submission, and observes the testaments of Patrick, shall obtain an hundred-fold
reward in the present world, and the kingdom
of heaven without end.

May we all reach that kingdom. May we
deserve it. May we inhabit it for ever and ever.
Amen. Finit.

I.—THE CASE OF THE PRIOR COLIDEORUM OF ARMAGH.

Universis* sancte matris ecclesie filiis, ad quos presentes litere, sive presens publicum instrumentum pervenerint seu pervenerit, Johannes, Dei et Apostolice sedis gratia, Archiepiscopus
Armachanus, Hibernie Primas, salutem in Domino sempiternam, Noverit vestra universitas quod
nos, die date presentium in notarii publici et testium subscriptorum presentia, ad ea que inter alia
nobis incumbunt pro jure visitacionis officio impendenda, in nostra ecclesia cathedrali metropolitica
ac primatiali Armachana constituti personaliter sedentes judicialiter pro tribunali, super officio
Prioris Colideorum dicte nostre ecclesie, cum Prior, quisquis fuerit, ex antiqua laudabili et approbata
consuetudine ejusdem ecclesie sit in loco Presentoris, et eapropter a nonnullis hesitato an hujusmodi
officium ex antiquis temporibus vel adhuc sit nec ne curatum, ad hujusmodi dubium removendum
per infrascriptos in hac parte productos in forma juris admissos et juratos inquiri fecimus diligenter.
Qui vero, videlicet Carolus Omellan Decanus, magister Salamon M^ccreanayr Cancellarius, Arthurus
M^ckathmayll Officialis de Tullaghoge, Thomas M^ckyllacrany, Nicholaus M^cgillamura, Donatus
Ohallian, et Johannes M^cgeerun, Colidei nostre ecclesie Armachane,† magister Philippus M^ckewyn
Herenacus de Darenoysse, fratres Willielmus Omoryssa Prior claustralis, et Johannes Ogoddane,
Canonici regulares, Ocoffy, Omartanan, et M^cgillamura, suarum nacionum Capitanei, et cives seniores et meliores quo supra, jurati dicunt supra sacramentum suum de communi omnium consensu,
referente dicto domino Decano Armachano, quod, attestantibus antiquis scripturis a centum annis
et amplius, et prout ab antiquioribus suis didicerunt et audiverunt, dictum officium Prioris Colideatus pro nullo fuit aut est curatum, adeo licet diversi ac nonnulli Priores temporibus suis successive et
divisim quilibet post alium beneficium curatum unacum dicto Prioratu pacifice tenuissent, non visi
aut cogniti fuerunt in suis beneficiis residere, sed pro dicte nostre ecclesie majoris Armachane honore
et in augmentationem divini cultus in eadem, unacum Colideis sub nomine Prioris permanere, nec
aliquem sciverunt preterquam Priorem modernum suo tempore celebrare, vel ratione Prioratus, aut
quod Presentoris officium exerceret, reputatum fore curatum, sed locum primum in mensa et in
exequendis ac regendis divinis officiis, ut in loco Presentoris, a Colideis ceteris et aliis infra et extra
reverentiam congruam sibi deberi, et super hoc fuit et est nulli dubium e converso, tam inter ecclesie
Canonicos et Colideos quam cives et alios convicinos, antiqua laudabilis et approbata consuetudo a
tanto tempore et per tempus cujus contrarii memoria hominum non existit, tenta cognita habita et
reputata. Etiam ex consuetudine consimili per predictam inquisitionem similiter comperto quod
Colideatus officium solum pro exercitio divinorum, in favorem dicte nostre ecclesie majoris Armachane ad augmentationem divini cultus in eadem, fuit et est officium atque ministerium nudum
nullo modo curatum, nec obstare poterit quin quilibet Colideus absque impeticione aliqua, sicut
hactenus sui consueverunt predecessores, unacum dicto officio Colideatus simul et‡ semel possit et
valeat beneficium curatum licite retinere, et ipsius inibi curam per alium similiter excercere. Et
quia nedum sic ut predictum est, sed etiam ex probatissimorum testium testimonio, et quod magis
est, sanctorum patrum antiquis cronicis, et predecessorum libris annalibus scrutatis et perlectis,

---

* Registrum Johannis Mey, lib. ii., fol. 11 *b*, p. 148.   † Ibid., fol. 12 *a*, p. 149.   ‡ Ibid., fol. 12 *b*, p. 150.

pure et plane invenimus necnon pacifice et quiete sine diminucione aliqua interruptione vel perturbacione consuetudinem talem fuisse et esse laudabilem et approbatam usitatam pariter et observatam. Nos igitur, premissis diligentissime consideratis, nedum quod a nonnullis nobis instantissime desuper fuerit supplicatum, sed pocius pro amore et honore dicte nostre ecclesie Armachane, que metropolitica et primatialis ac omnium per partes Hibernie ecclesiarum mater existit et magistra, cultum divinum cupientes inibi ampliare, atque quod eapropter sit institutum, ac hactenus fuerit observatum, facere ut congruit pro perpetuo adhiberi et inviolabiliter observari consuetudinem predictam laudabilem et approbatam, et quecunque inde secuta rata habentes et grata, sicuti sic fore decrevimus confirmavimus, et tenore presentium confirmamus, decreto hujusmodi mediante, pro perpetuo statuentes ut, vigore consuetudinis predicte, Prioris seu cujusque Colideatus officium curatum nullatenus senciatur teneatur vel alias reputetur quin quilibet beneficium curatum in casu predicto simul et semel cum Prioratus ac Colideatus officio possit et valeat libere et licite retinere, et ipsius inibi curam, dummodo in prefata nostra ecclesia Armachana personalem fecerit residenciam, ad suum debitum perficiendum, per alium similiter excercere. Quod si quid fortasse, alicujus inhiacione suggestione sive impetracione, in contrarium actum solicitatum fuerit aut adeptum, in dictum nostre ecclesie prejudicium ac ipso facto falso acquisitum, decernimusque ex nunc irritum fore et inane, ac impetrantem impetracionis intuitu eo ipso fuisse et esse tanquam dicte nostre ecclesie in suis libertatibus perturbatorem, excommunicationis vinculo innodatum, et pro tali, quousque* passis injuriam competenter satisfecerit ex commissis, publice fore nunciandum, &c.   Datum et actum in prefata nostra ecclesia Armachana xxiiii. die mensis Julii, sub anno ab incarnacione Domini secundum cursum et computacionem ecclesiarum Anglicane et Hibernicane M°. cccc^mo. xlv^to., Indictione viii^ta., pontificatus vero sanctissimi in Christo patris et domini nostri Domini Eugenii divina providencia Pape quarti anno xv°, hiis presentibus, reverendis et discretis viris fratre Patricio Odanguyssa Abbate Clochorensi, et magistro Jacobo Leche nostro Commissario generali, necnon domino Cormaco Oconnolan Vicario de Lessan, et Magonio Ocassede presbitero, etiam Patricio M^ckassaid Herenaco de Twyna, et Johanne Omellan clerico nostre diocesis Armachane, et multis aliis testibus in premissis vocatis specialiter et rogatis, &c.

In† causa appellacionis Prioris Colideorum, Examinacio testium xiiij. die Novembris [M°. cccc°. xlviii°.], frater Mauricius Oloucheran, Canonicus Regularis de Ardmacha et Sacrista, primus testis productus, admissus juramento et diligenter examinatus, deponit quod novit quatuor predecessores Prioris moderni qui aliunde beneficiati fuerunt, et hujusmodi beneficia unacum dicto Prioratu pacifice tenuerunt, nec fuit dignitas reputata, sed quod cum Colideis habet primum locum in mensa, et pre ceteris honoratur, Et solum deponit pro veritate.

Item frater Willelmus Omoryssa, Canonicus regularis et Prior claustralis monasterii apostolorum Petri et Pauli de Ardmachia, secundus testis productus, admissus juratus et diligenter examinatus, dicit et concordat ut supra, et addit quod pro aliquo tempore fuit conversatus testis qui loquitur in domo et familia cum dictis Colideis, et tempore quo intravit religionem tunc sibi benevolus et magister, dominus David M^cgillade qui tunc Prior fuerat Colideorum et Vicarius de Onellan, non bene placatus de introitu eo, quod ipsum voluit habere in Colideum, venit et genuflexit

---

* Ibid., fol. 13 a. p. 151.   * Ibid., fol. 15 a, p. 155.

O 2

coram apostolis Petro et Paulo, petendo quodammodo contra eum ab eisdem quod sic intrasset contra suum intentum, etc.; Et deponit ut supra.

Item dominus Nicholaus Oheremaid, tertius testis productus, admissus juratus et diligenter examinatus, dicit* et deponit de Priore ut supra, quod non habet nisi primum locum in mensa et majoris honoris, et eciam inceptor in execucione divinorum, et quod diversi predecessores fuerint beneficiati, ut supra; Et an dignitas est, de eo nescit, sed quod cause a curia consueverint sibi committi, et hoc credit ratione canonicatus eo quod Canonicus existit; Et solum deponit pro veritate.

Item dominus Patricius Olagan capellanus et apparitor, quartus testis et ultimus productus, admissus juratus et diligenter examinatus, deponit de dicto Priore, quod non habet nisi primum locum in mensa, et Precentoris magis honoratur et primus ac inceptor in divinis officiis, et dignitas alia non existit, quodque predecessores sui diversi fuerint aliunde beneficiati ut novit et audivit, et fuerunt pacifici; Et solum deponit pro veritate.

K.—NOTICES OF COLIDEI IN THE ARMAGH REGISTERS.

1364, Feb.   Odo [M'Dymin] Prior Communitatis Capituli Armachani. (Registrum Milonis Sweteman, fol. 36 *a*.)

1365, Aug. 20.   Odo M'doymyn, Prior Communitatis Capituli Armachani, one of the commissaries to visit the dioceses of Derry and Raphoe. (Ibid., fol. 28 *b*, 49 *b*.)

1366, Oct. 15.   Odo, Prior Communitatis Capituli Armachani, witnesses a commission from the Primate. (Ibid., fol 26 *b*.)

1366.   Odo, Prior Colideorum, admonished to expedite his journey to Rome, a hundred marks having been assigned to defray his expenses. (Ibid., fol. 23 *a*, 23 *b*.)

1366.   The Primate grants to Odo M'dymin, Prior Communitatis Capituli Armachani, as proctor for himself and the church of Armagh at the court of Rome, a pension of 20 marks out of the lands of Trientulcha, near Armagh, so long as he should be engaged at Rome on the said business. (Ibid., fol. 25 *b*.)

1366, Jan. 20.   The Primate certifies the Pope of the mission of Odo, Prior Communitatis Capituli Armachani, touching the wrongs of the church of Armagh and his own confirmation in the primacy. (Ibid., fol. 25 *a*.)

1367.   The Dean and Chapter inducted Patrick Orechi, a canon, as proctor for Odo M'doymyn, Prior Colideorum, then absent at Rome, into the dignity of Chancellor of the cathedral, vacant by the promotion of Patricius Okerulan to the deanry of Derry. License given to said Odo to hold the rectory of Tamlachtglyad (now Ballymore) previously enjoyed by him. (Ibid., fol. 37 *b*.)

1367.   In the progress of visitation of the diocese, the Dean and Chapter cited for the 4th of June; the abbot and convent of SS. Peter's and Paul's, and the Colidei for the 7th; and the clergy and people for the 12th. (Ibid., fol. 45 *b*.)

---

* Registrum Johannis Mey, fol. 15 *b*, p. 156.

1367, Sept. 18. Primate's remonstrance with Ohandeloyne [O'Hanlon], for injuries done to the Dean, the Canons, and Colidei. (Ibid., fol. 17 *b*.) Same day a letter sent to the Dean by the hands of Cristinus, a Colideus. (Ibid., fol. 18 *a*.)

1370, April 17. Citation to a visitation of the diocese inter Hibernicos served on Patrick Okorry, the Dean, for self, Chapter, and Colidei. (Ibid., fol. 43 *a*.)

1370. Progress of visitation: The Dean and Chapter, May 11th; the Colidei, May 13th; the clergy, May 16th. (Ibid., fol. 42 *a*.) So in 1375. (Ibid., fol. 45 *b*.)

1375, June 16. Arthur, John, and Magonius, Colidei, admonished, on pain of excommunication, to keep residence in the cathedral church. (Ibid., fol. 97 *a*.)

1406, Dec. 19. Primate Fleming granted the church of Dyrebruchisse alias Okaregan [now Killyman], which was appropriate to his mensa, to John Ocorre, Prior Colideorum, at the annual rent of two marks silver. (Registrum Fleming, fol. 7 *a*.)

1408. Letter of excommunication and interdict against Mauricius, son of Catholicus Oneyll, directed to the Dean, the Prior Colideorum, the Chapter, Colidei, and rest of clergy. (Ibid., fol. 15 *a*.)

1411. Mandate of the Primate to Thomas Olocheran, the Dean, and all and singular the Colidei, to admonish Thomas and Adam Olocheran, sons of the abbot of St. Peter's and St. Paul's, to desist from molesting Nicholas Ohelman. (Ibid., fol. 36 *b*.)

1411. Mandate of admonition to the Dean, Canons in residence, and Colidei. (Ibid., fol. 43 *b*.)

1411, March 11. John Hertylpool collated to the rectory of St. Patrick's church of Achloug [now Aghaloo], vacant by the death of John Ocor, Prior Colideorum. (Ibid., fol. 45 *b*.)

1415, July 45. Mandate of admonition to the Prior Colideorum and Colidei. (Ibid., fol. 57 *a*.)

1416, Oct. 30. John Ocassaly, Prior Colideorum, and Maurice Ofercheran, Chancellor. presiding in chapter (the Deanry being vacant), certify to the Pope the election of Robert Fitzhugh to the see of Armagh. (Registrum Swayne, lib. ii., fol. 16 *b*.)

1425. Letter of the Primate to Dionysius the Dean, and David, Prior Colideorum. (Ibid., lib. i., fol. 5 *b*.)

1427, Oct. 23. Commission from the Primate to Dionysius Oculean the Dean, conjointly with David Mcgillade, Prior Colideorum, to visit the diocese of Armagh. (Ibid., lib. i., fol. 27 *a*.)

1427, May 22. The lands of Derenoysse, Ballymycieny, Ballymaccolgayn, and Ballyhogan, in the parish of Derenoyse [now Derrynoose], belonging to the Prior and Colidei of Armagh, having been sequestrated by the Primate, for their neglecting to repair the chancel of Derenoyse, and for other omissions, the said Prior and Colidei broke the sequestration; whereupon they were warned to submit, the parishioners admonished not to pay their rents, four sequestrators were named, and. in case of continued contumacy, Odo and Maurice, the sons of Oneyll, were to be appealed to for the secular arm. (Ibid., lib. iii., fol. 78 *a*.)

1428, March 12. At an ordination held by the Primate in St. Peter's of Drogheda, John Mcgiernaid, Colideus of Armagh, was admitted to the priesthood. (Ibid., lib. i., fol. 55 *b*.)

1428. The common seal of the Chapter decreed to pertain to the custody of the Chancellor and Præcentor. (Ibid., lib. iii., fol. 132 *a*.)

1429, March 26. Patrick Occassaly, Colideus of the church of Armagh, ordained deacon ad titulum ejusdem," by the Primate, in St. Peter's of Drogheda. The same ordained priest, on the 26th of May, in the chapel of Termonfeghin. (Ibid., lib. i., fol. 56 *b.*)

1429, June 18. Salomon Mᶜcrenyr, Chancellor, and Magonius Ohynrachtaych, a Canon, the Primate's commissaries, received a letter by the hands of Philip Mᶜgeogayn, herenach of the church of Derrenoys on·behalf of the tenants, stating that the Colidei, asserting their canonical right to said church for their use, monopolized the issues and profits to that degree that the vicar had not enough left for his support; and the said commissaries were empowered to reapportion the revenues. William Mᶜgillade, Prior Colideorum, and his college of the church of Armagh, commonly called Colidei, were rectors of the church, and of the lands adjoining the same, being twenty miles by seven in extent; but scarcely any one could be prevailed on to accept the vicarage, and it had been for a long time vacant. On the 7th of October, the Prior and Colidei allocated the third part of all the tithes of Ballymaclemy citra montes, for the maintenance of a chaplain; but this being found insufficient, and the Prior and Colidei having granted no further augmentation, the commissaries added to the third part of Ballymaclemy and Ballycolgan, the third part of Balyhydocowa and Caranach, with half the third of all the tithes, &c., pertaining to said church. (Ibid., lib. i., fol. 48 *b.*)

1429, Nov. 4. David Mᶜgillade, Prior Colideorum, appointed a commissary by the Primate, to hold his visitation in ordinary. (Ibid., lib. i., fol. 36 *b.*)

1430, Sept. 25. David Mᶜgillade, Prior Colideorum, commissioned to examine into the grievances complained of by Maria ingen Mᶜinnab, Abbess of Ferta, in Armagh. (Ibid., lib. i., fol. 54 *a.*)

1430, May 17. Donald Okellechan, canon of Armagh, appeared before the Primate in his residence at Drogheda, and reported that the Prioratus Colideorum being vacant by the death of David Mᶜgillade, he had been elected into his place by the unanimous voice of the college. The notarial instrument of license executed to him on the occasion declares: "Dictus Prior, qui in exposicione verbi Dei et aliorum exponendorum plurimum facundus necessarius et utilis, necnon candelena peritus, existat, et ad officii exercitium et regimen, tamquam in loco Presentoris, sufficiens ac circumspectus; et ne propter exilitatem fructuum, cum ex emolumentis dicti Prioratus, qui dignitas existit, sicuti considerasset, absque alterius beneficii commoditatibus deficeret, ad sui condecentem statum uberius supportandum, prout predecessores sui Prioratus predicti per antiqua tempora diuturna unacum eodem Prioratu inconcusse beneficia curata detinuissent, ut ipse consimili modo perpetuam vicariam ecclesie parochialis de Twyna quam tunc possidebat, unacum dicto Prioratu libere at licite retinere, &c." (Registrum Prene, fol. 43 *b.*)

1432, Jan. 24. John Mᶜgeerun, Colideus of the church of Armagh, appointed by Archdeacon John Prene to collect his procurations. (Registrum Octaviani, fol. 31 *b.*)

1433. Eugenius Olorcan, Colideus of the church of Armagh, appointed by the Archdeacon to induct John Mᶜgeerun, Colideus of the same, into the rectory of the parish church of Carnesegyll [now Carnteel]. (Ibid., fol. 32 *b.*)

1434, Oct. 20. Donatus Okellachan, Prior Colideorum, a commissary of the Primate to hold the ordinary visitation. (Regist. Swayne, lib. i., fol. 27 *b.*)

1439, Jan. 9. Mandate of the Primate to Donaldus Okellaghan, Prior Colideorum, to induct and install John White in the Archdeaconry of Armagh. (Ibid., lib. iii., fol. 7 *b.*) Jan. 21, letters testificatory of said induction witnessed by Thomas Olucheran, Thomas M⸰kylcrany, David Okellachan, and Thadeus Ohallegan, Colidei of the church of Armagh. (Ibid., fol. 8 *a.*)

1441, May 19. Donaldus Okellachan. Prior Colideorum and Canon. David Okellaghan, vicar of Drumcrygh and Colideus. John Otownyr, priest and Colideus. (Registrum Prene, fol. 114 *b.*)

1441. The diocese placed under interdict, and the Prior and Colidei forbidden to celebrate mass and other divine offices, during the continuance of the same. (Ibid., fol. 155 *a.*)

1441, Oct. 30. License granted to David Okellachan, Colideus of Armagh, and vicar of Drumcrygh, for non-residence on his vicarage, his duties being discharged by a resident chaplain. (Ibid., fol. 112 *b*, 114 *b.*)

1441. In a sentence pronounced by the Primate, the order of the Armagh clergy is: the Dean, Abbot of St. Peter's and St. Paul's, Chancellor, Prior Colideorum, Official of Armagh, Canons, Colidei. (Ibid., fol. 122 *a.*)

1442, Nov. 7. Examination of Thomas M⸰killacrany, then eighty years of age, and Thomas Olucheran, Colidei of Armagh, in certain proceedings in the case of John, abbot of St. Peter's and St. Paul's. (Ibid., fol. 31 *a.*)

1448, Jan. 15. Commission of the Primate to the Dean and Prior Colideorum, in the matter of John M⸰geerun, a Colideus, who had killed a layman in self-defence, and was sentenced to pay as an eric 26 marks and a half in money or cows, authorizing a collection to be made for him in the deanries of Erthyr and Tulaghoge. (Registrum Mey, fols. 25 *a*, 27 *b*, 67 *a.*)

1450, Jan. 28. Commission to the Dean, Official, Prior, and other Colidei, especially Patrick Olagan, apparitor. (Ibid., fol. 22 *a.*)

1450, July 27. A license witnessed by Donaldus Okellachan, Prior Colideorum, "loco Precentoris." (Ibid.)

1455, Aug. 5. The Colidei lodged a complaint in court before the Primate against Cormac Oconnolan, vicar of Darenoyss, for detaining the third part of Ayogowen, with the profits appropriate to the rectory. (Registrum Prene, App. ii., fol. 13 *b.*)

1455, Aug. 13. Certain proceedings before the Primate witnessed by Nicholas Ohernayg, Patrick Olagan, apparitor, John Otonuir, "magister operis majoris ecclesie," and Malachias Offallagan, Colidei of said church. (Ibid., Append. ii., fol. 16 *b.*)

1458. License granted by Primate Bole to the Prior and Colidei to appoint a confessor. (Ibid., fol. 11 *a.*)

1458, May 5. Primate Bole confirms to the Colidei the privileges granted by his predecessor. (Registrum Bole, fol. 25 *b.*)

1460. Sentence of the Primate against Henry Oneyll and his brothers Odo and Mauricius, for injuries done to the Canonici Majores, the Colidei, and convent of St. Peter and St. Paul, of Armagh. (Registrum Prene, fol. 17 *b.*)

1462, Jan. 13. Collation of Magonius Ocoyne to the rectory of Tullaghnyskan, "in camera domini Primatis infra locum Colideorum Ardmachiæ." (Ibid., fol. 183 *b.*)

1462, Jan. 29. Certain proceedings, "in camera infra mansum suæ solitæ residentiæ apud Armachiam, viz., in loco Collideorum, coram Primate." (Ibid., fol. 201 *b.*)

1462, Feb. 19. Patrick Olagan, capellanus and Colideus of Armagh, appointed apparitor in the city and deanry of Erthyr, in place of Gregory M°gillacrany, deprived. (Ibid., fol. 194 *b.*)

1469, Sept. 20. The college of Colidei of the greater church of Armagh presented an appeal in said church, setting out that, whereas they were possessed of the rectory of Dompnaghmore, by virtue of an union made by the Primate, and confirmed by the Dean and Chapter, a certain clerk of Armagh, Tatheus Odonnegale, had procured a surreptitious presentation to the same, and sentence of deprivation against the Colidei. (Registrum Bole, fol. 36 *a.*)

1482, Jan. 22. Petrus Omulmoid, Prior Colideorum, a commissary of the Primate. (Registrum Octaviani, fol. 112 *a.*)

1484, July 16. Petrus Omulmoid, Prior Colideorum, Mauricius Omulmoid, "bajulator Canonis," and Odo Oconor, "magister operis ecclesie." (Ibid., fol. 268 *a.*)

1485, Jan. 23. Custody of the Deanry of Armagh committed to Petrus Omulmoid, late Prior Colideorum. (Ibid., fol. 73 *a.*)

1550, May 31. Primate Dowdall, by an instrument, from which the following is an extract, constituted the Dean of Armagh Master or Rector of the cathedral Colidei, in the room of Edmund Mecamayll, the late Dean : "Georgius, permissione divina Archiepiscopus Armachanus, &c., dilecto nobis in Christo Terentio Danyell, Decano ecclesiæ nostre metropolitice, &c. Tibi igitur, de cujus fidelitate circumspectione et industria plurimum in Domino confidimus, officium regiminis et gubernationis dictorum collegii et sacerdotum necnon Colledeorum et ceterorum ministrorum et servitorum ad divinum cultum in eodem collegio deservientium, sub nomine Magistri aut Rectoris collegii, et non Prioris, intuitu caritatis conferimus, et per presentes committimus et assignamus, inhibentes et prohibentes tibi ne terras aut redditus, decimas vel alios quoscumque fructus ad dictos Colledeos pertinentes alienabis vel ad tempus locabis sine nostro et dictorum Colledeorum consensu et voluntate." (Registrum Dowdall, p. 127.)

L.—OBITS OF COLIDEI, FROM THE ANTIPHONARY OF ARMAGH.

V. Kl. [Feb.] Hic in die sancte Agnetis virginis secundo, celebratis suis omnibus horis canonicis, licet intollerabili egritudine detentus, obiit vir omni probitate clarrissimus, dominus Edmundus M°Kamyl, Decanus Ardmachanus, ac Prior Collideorum sive conventus ecclesie majoris ac metropolitice Armachane, qui bona ipsius ecclesie secundum juris disposicionem et multo devotius pro suo tempore divisit, nam corpus suum in servitutem rediens, totam ipsius [ecclesiam] cum Dei adjutorio restauravit, nichilominus pauperibus omni die erogando necnon et hosbitalitatem satis honeste custodiendo ac servicium assiduum ecclesie reservando, Anno Domini MCCCCXLIX°.

XVII. Kl. [Septembr.] Hic obiit venerabilis vir dominus Johannes Mᵹıllaṁupᴅ quondam magister operum et Collideus hujus metropolitice ecclesie Ardmacane. Cujus anime propicietur Deus. MCCCCCLVI.

IV. Non. [Sept.] Obitus Rolandi m̃ ꝺıllaṁupa venerabilissimi viri, prudentis largique, humilis, affabilis, chari, amabilisque omnibus; qui erat quondam Rector ecclesiæ de Clonmor, Vicariusque Atri Dei, bacularius sacræ theologiæ, concionatorque ejusdem, ac Collideus metropolitice ecclesiæ Ardmacane, qui obiit festo sancti Columbæ ix°. Junii A°. D¹. 1570 : cujus animæ propitietur Deus. Amen. Perlegens dicat Pater noster, Ave, Credo.

III. Non. [Octob.]. Hic obiit dominus Nicolauus m̃ ꝺıllaṁupa quondam magister operum, ac Collideus hujus ecclesie metropoliticæ, vir bonus largus et amabilis, charusque omnibus, ac perfectus sacerdos, nec non perfectus in arte muscika. Anno Domini m.ccccc°.lxxiiii., vi°. Kalendas Octobris cujus anime propicietur Deus, et legens dicat Pater noster, Ave Maria, et Credo.—*MS. Trin. Coll., Dubl.*, B. 1. 1.

M.—Records of St. Andrews.

No. 1. — *The Registers of the Priory.*

Robert, an Englishman, and canon of St. Oswald's in Yorkshire, was brought to Scotland in company with five others to promulgate the Augustinian rule, and made abbot of Scone; whence he was promoted to the see of St. Andrews in 1122, and consecrated between 1125 and 1127. He carried out with great zeal the work which his predecessor had begun ;* and finding in king David a prince whose views regarding monastic discipline were coincident with his own, he founded and endowed at St. Andrews a priory of regular canons, to whom the hospital of the Keledei, together with their influence, was transferred, and in juxtaposition with whom the elder community became enfeebled, and eventually expired. This priory was founded in 1144. At an early stage of its existence the compilation of a book of muniments was taken in hands by one of the fraternity, in which were entered not only charters, but various historical matters, and, among the rest, the legend of St. Regulus, followed by an account of the church brought down to the writer's time. The original of this important collection, entitled the Magnum Registrum, has been missing ever since 1660 ;† and its loss would be irreparable if it had not been that some valuable extracts were made from it, and a table of its contents preserved.‡ Among these is the following account of the

---

* " Anno ab incarnatione Domini mcviii. ac tempore regis Malcolmi et Sanctæ Margaretæ, electus fuit Turgotus, prior Dunelmensis, in episcopum Sancti Andreæ ; consecratusque est Eboraci tertio Kalendas Augusti, et stetit per annos septem. In diebus illis totum jus Keledeorum per totum regnum Scotiæ transivit in Episcopatum Sancti Andreæ." Chron. Dunelmense ap. Selden Ad Lectorem, in Twysden's Hist. Angl. Script. Decem, p. vi. Also, Ussher, Brit. Eccl. Antiqq., cap. 15 (Works, vol. vi. p. 197).

† Sir James Dalrymple, Historical Collections, p. 106.

‡ In the present examination we have to deplore the loss of No. 11. " Petitio Kelideorum, et subjectio eorum Episcopo S. Andreæ." Sir James Dalrymple, though not remarkable in general for clearness of judgment, is in this case probably correct when he says, " If the contents of this were known, it would give great light to the whole matter." Hist. Collect., p. 284.

Keledei of St. Andrews.* Another very important register, or Liber Chartarum, which was compiled for this priory, is still in existence,† and it furnishes the principal portion of the charter evidence which is here brought forward in reference to the Keledei of this church.

No. 2.—*Historia Ecclesie Sancti Andree.*‡   A. D. 1144–1153.

Deleto igitur funditus Pictorum regno, et a Scotis occupato, vicissim res et possessiones ecclesiæ crescebant aut decrescebant, prout reges et principes devotionem ad sanctum Apostolum habebant. De quibus non est dicendum modo per singula, sed quæ ad nos spectant compendiose tractanda. Erat autem regia urbs Rymont,§ Regius mons, dicta, quam præfatus rex Hungus‖ Deo et sancto Apostolo dedit. Sublatis vero a præsenti vita Sanctis quorum supra mentionem fecimus, qui cum reliquiis beati Apostoli advenerant, et eorum discipulis atque imitatoribus, cultus ibi religiosus deperierat sicut et gens barbara et inculta fuerat.

Habebantur tamen in ecclesia Sancti Andreæ, quota et quanta tunc erat, tredecim¶ per succes-

---

* These extracts, copied from Sir R. Sibbald's transcripts, are preserved in the British Museum, Harl., No. 4628. Pinkerton says that the collection was written after 1708. Enquiry, vol. i., p. 451. The MS. is in folio, and the writing is in a good bold hand; but evidently the work of one who was ignorant of Latin, as the extract in the text above, which is printed with all its grammatical blemishes, sufficiently proves. It is much to be regretted that a record composed in an obscure and involved style should have its difficulties increased by the incapacity of successive scribes.

† Edited for the Bannatyne Club, with a valuable preface by Cosmo Innes, Edinb., 1841, under the title, "Liber Cartarum Prioratus Sancti Andree in Scotia. E Registro ipso in Archivis Baronum de Panmure hodie asservato."

‡ This narrative formed part of the "Historia," which stood No. 18 in the "Magnum Registrum" (fol. 58–99). In the existing transcript it is fol. 231 *b*. Pinkerton printed it in his Enquiry (vol. i., Appendix, p. 462), but with some inaccuracies, which added to the obscurity of the text. In estimating the character here given of the Keledei, we must bear in mind that the writer was a member of a rival community, whose advancement depended in a great measure upon the depression of the antecedent institution.

§ "Vertex Montis Regis, id est Rigmond." Extract in Pinkerton's Enquiry, vol. i., p. 499. In the chartulary the churchtown of St. Andrews is called Kilrimund, and the Irish Calendars notice Cıll Rıᵹmanaoh (Oct. 11). In the Annals of Tighernach (747) the prefix is *Cenn*, "head," instead of *cill*, "church," which answers to the word *vertex* above cited: "Mors Tuathalaín Abbatis Cind-rigmonaigh." So the Annals of Ulster, 746. The old name Rymont is still preserved in two hills of the parish, namely, West Balrymonth on the border of Cameron, and East Balrymonth adjoining Denino. In charters they are written Balrimund, Barrimunid, and Barrimunith.

‖ Hungus is the *Unnuist filius Urguist* of the Pictish Chronicle, and the *Oengus mac Fergusa rex Fortrenn* of the Irish Annals, whose death is placed by them at the year 834. St. Regulus may have been his contemporary, but it is incorrect to say that Hungus was the founder, because S. Cainnech, in the sixth century, built a church here, which had become a monastery before 747, in which year an abbot, who is mentioned in the preceding note, died.

¶ Thirteen, that is, twelve brethren and a prior, as in Monymusk. See *infra*, R., No. 14. Twelve, after the model of the apostolical college, was the prevailing number in early monastic institutions. (Reeves, notes to Adamnan's St. Columba, pp. 299–303). The original foundation of St. Benedict had twelve monasteries, and in each, twelve brethren under a superior. (S. Gregorii Dial., lib. ii., cap. 3—Opp., tom. ii., col. 220, ed. Bened.) Some writers suppose that the number stated here denotes so many successions, as Sir James Dalrymple (Hist. Collect., p. 123); and Toland (Nazarenus, Letter ii., p. 31). But the plural forms *vivunt*, *habent*, &c., in the narrative are sufficient to explode such an interpretation, which Goodall (Keith's Bishops, Prelim. Dissert., p. lx.), and subsequent

sionem carnalem,* quos Keledeos appellant, qui secundam (*sic*) suam æstimationem ęt hominum traditionem magis quam secundum sanctorum statuta patrum vivebant. Sed et adhuc similiter vivunt, et quædam habent communia, pauciora scilicet et deteriora, quædam vero propria, plura scilicet et potiora; prout quisque ab amicis suis aliqua necessitudine ad se pertinentibus, videlicet consanguineis et affinibus, vel ab iis quorum animæ charæ sunt, quod est animarum amici,† sive aliis quibus libet modis, poterit quis adipisci. Postquam Keledei effecti sunt, non licet eis habere uxores suas in domibus suis,‡ sed nec alias de quibus mala oriatur suspicio mulieres.§

Personæ nihilominus septem‖ fuerunt oblationes altaris inter se dividentes, quarum septem

Scotch writers dismiss as untenable. Possibly St. Bernard's account of the Armagh abuse—"nec parum processerat execranda successio, decursis jam hac malitia quasi generationibus quindecim," though not a case in point, may have suggested the erroneous interpretation. The words in the text simply mean that there was a society of thirteen, who were kept up by the transmission of the office either from father to son, or with limitation in certain families, instead of open election. An interesting entry in the Book of Armagh distinguishes between the *ecclesiastica* and *plebilis progenies* of a church. See Proceedings, vol. vi., p. 448.

* Van Hecke, the Bollandist, distinguishes between carnalis *generacio* and *successio.* (Acta SS., Octob., tom. viii., p. 166 *b.*) But the distinction is frivolous in the present case, as the estate of matrimony was no disqualification for Culdeeship. The expression includes sons and other kinsmen, and has reference to the old Celtic system, which limited certain monastic offices in particular families, and regulated the elections by the observance of a sort of ecclesiastical tanistry.

† So the words are in the MS., but Pinkerton disguised the expression by printing it *amiciarum amici*. Previously to my obtaining the true reading by a reference to what is now the original, I had conjecturally adopted it as an emendation of the text, supposing that the error was not attributable to him, but to his exemplar. I had so often met the Irish term *anmchara* (see e. gr. the Rule, in Evidence H., pp. 88, 90, *supra*) in the sense of a "soul-friend," or "spiritual adviser," i. e. "confessor," that at the first glance I was persuaded this clause was a paraphrase of it. This term, which was no doubt familiar to the ecclesiastics of a church just emerging from Celtic associations, was regarded as a Latin compound (which it radically is), and made *animacara*, declined in plural *animæcaræ;* and then to make it intelligible to a future or alien reader, the writer by way of explanation added parenthetically the words which have been so misunderstood. The passage has reference to the offerings made by the laity to those of the Keledei who were their confessors, respectively—*ab iis quorum animæcaræ sunt* (quod est *animarum amici*), signifying "by those whose anmchara s they (the Keledei) are. The profits of these Keledei flowed from three sources, gifts of friends, dues of confession, miscellaneous acquisitions.

‡ It is evident from this that the condition of matrimony was no disqualification for the office of a Keledeus, and such as were married men before their admission were likely to have families, from which, in process of time, persons would be chosen to fill up vacancies *carnali successione*. Van Hecke contends that this passage, instead of being an evidence that the Keledei were married men, is rather the reverse (Acta SS., *ut supra*, p. 166 *b.*); but he overlooks the fact that the having a wife was not incompatible with the office of a Keledeus, and that this exclusion of their wives from their houses (like the Dunkeld restriction) was exceptional, not general, having reference to their official residences, which they occupied when on duty.

§ Thus the MS.; but Pinkerton reads *mulieris*, and the Bollandist editor untowardly recommends it in the margin.

‖ These seven parsons, or beneficiaries, were over and above the thirteen Keledei, and appear to have taken the place of the superior officers of the ancient monastery, the bishop being one of them, and the hospital representing another. They occupied the position of Rectors, and their office had to a great extent become secularized and grown to be sinecure, while the Keledei were virtually the Vicars. Thus, in the subsequent taxation of the benefices belonging to the priory, the church of the Holy Trinity of St. Andrews is rated at 100 marks, while the Keledei who held the place of Vicars were taxed at 30. (See No. 15 *infra.*) When the chapter was recast, it was easy to transfer

portionum unam tantum habebat episcopus,* et hospitale unam; quinque vero reliquæ in quinque cæteros dividebantur, qui nullo† omnino altari vel ecclesiæ impendebant servitium,‡ præterquam peregrinus (*sic*) et hospites, cum plures quam sex adventarunt, more suo hospitio suscipiebant, sortem mittentes quis quos vel quot reciperet. Hospitale§ sane semper sex et infra suscipiebat. Sex (*recte* sed) quod nunc, donante Deo, postquam in manum Canonicorum devenit, omnes suscepit eo advenientes.

Personæ autem supra memoratæ reditus et possessiones proprias habebant, quas, cum e vitæ (*sic*) decederent, uxores eorum quas publice tenebant, filii quoque vel filiæ, propinqui vel generi, inter se dividebant: nihilominus‖ altaris oblationes cui non deserviebant; quod puduissent dicere, si non libuisset eis facere. Nec potuit tantum aufferri malum usque ad tempus fælicis memoriæ regis Alexandri, sanctæ Dei Ecclesiæ specialis amatoris, qui et ecclesiam beati Andreæ apostoli possessionibus et redditibus ampliavit, multisque et magnis muneribus cumulavit, libertatibus et consuetudinibus quæ sui regii muneris erant, cum regali possessione donavit. Terram etiam quæ Cursus Apri dicitur,¶ quam cum allatæ fuissent reliquiæ beati Andreæ Apostoli, rex Hungus, cujus

---

the altarages to the regular canons without interfering with the rights of the Keledei. These seven parsons enjoyed official estates as well as the altar oblations, and it is very probable that their lands formed the bulk of the landed property of the canons regular. "Episcopus, de terris personarum quæ abeuntibus eis in manum ejus obvenerant, quam libuit portionem consilio et assensu regis et filii ejus et ceterorum baronum qui aderant, fratri Roberto in manum tradidit." (Pinkerton, Enquiry, vol. i., p. 467.)

* See Nos. 7 and 8 *infra*, where the bishop's seventh is reserved. Bishop Arnald subsequently surrendered it; see No. 10. This parity of the bishop in emolument from the altar seems to be a vestige of the old Celtic system, in which the monastic bishop was a subordinate.

† So the MS., but *nullum* is preferable.

‡ It would seem from this that those five parsons were laymen, holding portions as it were of an impropriate rectory. Thus the Historia says: "oblationes in manibus laicorum, tam virorum quam mulierum, exceptæ, in usus ecclesiæ sunt receptæ." (Pinkerton, Enquiry, vol. i., p. 465.) Yet, in Bishop Arnald's grant the seven parsons are merely described as "non communiter viventes" (No. 10 *infra*.). Previously to 1144, the regular canons had acquired two of these parsonages (No. 3 *infra*), either by lapse, cession, or the cooption of the holders into their body.

§ The hospital was an important element in the old Celtic monasteries. At Armagh there was the *Lis Aeidhedh*, "Fort of Guests" (Four Mast., 1003, 1015, 1116, 1155), and at Clonmacnois, the *Tech-Aeidhedh*, "House of Guests," (*ib.*, 1031, 1093, 1106), each of which had lands, and an herenach.

‖ The use of nihilominus in this record is unusual, and it seems to be employed in the sense of *immo etiam*. See above, *Personæ nihilominus*, and again in the middle of No. 3 *infra*.

¶ When Bishop Robert wished to endow his new society of canons, but was unwilling to alienate any of the see estates, King David I. replied, "ut de terra illa, quæ Cursus Apri dicitur, quæ de Episcopatu non erat, quam rex Alexander frater ejus propter hoc Deo et sancto Andreæ devoverat, ut in ecclesia ejus religio constitueretur, sufficienter eis tribueret." (Pinkerton, Enquiry, vol. i., p. 467.) The earliest name of St. Andrews was *Mucros*, "Nemus porcorum." Cursus Apri in Gaelic would be cuṗṗach an ṫuiṗc: Wynton renders the name *Bairs Reake*. Boece preserves the tradition that it was so called from a great boar which frequented the neighbourhood, and after many efforts was slain by an armed multitude. (Histor. lib. xii.. fol. 263 *a*.) Dempster and Goodall, who were so desirous to appropriate Irish territories, might with equal reason and better appearance have changed a letter, and transferred the great Calydonian hunt from Ætolia to this scene of adventure. The Cursus Apri, (as appears from No. 22, *infra*), was the barony or tract comprehending the church lands of St. Andrews. For its extent, and the parishes contained in it, see Martine, Reliquiæ Divi Andreæ, pp. 93, 94; Lyon's History of St. Andrews, vol. i., p. 61.

supra mentionem fecimus, Deo et sancto Apostolo Andreæ dederat, et postea ablata fuerat,* ex integro instituit, eo nimirum obtentu et conditione ut in ipsa ecclesia constitueretur religio ad Deo deserviendum. Non enim erat qui beati Apostoli altari deserviret, nec ibi missa celebrabatur nisi cum rex vel episcopus illo advenerat, quod raro contingebat. Keledei namque in angulo quodam ecclesiæ, quæ modica nimis erat, suum officium more suo celebrabant.† Cujus donationis regiæ testes multi sunt superstites. Quam donationem et Comes David frater ejus concessit, quem rex heredem destinaverat, et in regno successorem, sicut est hodie.‡

No. 3.—*Carta Roberti episcopi de fundacione domus.* A. D. 1144.

Robertus Dei gratia Scottorum episcopus,§ omnibus, *et cetera.* Ecclesiam beati Andree apostoli, cui auctore Deo deservio, quoniam usque ad tempus nostrum permodica fuerat, Deo inspirante, ampliare studuimus ; sed quoniam non sufficit ad laudem nominis Domini lapidum congeriem congregare, nisi et procuremus vivos in Dei edificium lapides adunare, Canonicos ibidem ad Deo deserviendum sub regula canonicali beati patris Augustini constituimus : quibus et filium nostrum fratrem Robertum in partem laboris nostri assumentes, jure pariter et nomine prioris prefecimus, et ad victum et vestitum eorum ceteraque necessaria de possessionibus et redditibus nostris, consilio simul et concessione piissimi regis nostri David, necnon et filii ejus Henrici comitis et regis designati, nichilominus‖ et episcoporum, abbatum, comitum atque optimatum et fidelium suorum consilio porcionem quandam in perpetuam possidendam liberam et inconcussam indulsimus. Que autem donavimus et concessimus subscribenda dignum duximus : sunt autem hec, Barrimund, Struaithin Kinnines, Castdovenald, Drumckarach, Ledochin, Stradkines, Balhucca, Rodmanand, Pettultin, Kinastare, Chinemonie, Drumsac, Balemacdunechin, Egglesnamin, Ballothen, Sconin, molendinum de Kiiremund, molendinum de Puthachin, *etc.* De septem vero porcionibus que sunt altaris Sancti Andree ipsis Canonicis duas porciones¶ dedimus et concessimus, que pertinent duobus personagiis

---

* It had probably passed into lay occupation, like the church lands of Bangor in Ireland. See St. Bernard's Life of Malachi, chap. 5 (Messingham, Florilegium. p. 356 *a*).

† Bishop Gillan understands these words as implying that the Keledei "made use of a *Breviary* different from what was used afterwards by the *Canon Regulars* who invaded their Lands and Rights ;" and adds, "It is certain there were different *Breviaries* and *Missals* both in *England* and *Ireland :* and why not in *Scotland* also ?" (Remarks upon Sir J. Dalrymple's Hist. Coll., p. 130.)

‡ The foregoing has been printed by Pinkerton. (Enquiry, vol. i., pp. 462-467) ; Jamieson (Historical Account, pp. 378-388) ; and borrowed from him by the Bollandist Van Hecke (Acta SS., Octob., tom. viii., p. 166). But in neither case accurately.

§ In the Irish Annals, at 1055, 1093, we meet with the expression epꞃcob Clbɑn "Bishop of Scotland," and this title is confirmed by several Scottish records. See the interesting and oft-cited passage of the Historia in Pinkerton, Enquiry, vol. i., p. 464. Bishop Arnald styles himself *Scottorum episcopus* (Regist. Priorat. S. Andree, pp. 126. 127, 128) ; as also his successor, Richard. (Ibid., p. 12.)

‖ See the observations on the peculiar use of this word, in note § of the preceding page.

¶ These two shares seem to have been the portions of two parsonages which had lapsed by death. "Tunc dominus Episcopus, quasi sponte coactus, de terris personarum, quæ, abeuntibus eis in manum ejus obvenerant, quam libuit portionem, consilio et assensu Regis, &c., fratri Roberto in manum tradidit." (Pinkerton, Enquiry, vol. i.,

que ipsi habent, et hospitali ejusdem ville unam porcionem. Quod nimirum hospitale cum terris et possessionibus et redditibus eidem pertinentibus eisdem concessimus in susceptionem hospitum et peregrinorum, et ad ipsum hospitale medietatem decime carrucarum nostrarum et vaccarum et berchariarum et porchariarum et equariarum de parochia Sancte Trinitatis, et medietatem de nostro chan* ejus parrochie, et totam decimam de nostro chan de Bladebolg,† etc. Anno Dominice incarnacionis M°.c°.XL°.IIII°.‡

No. 4.—*Carta regis David ut Keldei de Kilrimont recipiantur,* etc. circ. A. D. 1144.

David rex Scotorum, *etc.* Sciatis me dedisse et concessisse priori et canonicis suis ecclesie beati Andree apostoli, ut recipiant Kelledeos de Kilrimont in canonicos secum cum omnibus possessionibus et redditibus suis, si voluerint canonici fieri; et si noluerint canonicari hii qui nunc vivunt habeant et teneant possessiones suas in vita sua; et post obitum illorum instituantur loco eorum tot canonici in ecclesia Sancti Andree quot sunt Kelledei, et omnia predia et omnes terre et elemosine eorum quas habent convertantur in usus canonicorum predicte ecclesie in perpetuam liberam et quietam elemosinam, *etc.*§

No. 5.—*Bulla Eugenii pape tercii.* A. D. 1147.

Eugenius *etc.*, Roberto priori ecclesie beati Andree in Scotia ejusque fratribus, *etc.*, prefatam ecclesiam, *etc.* sub beati Petri et nostra protectione suscipimus *etc.* Obeunte vero fratre nostro Roberto episcopo, nullus in ecclesia sancti Andree, que sedes episcopalis est, aliqua surreptionis astutia seu violentia preponatur, sed quem vos, communi consensu vel fratrum ecclesie vestre pars consilii sanioris secundum Deum canonice provideritis eligendum.‖ Statuimus etiam ut decedentibus Keledeis, loco eorum regulares canonici auctore Domino subrogentur,¶ *etc.* ANNO M°.c°.XLVII.**

---

p. 467) All the portions were subsequently transferred to the canons. See Nos. 7, 8, 10, *infra.* In 1156, Adrian IV. confirmed only two portions and that of the hospital (Regist., p. 52), but in 1163 Alexander III. confirmed the grant of all (ib., p. 55).

* This word, sometimes written *can, chanus,* and *kan,* is of frequent occurrence in early Scotch characters, being the Gaelic cáin, " a rent," " tribute."

† Bladbolg was a denomination of land belonging to the bishop, as appears from the recital in the Magnum Registrum. Pinkerton, Enquiry; vol. i., p. 470.

‡ Registrum Prioratus S. Andree, pp. 122, 123.

§ Ibid., p. 186.

‖ This ordinance took the election out of the hands of the Keledei, who under the old system enjoyed the right of choosing the bishop. Their claim, however, was afterwards revived. See Nos. 19–21, 23, 24, *infra.*

¶ The same provision is repeated in the bulls of Adrian IV., A. D. 1156 (Regist. Priorat., S. Andree, p. 52); Lucius III., A. D. 1183 (ibid., p. 60); Gregory VIII., A. D. 1187 (ibid., p. 65); Clement III., A. D. 1187 (ibid., p. 69); Innocent III., A. D. 1206 (ibid., p. 74); Honorius III., A. D. 1216 (ibid., p. 79); Innocent IV., A. D. 1248 (ibid., p. 101). Thus, for nearly a century the Keledei held their ground against papal, as they had previously done against regal, authority.

** Registr. Priorat. S. Andree, p. 49.

No. 6.—*Confirmacio regis David ecclesie S. Trinitatis de Dunfermelyn.* A. D. circ. 1148.

Do et concedo, assensu Henrici comitis, filii mei, *etc.,* Belacristin,* cum suis rectis divisis, in pratis et pascuis, excepta rectitudine quam Keledei† habere debent.‡

Controversia que versabatur inter monachos de Dunfermelyn et canonicos de Sancti Andrea super terra de Balcristin, in qua canonici de Sancto Andrea jus clamabant per Keledeos de tempore regis David avi mei in presentia mea terminata est. Ita quod monachi terram illam habeant, salva elemosina ipsis canonicis ab ipsis monachis de Dunfermelyn, quam Keledei habuerunt in terra illa tempore regis David.§

No. 7.—*Carta Roberti episcopi de oblacionibus altaris.* A. D. circ. 1156.

Robertus Dei gracia Sancti Andree episcopus, *etc.* Sciant omnes *etc.,* nos concessisse *etc.,* priori Sancti Andree et fratribus ibidem Deo servientibus omnes partes oblacionum altaris,‖ excepta septima, que de jure competit episcopo, liberas et quietas ab omni exactione immunes, *etc.*¶

No. 8.—*Communis confirmacio Malcolmi regis.* A. D. 1160.

Malcolmus Dei gratia Rex Scottorum, *etc.,* do et concedo *etc.,* porciones altaris preter septimam, que jure competit episcopo, *etc.*

Stradkines et aliam Stradkines** pro commutatione de Kynninis et de Lethin quas Kelledei habent.††

No. 9.—*Carta regis Malcolmi de conventione facta.* A. D. circ. 1160.

Malcolmus rex Scottorum *etc.,* Sciant *etc.* nos concessisse, et hac mea carta confirmasse con-

---

* Malcolm Cennmor had granted this denomination to the Keledei of Loch Levin (see P, No. 7, *infra*). On their suppression, it was transferred to the regular canons of St. Andrews.

† The name is written *Cheledei* in a confirmation charter. Regist. de Dunfermelyn, No. 3, p. 8.

‡ Registr. de Dunfermelyn, No. 2, p. 5. Repeated by Malcolm the Maiden, ib., No. 35, p. 19; by William the Lyon, ib., No. 50, p. 28; by Alexander II., ib., No. 74, p. 40; and by Alexander III., ib., No. 81, p. 46.

§ Registr. de Dunfermelyn, No. 59, p. 34.

‖ The seven *personæ* originally enjoyed these (see No. 2, p. 225 *supra*). Three portions were transferred before 1144. The bishop now grants six. In 1162–3, Bishop Arnald assigned and consolidated the whole seven.

¶ Registr. Priorat. S. Andree, p. 125. This charter is also preserved in a collection in the Advocates' Library. 15. 1. 18, No. 11.

** Strathkinnes and Nether Strathkinnes are situate in the north-west of the parish of St. Andrews.

†† Registr. Priorat. S. Andr., p. 206. There are like confirmations. Ernaldi episcopi circ. 1160 (ibid., p. 131); Alexandri III., A. D. 1163 (ibid., p. 54); Ricardi episcopi, circ. 1164 (ibid., p. 143); regis Willelmi, circ. 1167 (ibid., p. 214); Hugonis episcopi, circ. 1179 (ibid., p. 145); Rogeri episcopi, circ. 1190 (ibid., p. 150); Alexandri regis, 1228 (ibid., p. 233).

ventionem factam inter canonicos sancti Andree et Keldeos ejusdem ecclesie, scilicet de Stradkines* et de Lethin,† sicut cyrographum eorum ex utraque parte testatur, *etc.*‡

No. 10.—*Carta Arnaldi episcopi de tota oblacione altaris.*   A. D. 1162–3.

Omnibus *etc.* Arnaldus Dei gracia ecclesie sancti Andree apostoli humilis minister, salutem, *etc.* Quieti canonicorum in ecclesia beati Andree apostoli Deo serviencium in posterum consulentes, omnem oblacionem altaris sui, quam in septem partes divisam persone septem non communiter viventes tenuerunt quondam,§ predictis canonicis regularem vitam professis et in communem degentibus, totam, *etc.* concedendam esse decrevimus, quoniam qui altari deserviunt de altario vivere debent; neque secundum regulas clericales ibi oblacionum porciones fieri debent, ubi communitas vivencium unum facit quodammodo omne quod possidetur, *etc.*‖

No. 11.—*Cyrografum inter Hugonem episcopum et comitem Duncanum.*   A. D. 1178–1188.

Testibus, Erch[enbaldo] abbate, et Lamberto priore de Dunfermelyne, Abbate¶ Keledeorum Sancti Andree, Adam fratre comitis, *etc.***

No. 12.—*Conventio inter Priorem canonicorum et Kelledeos de Sancto Andree.*   A. D. 1199.

Hec est conventio facta inter Gilbertum priorem Sancti Andree et conventum ejusdem loci, et inter Kelledeos de Sancto Andrea, pro lite sopienda que inter illos erat de decimis; scilicet quod dominus prior et canonici concesserunt Kelledeis ut habeant et teneant sine omni calumpnia et contencione in perpetuum rectas decimas plenarias in terris suis,†† scilicet Kingasc,‡‡ Kinnakelle,§§ cum Petsporgin, et Petkennin,‖‖ Lethene,¶¶ cum Kininis, Kernes cum Cambrun;*** ceteris in manu

---

* The Strath or holm of the Kines, the stream called the Kinness Burn, which enters the inner harbour on the south of the city, now Strathkinnes, in the north-west of St. Andrews parish.

† Prior Lethem and Lamb's Lethem are two denominations in the east and south-east of the parish of Cameron.

‡ Registr. Prioratus S. Andree, p. 203.

§ See No. 2, p. 225 *supra.* This consolidation is confirmed in subsequent charters. Registr. Priorat. S. Andree, pp. 145, 215, 234.

‖ Registrum Prioratus S. Andree, p. 129.

¶ This style only occurs once elsewhere, namely, in the attestations of the supposed spurious charter of Malcolm Cennmor to Dunfermlin, where we find—" Testibus Ivo Kelledeorum Abbate, Macduffe Comite, Duncano Comite, Araldo Comite," *etc.*   Registr. de Dunfermelyn, p. 417, Preface, p. xxi.

** Regist. Priorat. S. Andree, p. 353.

†† The recital of the " terræ quas tenent Keledei," from the Magnum Registrum is somewhat different : " Kinkel, Kynnadanfihs, Kynnadyn Equ, Lethin, Kerin, Kerneis, Kynninis, Rathmergullum, Syreis, Baletath, Kaleturse (Boarhills?), Baleocherthyn, Pethkenyn, Kingerg." . Pinkerton, Enquiry, vol. i., p. 470.

‡‡ Now Kingask, on the sea-side in south of St. Andrews parish.

§§ Now Kinkel, a little north-west of last.

‖‖ Probably Pikie, in southern extremity of St. Andrews parish.

¶¶ Lethem in the east of Cameron parish.   Kernes is now Cairns, north-east of Lethem.

*** Now Cameron, giving name to Cameron parish, which, till 1645, formed part of St. Andrews.

canonicorum retentis, scilicet sponsaliis, purificacionibus, oblacionibus, baptismo, corporibus defunctorum, exceptis corporibus Kelledeorum, qui ubi voluerint sepelientur.* Preterea Kelledei habebunt omnes decimas et omnes obvenciones de Kilglassin,† excepto baptismo et corporibus defunctorum. Kelledei siquidem dederunt prefatis canonicis Trestirum‡ per rectas divisas suas imperpetuum, libere et quiete ab omnibus prout ipsi Kelledei liberius et quiecius villam illam habuerunt, *etc.* Testibus hiis domino Rogero episcopo, domino David fratre Regis, Johanne episcopo de Dunkeld, Janatha episcopo de Stratheren,§ Matheo episcopo de Aberdone, Radulfo electo de Brechin, Dunecano comite de Fif, et Malcolmo et Dunecano et David filiis ejus, Gilberto comite de Stratheren, et Malis fratre ejus, Gillecriste comite de Anegus, et filio suo Duncano, Murethach comite de Menetheth, Roberto filio domini Regis, Laurencio‖ filio Horm de Abernithin, Waldeuo filio Merlesuani, Adam filio Odonis, Macduf, Hugone dapifero, Duncano filio Adam de Syres, Buathac de Inchemorthach, Malcolmo filio Malpatric, Alano de Lacels, Bricio persona de Kellin, Galfrido de Malavilla, et pluribus aliis.¶

No. 13.—*Convencio de terra de Sconin et de Gariad.* A. D. circ. 1205.

Testibus, R. Archidiacono, Willelmo capellano de Dervisin, magistro Simono, Hugone senescaldo, Malcolmo judice, Johanne Kelledeo, Adam filio Odonis, etc.**

No. 14.—*Inter Taxaciones ecclesiarum Prioratus S. Andree.*

Ecclesia sancte Trinitatis [de Sancto Andrea],†† c. m^a., et inde Keledei R. pro . . . . xxx. m^a.

No. 15.—*Acta Commissariorum in causa litigata.* A. D. 1250.

Acta in ecclesia parochiali de Inuirkethin in crastino Sancti Leonardi anno gracie m.°cc.° quinquagesimo, coram domino abbate de Dunfermelin, capellano domini pape et cancellario domini regis Scocie, et domino R. thesaurario ecclesie Dunkeldensis, fungentibus auctoritate apostolica inter

---

* The arrangement at Monymusk on this head was not so liberal. See Evidence R, No. 14 *infra.*

† Now Kinglassie in south-east angle of St. Andrews parish.

‡ The priory exchanged Trestirum with the Archdeacon for other lands. Regist. Priorat. S. Andree, p. 315.

§ That is, the diocese of Dunblane. See p. 47 *supra.*

‖ This Laurence was lay abbot of Abernethy. See Evidence Q. No. 4 *infra.*

¶ Registrum Prioratus S. Andree, p. 318.

** Registrum Prioratus S. Andree, p. 329.

†† This church and its profits were enjoyed by Matthew the archdeacon; but, about the year 1170, bishop Richard granted the lands, chapels, oblations, and obventions of it to the priory of regular canons (Regist. Priorat. S. Andree, p. 132), which grant was confirmed by successive popes and bishops, (ibid., pp. 55, 58, 143, 151). All this time the Keledei enjoyed the vicarial profits, as appears from this entry, where they hold the same relation to this church that the vicars do to others in the list (ibid., p. 37). But bishop Gamelinus, about 1258, consolidated the rectory and vicarage, granting the whole to the regular canons, thus depriving the Keledei of their parochial status (ibid., p. 172.) This was and continues to be the parish church of St. Andrews: " Ecclesia parochialis civitatis Sancti Andree, Sancte Trinitatis videlicet" (ibid., p. 63); " Ecclesia parochialis sancte Trinitatis de Kyirimonthschyre" (ibid., p. 132). A new church which was built for it was consecrated by bishop David in 1243 (ibid., p. 348).

dominum priorem et conventum Sancti Andree ex una parte, et magistrum Adam de Malkarwistun gerentem se pro Preposito ecclesie Sancte Marie* civitatis sancti Andree, et Keledeos se gerentes pro canonicis, et eorum vicarios ex altera. Cum dies prenominatus prestitus ad publicandum sentenciam latam per priores de Sancto Oswaldo et de Kyrham in magistrum [A. de Malkarwistun,†] Ricardum Weytement, Willelmum Wischard, Robertum de Insula, Patricium de Muchard, Michaelem Ruffum, Michaelem Nigrum,‡ et quosque alios Keledeos gerentes se pro canonicis,§ et quosque alios inobedientes et rebelles ecclesie Sancte Marie Sancti Andree, et ad inquirendum utrum dicti Keledei et eorum vicarii divina celebraverint sic ligati, et ad statuendum quod canonicum fuerit super premissis. Prefati abbas et thesaurarius actis precedentibus inherentes, usi consilio jurisperitorum, sententiam latam per predictos priores de Sancto Oswaldo et de Kyrham in personas prenominatas, solempniter publicarunt, super inquisicione facienda utrum divina [celebraverint] sic ligati, testes admiserunt, et eorum dicta in scripta redigi fecerunt, et diem partibus prestiterunt, die Sabbati proxima post festum Sancti Andree in ecclesia [fratrum Predicatorum] de Pert, ad publicandum attestationes, ad dicendum (?) in testes et testificata, et ad ulterius procedendum secundum formam mandati apostolici: et licet [dicti judices] prenominatis Preposito et Keledeis, ob eorum manifestam contumaciam, de jure penam possent infligere, tamen penam eis infligendam usque ad diem partibus prestitam [distulerunt].‖

No. 16.—*Declaratio in curia papali.* A. D. 1250.

Omnibus presentes litteras inspecturis magister Guillelmus Parmen, domini pape capellanus, ac ejusdem contradictorum auditor, salutem in Domino. Noveritis quod cum Radulfus de Helig procurator amissus de speciali domini Pape mandato pro Preposito et Capitulo ecclesie Sancte Marie Sancti Andree in Scotia impetrasset litteras apostolicas sub hac forma: Innocentius episcopus etc., dilectis filiis Preposito et Capitulo ecclesie Sancte Marie Sancti Andree in Scotia salutem etc. Cum a nobis petitur quod justum est et honestum tam vigor equitatis quam ordo exigit rationis ut id per sollicitudinem officii nostri ad debitum perducatur effectum: eapropter dilecti in Domino filii, vestris justis postulationibus grato concurrentes assensu, ecclesias possessiones et alia bona vestra

---

* This is the earliest instance in which the Keledean church of St. Andrews appears under this title. That of Monymusk also bore the same name. Thus we see how opposed to fact is the sweeping assertion of Sir James Dalrymple, which has been copied by others, that " the common practice of the Culdees was to dedicate their principal churches to the Holy Trinitie, and not to the blessed Virgin or any saint." Histor. Collect., p. 248.

† He was witness to a composition dated 1245. (Registr. Priorat. S. Andree, p. 330.) In 1266, " Adam de Malkaruistun prepositus capelle sancte Marie civitatis Sancti Andree" attests a charter next after the bishop of Dunblane, and before the dean of Dunkeld and the official of St. Andrews. (Ibid., p. 311.) In earlier records he appears as a " clericus domini episcopi." (Ibid., pp. 169, 281.)

‡ The names of seven Keledei are here recited.

§ The constitution of these Keledei seems to have undergone some change previously to this time.

‖ Denmylne Charters, Advocates' Library, Edinburgh, 15. 1. 18. No. 30. The words here enclosed in brackets are now illegible, but are supplied from Sir R. Sibbald's copy as printed in his History of Fife, p. 78. An English translation is given in Lyon's History of St. Andrews, vol. ii., p. 307. See also Sir J. Dalrymple's Historical Collections, p. 283.

que impresentiarum rationabiliter possidetis, aut in futurum justis modis prestante Domino poteritis adipisci, sub beati Petri et nostra proteccione suscipimus, et ea vobis et ecclesie vestre auctoritate apostolica confirmamus et presentis scripti patrocinio communimus. Nulli ergo etc. Si quis autem etc. Datum Lugduni xii. Kalendas Septembres, pontificatus nostri anno septimo. Eisdem litteris Petrus de Sacello procurator prioris et capituli Sancti Andree cathedralis ecclesie in Scotia pro ipsis in audientia publica . . . . ea condicione absoluit, quod per predictas litteras nullum privilegia predictorum prioris et capituli Sancti Andree ecclesie cathedralis prejudicium [caperent], nec ad jurisdictionem executorum eorundem privilegiorum impediendum aliquatenus . . . . coram nobis. In cujus rei testimonium presentes literas fieri fecimus, et nostro communiri sigillo. Datum Lugduni ii. Id. Apriles pontificatus domini Innocentii pape IIII. anno septimo.*

No. 17.—*Prolatio actorum in causa litis pendentis.* A. D. 1253.

Universis etc. Johannes Dei gratia prior et conventus cathedralis ecclesie Sancti Andree in Scotia salutem. Noverit universitas vestra quod cum nos per fratrem Ricardum concanonicum nostrum et procuratorem nostrum ad sedem apostolicam constitutum literas apostolicas ad venerabilem patrem episcopum Brechinensem et religiosos abbatem de Abirbrothoc et priorem de May, impetrasse, continentes ut ipsi bone memorie David episcopum Sancti Andree, necnon Prepositum et Keledeos capelle Sancte Marie loci ejusdem, autoritate apostolica citarent peremptorie, ut infra tres menses post citacionis edictum per se vel procuratores ydoneos in presentia domini Pape se presentarent cum omnibus actis communibus ac munimentis pertinentibus ad causam que vertitur inter nos ex parte una et ipsos ex parte altera super prebendis dicte capelle et earum fructibus ac pertinenciis suis institucione seu collacione ipsarum, super hiis prout justum fuerit processuri, ac dicti episcopus abbas et prior predictos episcopum Sancti Andree, Prepositum et Keledeos juxta tenorem mandati apostolici citassent peremptorie, ut infra quindenum post festum apostolorum Petri et Pauli anno incarnacionis dominice M.CC.L. tercio in presentia domini Pape comparerent, etiam facturi etc. Nos dicto nostro episcopo ex hac luce sublato citacioni predicte ad instantiam nostram facte hac vice duximus supersedendum etc. Ita quod cum ecclesie vestre ut predictum est provisum fuerit de pastore, per aliam literam citatoriam jus nostrum dicta causa prosequi valeamus. Datum apud Sanctum Andream septimo idus Junii anno gracie, M.CC.L.° tercio.†

No. 18.—*Electio Willelmi Wischard in episcopum S. Andree.* A. D. 1273.

Consecratus est autem [Willelmus Wischard] apud Sconam, Idus Octobris, anno Domini MCCLXXIII., Keldeis‡ tunc ab electione exclusis.§.

---

* Denmylne Charters, Advocates' Library, Edinburgh, 15. 1. 18, No. 32. This document has been much defaced by the use of tincture of galls.

† Registrum Prioratus S. Andree, p. 26.

‡ This is the first time that the exclusion of the Keledei from the election is noticed, and from subsequent remarks in the Supplement of Fordun it would seem as if they had until this occasion enjoyed the privilege.

§ Joannis de Fordun Scotichronicon, lib. vi., cap. 43 (vol. i., p. 360, Ed. Goodall).

No. 19.—*Electio Willelmi Fraser in episcopum S. Andree.*   A. D. 1279.

Anno Domini MCCLXXIX. pridie Nonas Augusti electus est Willelmus Fraser, cancellarius regni, exclusis tunc etiam Keldeis, sicut et in electione præcedenti.*

No. 20.—*Electio Gulielmi de Lambirton in episcopum S. Andree.*   A. D. 1297.

Electus est [Willelmus de Lambirton] Non. Novembris, Anno Domini MCCXCVII., exclusis penitus Keldeis tunc, sicut et in duabus electionibus præcedentibus.† Propter quod Willelmus Cumyn, tunc Keledeorum præpositus, huic electioni se opponens, Romam adiit, et in præsentia domini Pape Bonifacii VIII. omnibus modis quibus potuit, electionem prædictam et ipsum electum impugnavit. Sed nihil profecit: nam, non obstantibus ipsius exceptionibus, dominus Papa ipsam electionem approbavit, electum confirmavit, ipsumque electum kalend. Junii A. D. MCCXCVIII. more debito consecravit. Et notandum est, quod jurisdictio sedis, ipsa vacante, penes capitulum totaliter remansit.‡

No. 21.—*Decisio contraversie inter Keledeos et episcopum de jurisdictione agri per Thomam Ranulphi guardianum citra mare Scoticum.*   A. D. 1309.

Et inventum est et solempniter in communi publicatum quod infra Cursum Apri non sunt nisi tres baronie, videlicet baronia domini episcopi S. Andree, baronia domini prioris S. Andree, et baronia Kalediorum. Que quidem baronie cum inhabitantibus immediate sunt subjecte Episcopo S. Andree et ecclesie, et nulli alio. Unde ratione dicte subjectionis, predicte baronie tam de jure quam de consuetudine approbata tenentur facere sectam curie dicti domini Episcopi et ibidem tam de visnetis et dictamentis interesse quam ad alia judicia de condempnatis facienda. Item inventum est quod si aliquod judicium infra curiam domini prepositi Kalediorum seu alicujus baronie infra Cursum Apri sit per aliquem falsatum, ad curiam domini Episcopi est appellandum, et ibi dictum judicium est determinandum et declarandum. *Etc.*§

No. 22.—*Electio Jacobi Ben in episcopum S. Andree.*   A. D. 1328.

Anno præmisso [MCCCXXVIII.] xiii. Kalend. Julii, processerunt ad electionem canonici Sancti Andree, exclusis penitus Keldeis, sicut in electionibus præcedentibus . . . . Contra autem electionem dominus Willelmus Cumyn, tunc præpositus Capellæ Regiæ,‖ se opposuit : sed suam appellationem veluti fingebat ; propter hoc curiam Romanam adire non prosecutus.¶

* Joannis de Fordun Scotichronicon, lib. vi., cap. 44 (vol. i., p. 361, Ed. Goodall).

† Among the lost documents in the Magnum Registrum is the " Relatio quid acciderit de contraversia post mortem Willielmi Phraser Episcopi, et instrumentum de eo."

‡ Joannis de Fordun Scotichronicon (vol. i., p. 361).

§ Registrum Prioratus S. Andree, Appendix to Preface, p. xxxi.

‖ St. Mary's de Rupe, the church of the Keledei, was occasionally called the " Capella regia civitatis Sancti Andree." Martine, Reliquiæ Divi Andreæ, pp. 24, 209, 215 ; Lyon, Hist. of St. Andrews, vol. i., pp. 26, 142 ; vol. ii., p. 148.

¶ Joannis de Fordun Scotichronicon, lib. vi., cap. 45 (vol. i., p. 362, Ed. Goodall).

No. 23.—*Electio Willelmi Bell in episcopum S. Andree.* A. D. 1332.

Electus est Willelmus Bell, decanus Dunkeldensis, exclusis tunc penitus Keldeis, nullumque jus in dicta electione vendicantibus seu impedimentum facientibus, per viam compromissi.*

24.—*Mandatum ad inducendum W. de Dalgernok.*—A. D. 1375.

Willelmus miseracione divina episcopus Sancti Andree dilecto nostro magistro Roberto Bell vicario ecclesie de Errale salutem cum benedictione divina. Quia ecclesiam parochialem de Seres Prepositure ecclesie Beate Marie civitatis Sancti Andree annexam, de jure et facto vacantem per mortem magistri Gilberti Armstrang ultimi rectoris ejusdem, ad presentacionem domini nostri Regis nostramque collacionem spectantem, discreto viro Willelmo de Dalgernok nobis per literas domini nostri Regis ad dictam ecclesiam de Seres presentato, intuitu contulimus caritatis, ac ipsum per annuli nostri tradicionem canonice investivimus de eadem, *etc.* Datum sub sigillo nostro apud Inchemurthach in festo conversionis Sancti Pauli apostoli, anno Domini millesimo tricentesimo septuagesimo quinto.†

N.—Records of Dunkeld.

No. 1.—John of Fordun,‡ and, after him, Wynton,§ and Dean Mylne,‖ following the chronicle in the great Register of St. Andrews,¶ refer the foundation of the church of Dunkeld to Constantine, son of Fergus, king of the Picts, who died in 820. The Pictish Chronicle,** and an ancient Saxon authority,†† ascribe it to Kenneth Mac Alpin, about 849. This chronological difference is not important; and the slight variation is noticed by Fordun, who gives the option of 227 or 244 years for the priority of Abernethy. From the Irish Annals we gather that, so early as the year 864, it was a place of ecclesiastical importance, and had a bishop, who took precedence of others of his own order in Pictland.‡‡ There are four other entries concerning this church in the same chronicles,§§ from which we may conclude that there was a close communication between it and Ireland. It is to be regretted that no register or chartulary of Dunkeld has descended to our time; but, in the absence of the information that such records would afford, we are fortunately supplied by Dean Mylne,—a writer at the close of the fifteenth century,—not only with the statement that this church was originally served by Keledei, but also with a valuable memorandum of their mode of life, and the measures which eventually led to their extinction.

* Scotichronicon (vol. i., p. 363).　　　　† Denmylne Charters, Advocates' Library, 15. 1. 18, No. 39.
‡ Scotichronicon, lib. iv., cap. 12 (vol. i., p. 189); lib. vi., cap. 40 (ibid., p. 356).
§ Cronykel, vi., 10.　　　　‖ See No. 2 *infra.*
¶ Thomas Innes, Critical Essay, vol. ii., p. 800.　　** Ibid., p. 783; Pinkerton, Enquiry, vol. i., p. 494.
†† Hickes, Thesaurus, vol. ii., p. 117; Reeves, Adamnan's Life of St. Columba, pp. 297, 316.
‡‡ See under Dunkeld, p. 41 *supra.*　　　　§§ Annals of Ulster, 872, 964, 1027, 1045.

No. 2.—Scripturum me de vestrae sedis initio, oportet primo retexere qualiter Constantinus Pictorum rex tertius, Divo Columbae totius tunc regni patrono devotus, monasterium insigne super ripam fluminis Tavensis, in locis illis quae nunc occupatis vos reverende pater, pro orto orientali, et vos Alexander pro mansione de Creif, in ejusdem divi Columbe honorem, ad Sancti Adampnani instantiam construxit et dotavit, circa annos domini septingentos viginti novem, post constructam ecclesiam de Abernethi ad annos ducentos viginti sex, novem menses et sex dies. at, ut aliorum est opinio, ducentos quadraginta quatuor.   In quo quidem monasterio imposuit viros religiosos, quos nominavit vulgus *Kelledeos*, aliter colideos, hoc est, colentes Deum ; habentes tamen, secundum orientalis ecclesiae ritum conjuges, a quibus dum vicissim ministrarunt, abstinebant ; sicut postea in ecclesia Beati Reguli, nunc Sancti Andreae, consuetum tunc fuit.   Sed dum placuit altissimo totius christianae religionis moderatori, crescenteque principum devotione et sanctitate. David rex sanctus. junior filiorum Malcolmi Canmor regis et Sanctae Margaretae reginae, mutato monasterio, in ecclesiam cathedralem erexit; et repudiatis Kelledeis, episcopum et canonicos instituit, seculareque collegium in futurum esse ordinavit, circa annos Domini mille centum et viginti septem. Primus tunc episcopus illius pro tempore monasterii abbas, et Regis postea consiliarius. erat.*

O.—RECORDS OF BRECHIN.

No. 1.—King David has the credit of founding the see of Brechin.   His part in the matter, however, seems to have been little more than that of giving endowment and perpetuity to an office which had existed in this church, at intervals, during many ages before his day.   Possibly his royal authority was exercised in assigning or defining a diocese for an ecclesiastic who had hitherto been rather an adjunct to, than the principal in, the monastic establishment of the place ; and thus giving to the bishop that local supremacy which outside the Celtic Church was generally enjoyed by the highest order of the ministry.   Of the early history of Brechin there is no record evidence, save the one brief but interesting notice wherewith the Pictish Chronicle dismisses Kenneth Mac Alpin, and closes its own recital.† The " Registrum Episcopatus Brechinensis" was edited by the late Patrick Chalmers of Auldbar, with preface by Cosmo Innes, and was presented to the Bannatyne Club by John Inglis Chalmers, " Aberdoniae, 1856."

---

* Vitae Dunkeldensis Ecclesiae Episcoporum, ab Alexandro Myln ejusdem Ecclesiae Canonico (Bannatyne Club, Edinb., 1831), pp. 4, 5.

† Hector Boece, under the reign of Malcolm II. (1001–1031) represents the Danes as assailing " Brethenum vetus Pictorum oppidum," and states that their leader having failed in taking the citadel. "infesto agmine in oppidum et sanctissimum templum ruit : quae caede, ruinis ac incendiis ita diruit, ut oppidum exinde pristinum decus nunquam recuperarit. Veteris vero fani praeter turrim quandam rotundam mira arte constructam nullum ad nostra secula remanserit vestigium."   Scotorum Historiae, lib. xi. (fol. 242 *b*, Par. 1575).   See p. 44. *supra.*

No. 2.—*Carta Willelmi regis confirmationis David regis.* A. D. 1165-71.

Willelmus rex Scotie *etc.* Sciatis me concessisse et carta mea confirmasse Episcopis et Keldeis de ecclesia de Brechin donationem illam quam dedit illis rex David avus meus per cartam suam de foro imperpetuum habituro in villa per dies dominicos adeo libere sicut Episcopus Sanctiandree forum habet. *Etc.**

No. 3.—*Confirmatio Turpini episcopi de Brechin de decima rethis.* A. D. 1178-1180.

Turpinus *etc.* Sciant *etc.* nos dedisse *etc.* ecclesie S. Thome martiris de Aberbrothoc *etc.*, decimam unius plenarii retis *etc.* Hiis testibus Hugone episcopo Sancti Andree, Bricio priore Kelledeorum de Brechin, W. archidiacano Sancti Andree, et Matussale decano, Andrea capellano, et Matheo sacrista ecclesie de Brechin, et insuper Gilbride comite de Anegus, et Dovenaldo Abbate de Brechin.†

No. 4.—*Carta ejusdem episcopi.* A. D. 1178-1198.

Universis *etc.* Turpinus Dei gratia episcopus Brechinensis salutem. Sciant *etc.* nos dedisse *etc.* ecclesie S. Thome de Abirbrothoc *etc.* unum toftum et croftum in villa de Strukatharach *etc.* Testibus Bricio priore de Brechin, Gillefali Kelde, Bricio capellano, Mathalan Kelde, Mackbeth Maywen.‡

No. 5.—*Carta Turpini episcopi Brechynensis de ecclesia de Veteri Munros.* A. D. 1178-1198.

Testibus M. episcopo Aberdonense, Archenbaldo abbate de Dunfermelyn, Priore de Brechyn, Andrea capellano de Brechyn, Roberto capellano Regis, Hugone clerico Regis, Ricardo de Prebenda, Ricardo de Aberbrothoc.§

No. 6.—*Carta Turpini episcopi de ecclesia de Kateryn.* A. D. 1178-1198.

Hiis testibus, Gregorio archidiacono nostro, et Matheo decano de Brechyn, Andrea presbytero, et magistro Ysaac de Brechyn, Roberto abbate de Scone, *etc.*¶

No. 7.—*Carta de Terra de Balegillegrand.*** A. D. 1202.

Dovenaldus Abbe de Brechyn†† omnibus *etc.* Sciant *etc.* me pro salute animarum *etc.*, et

* Regist. Episcopat. Brechinens., No. 1 (vol. i., p. 3). Recited in Nos. 38, 69 (ib., pp. 57, 139).
† Regist. Vetus de Aberbrothoc, No. 193 (p. 134); Regist. Episcopat. Brechinens., No. 216 (vol. ii., p. 269).
‡ Regist. Vetus de Aberbrothoc, No. 75 (p. 50); Regist. Episcopat. Brechinens., No. 220 (vol. ii., p. 270).
§ Regist. Vetus de Aberbrothoc, No. 173 (p. 121); Regist. Episcopat. Brechinens., No. 195 (vol. ii., p. 255).
[In another charter he is styled *persona.* Regist. Vet. de Aberbrothoc, No. 178 (p. 124).
¶ Regist. Vetus de Aberbrothoc, No. 177 (p. 123); Regist. Episcopat. Brechinens., No. 201 (vol. ii., p. 256).
** The royal confirmation of this charter is witnessed by Florentius, bishop elect of Glasgow, 1202. (Keith. Bishops. p. 236).
†† He witnesses a charter of bishop Turpin as "Dovenaldus Abbas de Brechin" (No. 3 *supra*). He was evi-

anima patris mei Samsonis *etc.* dedisse *etc.* ecclesie beati Thome martiris de Abirbrothoc *etc.* illum davach qui vocatur Balegillegrande *etc.* tenendum in liberam *etc.* elemosinam *etc.* Hiis testibus, Radulpho episcopo Brechynensi, Gregorio archidiacono de Brechyn, Malbrido priore Keledeorum de Brechyn, Andrea persona de Brechyn, Willelmo Cumyn justiciario domini Regis, Willelmo filio Orm, Stephano de Blare, Roberto Mansel.*

No. 8.—*Confirmacio Radulphi episcopi Brechynensis de ecclesia de Veteri Munros.* A. D. 1202–1218.

Testibus Wydone abbate de Lundors, Gregorio archidiacono nostro. Willelmo de Boscho cancellario domini Regis, Petro capellano nostro, Andrea de Brechyn, Mallebryd Priore de Brechyn, Alexandro de Mouhaut, Roberto filio Edgari, et T. filio ejus.†

dently a layman, but possessed of church property. Samson his father was probably the "Samson episcopus de Brechin," who attests various charters of St. Andrews in the time of king Malcolm and the bishops Arnold and Richard, 1158–1165. Mr. Innes, finding in the Register of Dunfermlin a "Leod abbas de Breichin," among the lay witnesses to a charter of king David (No. 3, p. 8), and "Leod de Brechin" similarly placed in the Register of St. Andrews (p. 182); and further, meeting with "Dovinalde nepos Leod" in a composition under king David (ibid., p. 118), connected them with the grantor in the present document, and constructed a conjectural succession thus: Leod, abbot of Brechin, father of Samson, father of Dovenald, abbot of Brechin. But Dovinalde, grandson of Leod, was a cleric and juror at an arbitration in Fife, with which he was locally connected, before 1130, whereas Leod of Brechin was his contemporary, and the present Dovenald makes his grant seventy years later. Mention is made, at 1227, of a Gilandreas Mac Leod (Reg. Vet. de Aberbroth., No. 229, p. 163), to whom king Alexander, in 1232, grants certain lands, "salvis clericis de Breychin rectitudinibus suis, et salvis Abbati de Breychin annuatim decem solidis de Kinnebred." He also confirms to him and his issue by "Forthelech filia Bricii judicis," his wife, certain other possessions. (Regist. Episcopat. Brechinens., No. 2, vol. i., p. 3.) The Registrum Vetus de Aberbrothoc furnishes the names of two other *Abbes* or *Abbates*, who took their title from Brechin, whose connexion is shown in the following table:—

MALISIUS.

JOHANNES.	MALCOLMUS
"Johannes Abbe, filius Malisii," makes a grant to Abroath, Morgund, and John, his sons, with Malcolm his brother, being witnesses, A. D. 1204–1211. (Reg. V. de Aberbroth., No. 72, p. 47) "Johannes Abbas filius Malisii." (Ib., No. 73, p. 48.) In 1219 Johannes Abbas de Brechyn was a lay witness. (Ib., No. 228, p. 163.)	Witnesses, as brother, the grant of Johannes; and, as uncle, that of Murgund.

MURGUNDUS.	JOHANNES
"Murgundus filius Johannis Abbe" confirms his father's donation, and "Johannes Abbe pater meus" witnesses the "confirmacio Murgundi Abbe." (Reg. Vet. de Aberbroth., No. 74, p. 48.) Thus an official title seems to have become a family name, like *Mac nAb.*	Witnesses, as son, the grant of Johannes Abbe, and, as brother, that of Murgundus.

* Regist. Vetus de Aberbrothoc, No. 74 (p. 49).

† Regist. Vet. de Aberbrothoc, No. 174 (p. 122); Regist. Episcopat. Brechinens., No. 198 (vol. ii., p. 256). These witnesses appear in the same order in other charters of the same bishop. Reg. Vet. de Aberbr., No. 179 (p. 125), No. 180 (p. 125–6), No. 181 (p. 126), No. 182 (p. 126–7), No. 183 (p. 127), No. 184 (p. 128).

No. 9.—*Confirmacio Radulphi episcopi de Brechyn de omnibus ecclesiis.* A. D. 1202–1218.

Hiis testibus* Guidone abbate de Lundors, Gregorio archidiacono nostro, Willelmo officiali nostro, Matheo decano nostro, et Andrea de Brechin, Alexandro de Muhaut, et magistro Ysaac clericis nostris, *etc.*†

No. 10.—*Confirmacio Capituli de Brechyn de ecclesiis.*‡ A. D. 1202–1218.

Universis *etc.* M. Prior et Kelledei, ceterique clerici de capitulo Brechinensis ecclesie salutem. Universitati vestre notum facimus Nos donaciones et concessiones ecclesiarum Deo et monasterio beati Thome martiris de Aberbrothoc *etc.*, a felicis memorie Turpino et Radulpho Brechinensis ecclesie episcopis canonice collatas, râtas et gratas habere, et eisdem donacionibus et concessionibus, sicut in eorum cartis liberius *etc.*, continentur, consilium prebere et assensum. Et in hujus rei testimonium presenti scripto sigillum ecclesie nostre duximus apponendum. Testibus G. archidiacono, Hugone de Sigillo, Matheo decano, Andrea capellano, Petro capellano, Ranulfo capellano de Maringtun, Ada Blundo, et Roberto clerico filio Ade Senescalldi.§

No. 11.—*Carta Radulphi episcopi Brechinensis de procurationibus faciendis.* A. D. 1202–1214.

Testibus Gregorio archidiacono, Willelmo capellano, Andrea capellano de Brechin, Matheo decano, Petro capellano nostro, Malbrido priore Kelledeorum de Brechin, Willelmo de Kerneil persona de Dunde, Henrico capellano de Munros.‖

No. 12.—*Confirmacio Capituli de Brechin de Procuracionibus.*¶ A. D. 1204–1214.

Universis *etc.* M. Prior et Kelledei ceterique de capitulo Brechinensis ecclesie salutem. Sit universitati vestre notum, Radulfum Dei gratia Brechinensem episcopum, consilio nostro et assensu, monachis de Aberbrothoc caritatis intuitu concessisse ut quandocunque ad quasdam ecclesias eorum in diocesi ejus sitas visitandas ex officio venerit, videlicet ad ecclesiam de Maringtun, vel ad ecclesiam de Gutherin, vel ad ecclesiam de Pannebride, vel ad ecclesiam de Muniekkin, vel ad ecclesiam de Dunectin, ad nullam eorum hospitalitatis ei exhibeatur procuracio, sed tantum ad abbaciam, ubi hoc decencius et honestius fieri potest. Nos eciam concessionem istam, sicut in carta predictorum monachorum melius continetur, omnino ratum et gratum habemus. Et in hujus rei testimonium presenti scripto ecclesie nostre sigillum dignum duximus apponendum. Teste capituli nostri universitate.**

---

* The prior and Keledei do not attest this charter, because they appear as principals in a separate confirmation ; but the archdeacon, official, and dean, are witnesses, because they were not then members of the chapter, as is proved by their being witnesses to the confirmation charters granted by the Prior, Keledei, and *other clerks of the chapter of Brechin*, as appears in No. 10 *supra.*

† Regist. Vet. de Aberbrothoc, No. 185 (p. 128-9); Regist. Episcopat. Brechinens., No. 205 (vol. ii., pp. 258-9).

‡ Printed by Goodall in his Dissertation (Keith's Bishops, p. lviii.).

§ Regist. Vet. de Aberbrothoc, No. 188 (p. 130); Regist. Episcopat. Brechinens., No. 206 (vol. ii. p. 259).

‖ Regist. Vet. de Aberbrothoc, No. 189 (p. 131); Regist. Episcopat. Brechinens., No. 208 (vol. ii., p. 260).

¶ Printed by Goodall in his Dissertation (Keith's Bishops. p. lvii.).

** Regist. Vet. de Aberbrothoc, No. 192 (p. 133); Regist. Episcopatus Brechinens.. No. 209 (vol. ii.. p. 261).

No. 13.—*Confirmacio episcopi Hugonis de Brechin de decima rethis.* A. D. circ. 1218.

Testibus Willelmo de Bosco cancellario domini Regis, Gregorio archidiacono nostro, Malbride priore Kelledeorum nostrorum, magistro Simone de Sancto Andrea, Alexandro de Muhaut, Roberto, Petro, Willemo capellanis nostris, et capitulo nostro.*

No. 14.—*Confirmacio ejusdem episcopi de tofto.* A. D. circ. 1218.

Testibus *etc.*, Mallebryd priore Keledeorum nostrorum, *etc.*, et capitulo nostro.†

No. 15.—*Confirmacio ejusdem de ecclesia de Veteri Munros.* A. D. circ. 1218.

Testibus *etc.* Mallebrydo priore Keledeorum nostrorum, *etc.*, et capitulo nostro.‡

No. 16.—*Confirmacio ejusdem de omnibus ecclesiis.* A. D. circ. 1218.

Testibus Roberto electo Rossensi, Guidone abbate de Lundors, Willelmo abbate de Scone, Willelmo de Bosco cancellario domini regis, Gregorio archidiacano nostro, Malbrido priore Kelledeorum nostrorum, *etc.*, et capitulo nostro.§

No. 17.—*Confirmacio ejusdem de procuracionibus faciendis.* A. D. circ. 1218.

Hiis testibus, *etc.*, Malbrido priore Kelledeorum nostrorum, *etc.*, et capitulo nostro.‖

No. 18.—*Confirmacio Gregorii episcopi de Brechin de decima unius plenarii rethis.*—A. D. 1219–1222.

Testibus domino Bricio Moraviensi episcopo, Willelmo de Bosco cancellario, Malbrido priore Kelledeorum nostrorum, magistro Henrico de Norham officiali nostro, Freskino Moraviensis ecclesie decano, *etc.*, et toto capitulo nostro.¶

No. 19.—*Confirmacio ejusdem de tofto.* A. D. 1219–1222.

Testibus domino Bricio episcopo Moraviensi, domino Willelmo de Bosco cancellario, Mallebryd priore Keledeorum nostrorum, magistro Henrico de Norham officiali nostro, Fertheskyno Moraviensis ecclesie decano, *etc.***

No. 20.—*Confirmacio ejusdem de ecclesia de Veteri Munros.* A. D. 1219–1222.

Testibus *etc.*, Malbrido priore Kelledeorum nostrorum, *etc.*††

---

* Regist. Vet. de Aberbrothoc, No. 195 (p. 134); Regist. Episcopat. Brechinens., No. 218 (vol. ii., p. 270).
† Regist. Vet. de Aberbrothoc, No. 78 (p. 52); Regist. Episcopat. Brechinens., No. 222 (vol. ii., p. 271).
‡ Regist. Vet. de Aberbrothoc, No. 175 (p. 122); Regist. Episcopat. Brechinens., No. 199 (vol. ii., p. 256).
§ Regist. Vet. de Aberbrothoc, No. 186 (p. 129).
‖ Regist. Vet. de Aberbrothoc, No. 190 (p. 132); Regist. Episcopat. Brechinens., No. 210 (vol. ii., p. 261).
¶ Regist. Vet. de Aberbrothoc, No. 196 (p. 135); Regist. Episcopat. Brechinens., No. 219 (vol. ii., p. 270).
** Regist. Vet. de Aberbrothoc, No. 79 (p. 52); Regist. Episcopat. Brechinens., No. 223 (vol. ii., p. 271).
†† Regist. Vet. de Aberbrothoc, No. 176 (p. 123); Regist. Episcopat. Brechinens., No. 200 (vol. ii., p. 256).

No. 21.—*Confirmacio ejusdem de omnibus ecclesiis.* A. D. 1219–1222.

Testibus *etc.*, Malbrido priore Kelledeorum nostrorum, *etc.*, et toto capitulo nostro.*

No. 22.—*Confirmacio ejusdem de procurationibus faciendis.* A. D. 1219–1222.

Testibus *etc.*, Malbrido priore Kelledeorum nostrorum, *etc.*, et toto capitulo nostro.†

No. 23.—*Ordinacio Albini episcopi Brechynensis super vicariis dicte diocesis.* A. D. 1248.

Omnibus *etc.* Noverit universitas vestra nos *etc.*, de communi consensu et assensu capituli nostri, ratas et gratas habere et hac carta nostra confirmare donaciones et concessiones ecclesiarum *etc.* a predecessoribus nostris factas Deo et monasterio de Aberbrothoc.‡

No. 24.—*Confirmacio capituli Brechinensis de eisdem.* A. D. 1248.

Omnibus *etc.* Willelmus decanus, et capitulum Brechynense *etc.* Noverit universitas vestra nos de communi consensu et assensu tocius capituli nostri ratas et gratas habere *etc.*, *ut supra.*§

No. 25.—*Composicio facta inter ecclesiam Brechynensem et monasterium de Aberbrothoc.* A. D. 1248.

Omnibus *etc.* Albinus *etc.* Brechynensis episcopus, et Willelmus decanus, necnon et capitulum ejusdem loci, salutem *etc.* Cum orta esset contencio inter nos et ecclesiam nostram ex una parte et Abbatem et monachos de Aberbrothoc et eorum monasterium ex altera, *etc.*‖

No. 26.—*Declaracio episcopi Brechinensis unacum toto capitulo de qualitate prebendarum ejusdem.* A. D. 1372.

Universis *etc.* Ubi undecim beneficia¶ in canonicatus in predicta ecclesia antiquitus fundata comperimus et creata. Quorum quatuor sunt dignitates, videlicet Decanatus, Cantoria, Cancellaria, et Thezauraria, quintum vero videlicet Archidiaconatus officium est in ecclesia predicta *etc.* Reliqua vero sex beneficia, videlicet Vicaria, Pensionaria, Subdiaconatus, Kilmoir, Butirgill, et Guthrie, simplices prebendas reperimus et compassibiles cum beneficio curato et cum alio qualicunque *etc.***

---

* Regist. Vet. de Aberbrothoc, No. 187 (p. 130).

† Regist. Vet. de Aberbrothoc, No. 191 (p. 132); Regist. Episcopat. Brechinens., No. 211 (vol. ii., p. 261).

‡ Regist. Vet. de Aberbrothoc, No. 239 (p. 174); Regist. Episcopat. Brechinens., No. 213 (vol. ii., p. 264).

§ Regist. Vet. de Aberbrothoc, No. 240 (p. 175); Regist. Episcopat. Brechinens., No. 212 (vol. ii., p. 262).

‖ Regist. Vet. de Aberbrothoc, No. 243 (p. 179); Regist. Episcopat. Brechinens., No. 212 (vol. ii., p. 262).

¶ These eleven canonries no doubt numerically represented the ancient Keledean foundation, to which was to be added, for the twelfth, the Bishop's portion; for elsewhere he appears as rector and prebendary of Brechin. Regist. Episcopat. Brechinens., No. 45 (vol. i., p. 67).

** Regist. Episcopat. Brechinens., No. 15 (vol. i., p. 19).

P.—RECORDS OF LOCHLEVEN.

No. 1.—St. Serb, or Serf, called Servanus in ecclesiastical writings, and Sare in vulgar use, was the reputed founder of the ancient monastery on the Inch of Lochleven. His history is very obscure, and his Life, the only copy of which now known to exist is preserved in Dublin,[*] is full of anachronisms and absurdities. He is stated therein to have been the son of " Obeth filius Eliud," a noble king in the land of Chanaan, and his wife " Alpia filia regis Arabie," and for twenty years to have been a bishop in his native country, but that subsequently he travelled westwards, and reached Scotland, where he received Palladius on his arrival, and became his fellow-labourer. Two points, however, in his history seem to be authentic, namely, that he baptized and educated St. Kentigern of Glasgow, and that Culenros, now Culros, on the Forth, was his principal church, where he died, at an advanced age, about the year 540.[†] Those who represent the Culdees as a distinct order delight in assigning their origin to St. Serf, and describe their system as cradled in Culros and matured in Lochleven.[‡] But this is only one of the many errors which have been current on the subject of the Culdees.

Of St. Serf's connexion with Lochleven, the earliest evidence on record is a little collection of charters now incorporated with the Register of St. Andrews. The compiler states that he judged it advisable to set out with brevity, but in a collected and lucid form, divested of all preambles and verbiage, the contents of an old volume written " antiquo Scotorum idiomate," relating to the church of St. Servanus of the island of Lochlevine. This collection had come into the possession of the Priory of St. Andrews, when the island and its appendages were made over to that house. The original record, if now existing, would be of extreme value, not only for historical but philological purposes, and would somewhat resemble in nature, but greatly transcend in importance, the Gaelic memoranda which are enrolled in the Book of Deir. In its absence, however, we possess a very

---

[*] Primate Marsh's Library, Cl. V. 3. Tab. 4. No. 16. It occupies fols. 1 to 6, in the quarto MS. which contains Jocelin's Life of St. Kentigern. See p. 27 *supra*, note [*]. This may have been the authority from which Archbishop Ussher made his extracts, Brit. Eccl. Antiqq., cap. xv. (Works, vol. vi., pp. 214, 215). The legend in the Breviary of Aberdeen commemorates St. Servanus at July 1, and adds, " Est et alius sanctus Servanus nacione Israeliticus, qui temporibus beati Adampnani abbatis in insula Petmook multis miraculis claruit, prout gesta per eum in ejus vita lucidius complectuntur." Propr. SS. Part. Estival. fol. 16 *b a.* The *insula Petmook* is St. Serf's Isle in Loch Leven, which belongs to the parish of Portmoak.

[†] The Irish tract " De Matribus Sanctorum Hiberniæ," which Colgan ascribes to Ængus the Culdee, contains the earliest notice of this saint: Ɑlma ınʒen ꝑıʒ Cꝑuıchnech mɑtɑıꝑ Ŝeıꝑb mec Pꝑoıc ꝑıʒ Cɑnɑnꝺ eıʒeıꝑcı. Ɑcuꝑ ı�ñe ꝑın ın ꝑꝑuıc ꝑenoıꝑ conʒeb Cuılenꝺ�ñoꝑ hı Sꝑɑıch hı�ñenꝺ hı Comʒellʒɑıb ıɑꝑ ꝑłɑb Nochel ɑcuꝑ muı� nʒıubɑn. " Alma, daughter of the king of Cruithne, *was* mother of Serb, son of Proc, king of Canaan of Egypt; and he is the venerable old man who possesses [i. e. is patron of] Cuilennros [Culros] in Srath Hirenn in the Comgells, between Sliabh nOchel [the Ochill Hills] and the sea of Giudi [the Frith of Forth]." Book of Lecan, fol. 43 *bb*. The Latin Life points to the same position in these words: " Habitent [socii tui] terram Fif, et a monte Britannorum ad montem qui dicitur Okhel."

[‡] As, for example, the editor of the Ordo Monasticus, in Brockie's edition of Holstenius' Codex Regularum, vol. ii., pp. 63, 64.

valuable substitute, which has been faithfully printed by the Bannatyne Club,* and from their publication transferred to these pages.

No. 2.—*De primo rege qui dedit insulam de Lochlevin.* A. D. circ. 842.

Brude filius Dergard,† qui ultimus regum Pictorum secundum antiquas tradiciones fuisse recolitur, contulit insulam Lochleuine‡ Deo omnipotenti et sancto Servano, et Keledeis heremitis§ ibidem commorantibus et Deo servientibus et servituris in illa insula. Et prefati Keledei dederunt locum cellule episcopo Sancti Andree sub tali forma : quod episcopus exhiberit eis victum et vestitum. Et ne ignoretur quis contulit episcopo locum ibi, Ronanus‖ monachus et abbas,¶ vir admirande sanctitatis, primo concessit precario** locum ibi episcopo, scilicet Fothath filio Bren,†† qui nunc et tunc per totam Scociam fuit celebris et satis commendabilis vite. Prefatus episcopus dedit benediccionem suam plenarie omnibus hiis qui observarent convencionem istam et amiciciam initam inter episcopum et Keledeos, et versa vice dedit malediccionem suam omnibus episcopis qui infirmarent et revocarent prefatam convencionem.‡‡

No. 3.—*Qualiter Machbet filius Finlach et Gruoch dederunt sancto Servano Kyrkenes.* A. D. 1037–1054.

Machbet filius Finlach§§ contulit pro suffragiis orationum, et Gruoch filia Bodhe,‖‖ rex et regina

---

* Registrum Prioratus S. Andree. pp. 113-118. They had previously, but not with such accuracy, been printed by Crauford, in his Officers of State, Appendix, pp. 428-432 ; by Bishop Gillan, in his Remarks on Sir James Dalrymple's Historical Collections, pp. 160-162 ; and by Dr. Jamieson, in his Historical Account of the Culdees, pp. 369-373. Pinkerton also gives the imperfect and incorrect version which is contained in the extracts from the Magnum Registrum, Enquiry, vol. i., pp. 468, 469.

† Wynton identifies the founder with Brude mac Derili, St. Adamnan's contemporary, who died in 706 ; but this is too early. Brude VII., called by Fordun Brude filius Feredech (Scotichr.. iv., 13) reigned in 842 for one year. The chronological note of his being the last king of the Picts is a stronger traditional feature than his parentage.

‡ In Gaelic *Loch Leamhna,* "Lake of the Elm." The River Leven flows out of it on the south-east. The island called the Inch, about seventy acres in extent, now included in the parish of Portmoak, contains the site of the primitive monastery.

§ This epithet contrasts strongly with the description of the Keledei of St. Andrews, and shows that, while the name was preserved, the discipline of the Keledei became greatly relaxed in the course of time.

‖ We have no other record of this individual. An abbot of Ceann-Garadh (Kingarth), of this name, died in 732.

¶ This expression savours of a period when hereditary abbotships were enjoyed without the qualification of either vows or holy orders.

** This adverb denotes that the grant was made by a *precaria,* a quasi mode of alienation of church property, which was recognised under the Roman law. See Calvinus, Lexicon Juridicum, and especially Du Cange (ed. Henschel) under *Precaria.*

†† According to the Four Masters " Fothadh son of Bran, scribe, and bishop of the islands of Alba," died in 961. He is the second of the recorded bishops of St. Andrews. See Reeves's St. Columba, p. 394. See pp. 51, 52 *supra.*

‡‡ Registrum Prioratus S. Andree, p. 113.

§§ Macbeathaidh mac Finnlaich was slain, according to the Irish Annals, in 1058.

‖‖ This is the only ancient record of the name of Macbeth's queen. Pinkerton, followed by the Hon. A. Herbert, states that her name is found in the Chartulary of Dunfermlyn (Enquiry, ii., p. 197 ; Irish Nennius, p. lxxx.). but

Scotorum, Kyrkenes Deo omnipotenti et Keledeis prefate insule Lochleuine, cum suis finibus et terminis. Hii enim sunt fines et termini de Kyrkenes* et villule que dicitur Pethmokanne : de loco Moneloccodhan usque ad amnem qui dicitur Leuine, et hoc in latitudine. Item a pubblica strata que ducit apud Hinhirkethy, usque ad Saxum Hiberniensium,† et hoc in longitudine. Et dicitur Saxum Hiberniensium quia Malcolmus rex,‡ filius Duncani concessit eis salinagium quod Scotice dicitur Chonnane. Et venerunt Hibernienses ad Kyrkenes ad domum cujusdam viri nomine Mochan, qui tunc fuit absens, et solummodo mulieres erant in domo, quos oppresserunt violenter Hibernienses, non tamen sine rubore et verecundia. Rei etiam eventu ad aures prefati Mochan pervento, iter quam tocius domi festinavit, et invenit ibi Hibernienses in eadem domo cum matre sua. Exhortacione etenim matri sue sepius facta, ut extra domum veniret, que nullatenus voluit, set Hibernienses voluit protegere, et eis pacem dare. Quos omnes prefatus vir, in ulcionem tanti facinoris, ut oppressores mulierum et barbaros et sacrilegos in medio flamme ignis una cum matre sua viriliter combussit. Et ex hac causa dicitur locus ille Saxum Hiberniensum.§

No. 4.—*De libertate Kyrkenes collata a rege Macbet filio Finlac, et a Gruohc regina.* A. D. 1037–1054.

Cum omni libertate collata fuit villa de Kyrkenes Deo omnipotenti et Keledeis, absque omni munere et onere et exaccione regis et filii regis, vicecomitis et alicujus, et sine refectione pontis, et sine excercitu et venacione, set pietatis intuitu et orationum suffragiis fuit Deo omnipotenti collata.‖

No. 5.—*A quo data est villa de Bolgyne heremitis de Lochlevin.* A. D. 1037–1054.

Cum summa veneracione et devocione Makbeth rex contulit Deo et sancto Servano de Lochleuyn et heremitis ibidem Deo servientibus Bolgyne¶ filii Torfyny cum omni libertate et sine onere exercitus regis et filii ejus, vel vicecomitis, et sine exactione alicujus, set caritatis intuitu et orationum suffragiis.**

they are in error. The Annals of Ulster, at 1038, make mention of *Mac mic Boete mic Cinaedha,* "grandson of Boethe son of Cinaedh," who was nephew to dame Gruoch. "Lulach nepos filii Boide" is named in the list of kings from the Magnum Regist. of St. Andrews. Innes, Crit. Essay, vol. ii., p. 791. See Irish Nennius, p. lxxx.

* This place, which retains its name, is situated a little south of Lochlevin.

† In No. 13 *infra,* we find "Morrehat vir venerande senectutis et Hiberniensis," a person of distinction in Fife. The Irish relations of this county were renewed in 1237, when Hugh de Lacy, Earl of Ulster, granted the churches of *Ruskath* (now Roosky) and *Karlingeford,* with all the churches and chapels of *Coling* (Cooley, the principal part of the barony of Lower Dundalk) to the church of St. Andrews. Regist. Priorat. S. Andree, p. 118.

‡ That is Malcolm Cennmor. His reign commenced in 1056 ; and the Irish Annals, which call him "*Maelcolaim mac Dunchadhc,* supreme king of Alba," place his death at 1093. Dunchadh or Donnchadh, which is the genuine form, is generally made Duncan in Scottish Records.

§ Registrum Prioratus S. Andree, p. 114.   ‖ Ibid.

¶ There is a Balgonie, on the south bank of the Leven, in the parish of Markinch ; also a Balgonie, and Mickle Balgonie, in the parish of Auchterderran, south of Loch Leven.

** This grant does not form one of the series, but is given apart in the transcript, at p. 12 of the Regist. Priorat. S. Andree.

No. 6.—*De collacione et libertate de Petnemokane.* A. D. 1098–1107.

Edgarus filius Malcomi, rex Scocie, contulit in elemosinam Deo omnipotenti et predictis Keledeis Petnemokanne cum omnibus libertatibus, sicut prenotatum est in capitulo precedenti.*

No. 7.—*De villa de Ballecristyn et ejus libertate.* A. D. 1070–1093.

Malcolmus rex et Margareta regina Scocie contulerunt devote villam de Ballecristin† Deo omnipotenti et Keledeis de Louchleuen cum eadem libertate ut prius.‡

No. 8.—*De libertatibus villarum de Kyrkenes et de Pettenmokan.* A. D. 1094–1096.

Douenald filius Conchat§ regis dedit omnimodam libertatem duabus villis, scilicet de Kyrkenes et de Pettenmokane cum ceteris regibus, scilicet, Duncano rege,‖ Edgaro, et Alexandro, et David fratribus ejusdem, et omnibus villis quascunque tunc habuerunt vel postea habere potuerunt.¶

No. 9.—*De donacione de Admore et ejus libertate.* A. D. 1093–1107.

Edelradus** vir venerande memorie filius Malcolmi regis Scocie, abbas de Dunkelden†† et insuper comes de Fyf, contulit Deo omnipotenti, et sancto Servano et Keledeis de insula Louchleuen, cum summa reverencia et honore, et omni libertate, et sine exaccione et peticione cujusquam in mundo, episcopi vel regis, vel comitis, Admore‡‡ cum suis rectis terminis et divisis. Et quia illa possessio fuit illi tradita a parentibus suis cum esset in juvenali etate, itcirco cum majori affeccione et amore illam optulit Deo et sancto Servano et prefatis viris Deo servientibus et ibidem servituris. Et istam collacionem et donacionem primo factam confirmaverunt duo fratres Hedelradi, scilicet David, et Alexander, in presentia multorum virorum fidedignorum, scilicet Constantini comitis de Fyf, §§ viri

* Registrum Prioratus S. Andree, p. 115.

† Now Balchristie, in the parish of Newburn, far off on the south-east. The remains of a church are recorded as having been here. New Stat. Ac., vol. ix., Fife, p. 125; Old Stat. Ac., vol. xvi., p. 136. Balcristen was granted and confirmed in numerous charters to Dunfermlin, " excepta rectitudine quam Keledei habere debent;" and when the possessions of Lochlevin were transferred to the Priory of St. Andrews, the Keledean interest in it passed to the canons; so that in a subsequent arbitration, while the land was awarded to Dunfermlin, it was "salva elemosina ipsis canonicis." Regist. Dunferm., p. 34.

‡ Registrum Prioratus S. Andree, p. 115.

§ Commonly known as Donald Bane, brother of Malcolm Canmore. Conchat is so written for Donchat (in Irish Donnchadh), the original Mac Donchat causing an assimilation of the initial D, just as Mac Donnell is often written Mac Connell; and when the translator rendered the Mac by filius, he left the assimilated Conchat unrestored.

‖ That is Dunchadh, the eldest and illegitimate son of Malcolm Canmore.

¶ Registrum Prioratus S. Andree, p. 115.

** Ethelred was one of the six sons whom Queen Margaret bore to Malcolm Cenmore. He died before his brother's accession, and was buried in the old church of St. Andrews in Kilreymonth. Fordun, Scotichron., v. 28.

†† The abbacy of Dunkeld had passed into lay hands before this, and was enjoyed by Crinan, or rather Cronan, father of king Duncan who was slain by Macbeth. See p. 42 supra.

‡‡ Now Auchmore on the Leven. §§ Douglas places his death at 1127 or 1129. Peerage, vol. i., p. 578.

discretissimi et Nesse et Cormac filii Macbeath et Malnethte* filii Beollani, sacerdotum de Abyrne-thyn, et Mallebride alterius sacerdotis, et Thuadhel† et Augustini sacerdotis, Keledeorum,‡ Berbeadh, rectoris scolarum§ de Abyrnethyn, et coram cetibus totius universitatis tunc de Abyrnethin ibidem degentibus, et coram Deo omnipotenti et omnibus sanctis. Et ibi data est plenarie et universaliter ab omnibus sacerdotibus clericis et laicis maledictio Dei omnipotentis et beate Marie virginis et omnium sanctorum, ut Dominus Deus daret eum in exterminium et perdicionem, et in omnes illos quicunque irritarent et revocarent et diminuerent elemosinam de Admore, omni populo respondente, Fiat, Amen.‖

No. 10.—*De donacione ecclesie de Marckinche per Maldun episcopum.* A. D. 1034–1055.

Maldunus¶ episcopus sancti Andree contulit ecclesiam de Marchinke** cum tota terra honorifice et devote Deo et sancto Servano, et Keledeis de insula Louchleuen, cum prefata libertate.††

No. 11.—*De concessione ecclesie de Sconyn per Tuadal episcopum.* A. D. 1055–1059.

Tuadal‡‡ episcopus Sancti Andree contulit ecclesiam de Sconyn§§ prefatis viris religiosis devote et integre cum omni libertate et honore pro suffragiis oracionum.‖‖

No. 12.—*De ecclesia de Hurkyndorath.* A. D. 1059–1093.

Modach¶¶ filius Malmykel vir piissime recordacionis, episcopus Sancti Andree, cujus vita et doctrina tota regio Scotorum feliciter est illustrata, contulit Deo et Sancto Servano, et Keledeis heremitis apud insulam Louchleuen in scola virtutum ibidem degentibus, devote et honorifice, cum

---

* More correctly Malsnechte. We find Malsnecte mac Lulaig, and Malsnacht in the Regist. Priorat. S. Andree, pp. 59, 152, 179.

† A corrupt form of *Tuathal*.

‡ Concerning the Keledei of Abernethy. see p. 54 *supra*, and EVIDENCE Q *infra*.

§ For an account of this officer, see the valuable paper of Mr. Joseph Robertson, in Miscellany of the Spalding Club, vol. v., p. 68.

‖ Registrum Prioratus S. Andree, pp. 115, 116.

¶ He is the eighth bishop of St. Andrews on the Scotch lists, and is called by them *Maldwinus filius Gillandris.* Supplement to Scotichron., vi., 24. His death is thus recorded by Tighernach at 1055, ꞇⰰⰻⰾⰺꞓⰻ mac ᵹⰻⰾⰾⰰ OⰑⱀⰰⰻⱀ eⱂⱂⰽⱂ Ⱀⰾⰱⰰⱀ, ⰰⰽⱂⱃ ⱁⱂⰱⰰⱀ ᵹⰰeⰱeⰾ ⱁ ꞈⰾeⰻⱂⰽⰻⰱ ⰻⱀ Cⱈⱂⰻⱂꞇⱁ ꞟⱑⰻeⱀⰻꞇ, " Maelduin son of Gillaodrain, bishop of Alba, and the glory of the clergy of the Gaedhil, slept in Christ." The Chronicon Scotorum and Four Masters have a similar entry at this year, but they, conformably with Scotch records, call him " son of Gilleandreas."

** A parish now called Markinch, situate in Fife to the east of Loch Leven.

†† Registrum Prioratus S. Andree, p. 116.

‡‡ Called Tuthald in the catalogue of the bishops of St. Andrews. He succeeded Malduin, and sat four years.

§§ Now Scoonie parish, in the county of Fife, further east of Markinch.

‖‖ Registrum Prioratus S. Andree, p. 116.

¶¶ This name does not occur in the catalogues of the bishops of St. Andrews, and it is probably an error or an alias for Fothadh. See Ruddiman's Preface to Anderson's Diplomata. The eulogium passed on him here agrees with the entry of the Annals of Ulster at 1093, ꝼⱁꞇⱈⱆⰱⱃ ⰰⱂⰱeⱂⱂꞓⱂ Ⱀⰾⰱⰰⰻⱀ ⰻⱀ Cⱈⱂⰻⱂꞇⱁ ꞟⱑⰻeⱀⰻꞇ, " Fothadh, high-bishop of Alba, rested in Christ."

prefatis libertatibus ecclesiam de Hurkenedorath.* Iste sunt antique prestaciones et canones, quas prefate ecclesie solvebant antiquitus, scilicet triginta panes decoctos cum antiqua mensura farine ibi apposita, et triginta caseos quorum quilibet facit chudreme, et octo male de braseo, et derchede male et chedher male.†

No. 13.—*Perambulacio inter terras de Kyrknesse et Lochore.*‡ A. D. 1122–1129.

Fornax et incendium tocius iniquitatis, scilicet Robertus Burgonensis§ miles, gravaminibus et injuriis prefatos viros religiosos nequiter et calumpniose vexavit et fatigavit, volens precise fervore sue rapacitatis et infrenate tyrannidis, ab eis auferre quartam partem de Kyrkenes. Consilio inito a fratribus juxta simplicitatem suam accesserunt ad presentiam regis David, supplicantes ei ut justum judicium faceret inter eos et prefatum Robertum. Tandem rex, misericordia motus, misit nuncios suos per provinciam de Fyf et Fothrithi,‖ et convocavit hominum multitudinem in unum locum, scilicet Constatinum¶ comitem de Fyf, virum discretum et facundum cum satrapys et satellitibus et exercitu de Fyf, et Macbeath thaynetum** de Falleland,†† et primicerios et duces et lumnarcas‡‡ exercitus episcopi, et Soen ducem . . . . . . cum familia sua. Et tunc temporis fuerunt duces excercitus episcopi Budadh et Slogadadh;§§ et hii omnes sunt testes hujus alter-

* Now Auchterderran parish, situate a little to the south-east of Loch Leven.

† Registrum Prioratus S. Andree, p. 117.

‡ In Ballingry parish, a little south-west of Kirkness. This would seem to have been the estate of Robertus Burgonensis.

§ Robertus Burguine witnesses a charter of king David (Reg. S. Andr., p. 183); Robertus Burg. another of the same king (Reg. Dunferm., p. 4); Robertus Burguillun (ib., p. 10); Robertus Burgeis (ib., p. 13): so also in the Chartulary of Scone.

‖ These two territories comprised the present counties of Fife and Kinross, and their respective boundaries are shown by the distribution of the parishes in the old deanries of Fyf and Fothri (Reg. S. Andree, pp. 32, 33). The south-west half of the united counties formed the territory of Fothribh. The Register of Dunfermlyn frequently couples Fyf and Fothrif, and also mentions the *parochia tota Fothrif* (pp. 6, 20, 29, 152). The word Ꝓothꝥιb in Irish means "a forest," and Cuil-Fothribh in Dalaradia is interpreted "corner of the forest." Calend. of Donegal, Aug. 1; Book of Lecan, fol. 184 *bb*; Ogyg. iii., 51 (p. 293). We find a Domnach-Fothairbe in Hy-Tuirtre, Vita Trip. S. Patricii, ii. 140 (Trias Th., p. 148 *b*). The Fothrick Moors in the west of Fife preserve the name (Sibbald's Fife, p. 2): an "Ecclesia de Forthir" appears in the taxation of the deanry (Reg. Pr. S. Andree, p. 33), which was a parish composed of adjacent portions of the modern Markinch, Kettle, and Falkland. In the north of Markinch is *Kirkforthar*, and in the contiguous part of Kettles is *Forthar*.

¶ He and Rob. Burg. witness early charters of king David (Reg. Dunferm., pp. 4, 13); he had died previously to some subsequent charters of the same sovereign (ib., p. 16).

** *Thainus* (Reg. Aberbr., p. 27) or *Theinus* (Reg. S. Andr., pp. 181, 192) is the usual form by which the Saxon *Thane* is latinized. Ϲοιꝛech was the Gaelic term which it denoted; and in the Book of Deir we find the two classes of nobles coupled together: the *Mormaer* or Earl and the *Toiseach* or Thane.

†† Falkland parish in Fife has an ancient castle. New Stat. Ac., vol. ix., p. 923.

‡‡ In the original it is lūnarca, possibly by an error for *liminarca*. See Du Cange, *sub voc.*

§§ Lyon, understanding *episcopi* as a nominative plural, unwarrantably creates "two Culdean bishops." Budadh and Slogadadh, "who certainly belonged to no fixed dioceses." Hist. of St. Andrews, vol. i., p. 86; vol. ii., p. 278. As military officers of the bishop, their names were in excellent keeping with their vocation, for *Budadh* (recte Ꝋuaꝋach

S

cacionis et dissensionis. Tantem fuit compromissum in tres viros legales et idoneos, scilicet Constantinum comitem de Fyf magnum judicem in Scocia, et Dufgal* filium Mocche, qui fuit senex justus et venerabilis, et Meidoinneth† filium Machedath judicem bonum et discretum. Set iste Dufgal primo pronunciavit sentenciam pro monachis, id est Keledeis, et contra protervitatem et calumpniam Roberti Burgonensis, quia alii judices detulerunt Dufgal propter sui senectutem et juris periciam, et ita fuit decisum istud negocium sentencionaliter et per juramentum. Isti sunt clerici qui juraverunt super finibus ville de Kyrkenes, Duftah‡ sacerdos et abbas, et Sarran filius Sodelne,§ et Eugenius monachus, et Douinalde nepos Leod,‖ et Morrehat¶ vir venerande senectutis et Hiberniensis, et Cathan senex. Et sic victus fuit predictus R. coram omnibus.

No. 14.—*Donacio monasterii de Lochlewyn Roberto priori Sancti Andree, per Robertum episcopum.*
A. D. 1144–1150.

Omnibus sancte matris ecclesie filiis, Robertus,** Dei gratia minister humilis ecclesie Sancti Andree, salutem et episcopalem benedictionem. Sciant omnes tam presentes quam absentes, nos dedisse et concessisse ecclesie Sancti Andree et Roberto priori, abbaciam de insula Lochleuene, cum omnibus ad eam pertinentibus, ad canonicos regulares constituendum in ea; hoc est cum Findahin et omnibus suis apendiciis; et cum Portemuoch et suis apendiciis; et cum molendinis ad pontem; et cum uno molendino in terra Findachin; et Chircnes cum suis apendiciis omnibus; et cum dimidia villa de Urechehem cum suis apendiciis; et villa ecclesiastica de Sconin et suis apendiciis; et cum viginti melis casei et uno porco de Marchinche; et cum viginti melis casei et quatuor melis de breis et uno porco de Ecmor; et cum viginti melis ordei de Balechristin; et cum viginti melis casei et uno porco de Bolgin filii Thorfini; et cum decimis de domo nostra de insula;

Four Mast., 895, 905, 906, 960), signifies "Victorious," and *Slogadadh* (recte Slożaḃach or Sluaiżeḃoch, Four Mast., 784, 885) "a Hoster." See Buathac, p. 113 *supra.* In the Chron. Pict. we find "Leot et Sluagadach exierunt ad Romam," 956–970 (Pinkerton, Enquiry, vol. i., p. 497); and in the Regist. Priorat. S. Andree, "terra Helen quam Slothagth tenuit" (p. 59), Sluthagh (p. 140), Sluthadi (p. 146), Slodah (p. 152).

* "Dufgal qui fuit senex" resembles Sean Ḃubhżaill Sżoine, "Old Dubhgall of Scone," who is mentioned in the Irish tract on the "Men of Alba," preserved in the Book of Ballymote, and Mac Firbis's Geneal. MS. Old Dubhgall was father of Raingce, whose son, Cusidhe, was progenitor of the Clann Considhe in Bib, i. e. Fife. But he occurs far too high in the pedigree to admit of his being a contemporary with king David. See the Genealogical Table of the Dalriadic kings in Reeves's St. Columba, opposite p. 438.

† Probably a corruption of Meldomnach, for Maelḃomhnaiżh.

‡ That is Ḃubhchach, now Duffy. His title in the text is another proof of the spread of lay abbacies, when it became necessary to specify his clerical character.

§ Better *Sodelue.* Sodelbh (from po-ḃelḃ, "good-visage"), latinized *Pulcheria*, was a woman's name.

‖ He has been identified with Dovenaldus son of Samson, abbot of Brechin in 1202, but the interval is too great to admit of identity. See note on EVIDENCE O, No. 7, p. 120 *supra.*

¶ Probably Muiṁċepcach. The episcopal residence of Inchmurthach in the southern extremity of St. Andrews parish is called in one instrument *Inchmurahat.* (Reg. Priorat. S. Andree, p. 179.)

** In the confirmation of Pope Alexander III. (1163) we find among the possessions, "ex donacione Roberti episcopi abbatiam de insula Louchlevene cum omnibus ad eam pertinentibus" (Reg. Priorat. S. Andree, p. 55).

et cum decimis tocius redditus quem recepturi sumus ad eandem domum; et cum vestimentis ecclesiasticis, quæ ipsi Chelede* habuerunt; et cum hiis libris,† id est, cum Pastorali, Graduali, Missali, Origine, Sentenciis abbatis Clareuallensis, tribus quaternionibus de Sacramentis, cum parte Bibliotece, cum Leccionario, cum Actibus Apostolorum, textu Evangeliorum, Prospero, tribus libris Salomonis, glosis de Canticis Canticorum, Interpretacionibus dictionum, collectione Sentenciarum, exposicione super Genesim, Excepcionibus ecclesiasticarum Regularum. Hiis testibus, Gregorio episcopo de Duneheldin, et Guillelmo abbate de Sancta Cruce, et Thoraldo archidiacono, et Matheo archidiacono, Aiulfo decano, magistro Thoma, magistro Herberto, Ricardo capellano episcopi.‡

No. 15.—*Carta regis David de insula de Lochleven.* A. D. 1144-1150.

David rex Scottorum episcopis abbatibus comitibus vicecomitibus et omnibus probis hominibus tocius terre sue salutem. Sciatis me concessisse et dedisse Canonicis Sancti Andree insulam de Lochleuene, ut ipsi ibi instituant ordinem canonicalem; et Keldei§ qui ibidem inventi fuerint, si regulariter vivere voluerint, in pace cum eis et sub eis maneant; et si quis illorum ad hoc resistere voluerit, 'volo et precipio ut ab insula eiciatur. Testibus, Roberto episcopo Sancti Andree, Andrea episcopo de Cathenes, Waltero cancellario, Nicholao clerico, Hugone de Moreuille, Waltero filio Alani, apud Berwic.‖

No. 16.—*Confirmacio Adriani pape quarti de eodem.* A. D. 1156.

Inter alia Abatiam de Lohuleuene cum ecclesiis et terris et chan ad eam pertinentibus, etc.¶

---

* This form of the name, which is almost identical with the Irish celede, is unique in Scottish records. We find it latinized *Cheledei* in the Register of Dunfermlin, No. 3, p. 8.

† Reference to the contents of this little Culdean library is to be found in Jamieson's Culdees, p. 377; the preface to the Regist. Priorat. S. Andree, p. xvi.; Lyon's Hist. of St. Andrews, vol. ii., p. 271; Innes's Scotland in the Middle Ages, p. 333. The character of the books is just what might be expected in a small monastic establishment of that date, and the ritual works are those which were in general use. 1, a *Pastorale*, or Ritual; 2, a *Graduale*, or Antiphonary; 3, a *Missale*, or Liturgy book; 4, an *Origo*, or *Origines*,—if the former, some tract like the popular "Origo Mundi;" if the latter, some of the writings of Origen (whose name is sometimes written *Origines* instead of *Origenes*,—see Panzer); 5, the *Sententiæ* of St. Bernard; 6, a Treatise on the Sacraments, in three staves; 7, a portion of the Vulgate Bible; 8, a *Lectionarium*, or book of Epistles and Gospels; 9, the Acts of the Apostles; 10, the Four Gospels; 11, a *Prosper*, probably some work of Prosper Aquitanus; 12, three Books of Solomon; 13, Glosses on Solomon's Song; 14, Interpretations of words; 15, a collection of *Sententiæ*, or religious maxims; 16, Exposition of Genesis; 17, Excerpts of Ecclesiastical Rules.

‡ Registrum Prioratus S. Andree, p. 43; Jamieson's Culdees, p. 375; Keith's Bishops, p. 557 (ed. 1824).

§ In the original charter the word is written *Keledei*. The contraction of the word in the after copy indicates a step towards the modern pronunciation. See EVIDENCE R, No. 14, p. 138, *infra*.

‖ Registrum Prioratus S. Andree, p. 188. It was previously printed in Crawford's Officers of State, p. 6 c; Keith's Bishops, p. 9. A facsimile of the original charter, which belonged to the University of St. Andrews, is engraved in Anderson's Diplomata Scotiæ, tab. xii. and xiii.; also in the preface to the Register of S. Andrews, p. xvi., where a facsimile of its apograph in the Register is added.

¶ Registrum Prioratus S. Andree, p. 51.

No. 17.—*Concessio nostra Canonicis sancti Servani intra lacum de Lewin.* A. D. 1248.

Universis *etc.* Joannes prior et conventus Sanctiandree *etc.* Quamvis pie memorie David et Villelmus reges Scotie, et Robertus et Ricardus episcopi Sanctiandree, pio religionis affectu dederunt et confirmaverunt nobis et successoribus nostris abbaciam Keledeorum intra lacum de Lewin cum omnibus suis annexis connexis, disposicionemque religionis in eadem, *etc.*; Noverit vestra universitas nos exilitate bonorum prioratus nostri de Loichlewin considerata, ac quieti fratrum et canonicorum nostrorum ordinis S. Augustini ibidem institutorum et commorantium caritate fraterna providere volentes *etc.* concessisse *etc.* Deo et ecclesie sancti Servani intra lacum de Lewin *etc.* totam et integram insulam sancti Servani in dicto lacu situatam, cum jure piscandi in eodem, et omnibus commoditatibus suis, *etc.**

Q.—Records of Abernethy.

No. 1.—John of Fordun had access to "a certain chronicle of the church of Abernithy," but it has long since perished, and all that remains to justify the traditional belief as to the antiquity of this foundation consists of a short notice in the Chronicon Pictorum, some statements in the Scotichronicon, some charters in the Registrum Vetus of Arbroath, and a round tower. Towards the close of the twelfth century, William the Lyon granted to the abbey of St. Thomas the Martyr, at Aberbrothoc, the church of Abernethy with its appurtenances; and this donation, with its consequent developments, gave rise to a series of proceedings, the records of which find a place in the Register of that house. They are printed in the "Registrum Vetus de Aberbrothoc," which was edited for the Bannatyne Club, by Mr. Cosmo Innes, and the late Mr. Patrick Chalmers of Auldbar, Edinburgh, 1848.

No. 2.—Necton Morbet† filius Erip xxiv [annis] regnavit. Tercio anno regni ejus Darlugdach‡ abbatissa Cille-dara, de Hibernia exulat pro Christo§ ad Britanniam. Secundo anno adventus sui, immolavit Nectonius Aburnethige Deo et sancte Brigide, presente Dairlugtach; que cantavit Alleluia super istam hostiam. Optulit igitur Nectonius magnus filius Wirp, rex omnium provinciarum Pictorum, Apurnethige sancte Brigide usque ad diem judicii, cum suis finibus, que posite sunt a lapide in Apurfeirt usque ad lapidem juxta Cairfuill, id est Lethfoss; et inde in altum usque ad Athan. Causa autem oblationis hoc est: Nectonius invite iulie vivens,‖ fratre suo Drusto expul-

---

* Registrum Prioratus S. Andree, p. 121.　　　　　† Recte *Mor-brec.*

‡ She was successor of St. Brigid at Kildare; and the festivals of both are on the same day. See Colgan, Actt. SS., p. 229; and Martyrol. of Donegal, at Feb. 1.

§ Innes and Pinkerton erroneously read *Cilla Darade,* and *proximo.* See Irish Nennius, p. 162.

‖ Innes reads this, *in uite iulie manens,* suggesting as an emendation "in exilio manens." Pinkerton reads *in Vita Julia manens,* observing, "Videtur latina interpretatio alicujus nominis Hibernici."

sante se usque ad Hiberniam, Brigidam sanctam petivit ut postulasset Deum pro se. Orans autem pro illo dixit, Si pervenies ad patriam tuam Dominus miserebitur tui, regnum Pictorum in pace possidebis.*

No. 3.—Isti quoque regi Brudeo successit Garnard filius Dompnach, sive Makdompnach, qui fundavit et ædificavit ecclesiam collegiatam de Abirnethy. Postquam illuc introduxit beatus Patricius sanctam Brigidam, sicut in quadam chronica ecclesiæ de Abirnethy reperimus, cum suis novem virginibus in Scotiam : et obtulit Deo et beatæ Mariæ, et beatæ Brigidæ, et virginibus suis, omnes terras et decimas quas Prior et Canonici habent ex antiquo. Istæ vero novem virgines infra quinque. annos decesserunt, et ex parte boreali dictæ ecclesiæ sunt sepultæ. Et in illa ecclesia fuerunt tres electiones factæ, quando non fuit nisi unus solus episcopus in Scotia. Tunc fuit locus ille sedes principalis, regalis et pontificalis, per aliquot tempora, totius regni Pictorum. Ipsa autem ecclesia fundata erat ante ecclesiam Dunkeldensem ducentis viginti septem annis novem mensibus et sex diebus.† In alia chronica reperi ipsam præfundatam fuisse ecclesiæ Dunkeldensi CCXLIV. annis.‡

No. 4.—*Carta Laurencii de Abernythy de ecclesia de Abernythy.* A. D. 1189–1199.

Laurencius filius Orm de Abirnythy omnibus hominibus et amicis suis salutem. Sciant presentes et futuri me quietum clamasse pro me et heredibus meis Deo et ecclesie sancti Thome de Abirbrothoc et monachis ibidem in perpetuum omne jus quod habui vel quod clamare potui in advocacione ecclesie de Abirnythy cum istis pertinenciis suis, scilicet cum capella de Dron, et cum capella de Dunbulcc, et cum capella de Erolyn, et cum terra de Belache et de Petenlouer, et cum medietate omnium decimarum proveniencium ex propria pecunia mea et heredum meorum ; quarum alteram medietatem habebunt Keledei de Abirnythy, et cum omnibus decimis territorii de Abirnythy, et cum omnibus justis pertinenciis ejusdem ecclesie, preter illas decimas que spectant ad ecclesiam de Flisk, et ad ecclesiam de Cultram, et preter decimas de dominio meo de Abirnythy quas Keledei de Abirnythy habent et semper habere solebant ; scilicet de Mukedrum et de Kerpul, et de Balehyrewelle et de Ballecolly et de Invernythy ex orientali parte rivuli, *etc.*§

No. 5.—*Carta domini Regis de ecclesia de Abernythyn.* A. D. 1189–1196.

Willelmus Dei gratia Rex Scottorum *etc.* Sciant *etc.* me dedisse *etc.* Deo et ecclesie sancti Thome de Abirbrothoc et monachis ibidem Deo servientibus in liberam puram et perpetuam elemosinam ecclesiam de Abirnythyn cum istis pertinenciis *etc. ut supra,* et cum medietate omnium decimarum proveniencium ex propria [pecunia] Abbatis de Abirnythyn, quarum alteram medietatem habebunt Keledei de Abirnythyn *etc. ut supra,* preter *etc. ut supra,* et preter decimas de

---

* Chronicon Pictorum, ap. Innes, Critical Essay, vol. ii., p. 778 ; Pinkerton, Enquiry, vol. i., pp. 486, 493.
† See the extract from Mylne, EVIDENCE N, No. 2, p. 118 *supra.*
‡ Fordun, Scotichronicon, lib. iv., cap. 12 (vol. i., p. 188).
§ Registrum Vetus de Aberbrothoc, No. 35, p. 26.

dominio ipsius Abbatis, quas Keledei de Abirnythi habere solebant, scilicet de Mukedrum *etc. ut supra.* *

No. 6.—*Carta Symonis episcopi Dumblanensis de ecclesia de Abernythy.* A. D. 1189–1196.

Symon Dei gratia Dumblanensis episcopus *etc.* Sciant *etc.* nos ad peticionem Domini Willelmi illustris Scocie regis dedisse *etc.* Deo et ecclesie sancti Thome martiris de Aberbrothoc *etc.* ecclesiam de Abernythy *etc. ut supra,* et liceat eis capellanos quos voluerint in eadem ecclesia constituere, salvis synodalibus, *etc.*†

Sequuntur confirmaciones Jonathe episcopi Dumblanensis, A. D. circ. 1200; et Abrahe Dumblanensis episcopi, A. D. 1211–1214, sub iisdem verbis.‡

No. 7.—*Sententia Abrahe episcopi Dumblanensis super decimis de Abernythy.* A. D. 1211–1214.

Abraham *etc.* Cum coram nobis super quibusdam decimis, scilicet Petkarry, Petyman, Malcarny, Petkorny, Pethwnegus, Galthanin, per rectas divisas suas quas abbas et conventus de Aberbrothoc asserebant ad ecclesiam eorum de Abernythy jure parochiali spectare, inter eosdem Abbatem et monachos et Priorem et Kelledeos de Abernythy questio movetur, lite inter partes contestata *etc.* predictas decimas predicto Abbati, qui procurator monachorum erat, *etc.* diffinitive adjudicavimus; predicto Priori, qui procurator erat Kelledeorum, nomine Kelledeorum de Abernythy super eisdem decimis perpetuum silencium imponentes. Quam sentenciam de consensu et voluntate predictorum Kelledeorum execucioni fecimus demandari, *etc.*§

No. 8.—*Sententia ejusdem episcopi super eisdem decimis.* A. D. 1211–1214.

Universis *etc.* Abraham *etc.* Universitati vestre notum fieri volumus litem illam que inter dompnum Abbatem de Aberbrothoc *etc.* ex una parte et Priorem et Kelledeos de Abernythy ex altera, super decimis quarundam terrarum parochie de Abernythy, diu tam in curia domini nostri W. illustrissimi Regis, quam in ecclesiastica coram nobis noscitur agitata, coram nobis et in curia nostra multis eciam viris nobilibus ex parte dicti domini Regis, ad finem ejusdem litis audiendum destinatis, sub hac forma sentencia diffinitiva esse extinctam: Quod dicti Abbas et conventus dictam ecclesiam de Abernythin adeo plenarie integre et pacifice habebunt et possidebunt, sicut melius et plenius predecessores dictorum Abbatis et conventus habuerunt *etc.* Dicti etiam Abbas et conventus et dicti Prior et Kelledei in predictam sententiam legittime consenserunt, et sacramentum fidei prestiterunt quod nunquam contra predictam sentenciam vel ipsius exsecutionem aliqua occasione venirent, *etc.*‖

No. 9.—Hoc anno [1272] factus est prioratus de Abirnethy in Canonicos Regulares, qui prius fuerunt Keldei.¶

---

* Registrum Vetus de Aberbrothoc, No. 34, p. 25.   † Ibid., No. 211, p. 145.
‡ Ibid., Nos. 212, 213, pp. 146, 147.   § Ibid., No. 214, p. 147.
‖ Ibid., No. 215, p. 148.
¶ Fordun, Scotichronicon, lib. x., cap. 33 (vol. ii., p. 120).

R.—RECORDS OF MONYMUSK.

No. 1.—The parish of Monymusk is situated on the River Don, north-west of Aberdeen. Its place in history is due to its connexion with St. Andrews, for as to the story of its foundation by Malcolm Cennmor, it rests upon the doubtful authority of a boundary charter,* and the more questionable assertion of Hector Boece.† The declarations of title, and the controversies which grew out of its relations with the church of St. Andrews, rendered it a matter of importance to have its early muniments preserved, and accordingly a small collection of its charters were transferred into the Register of the Priory, where they remain in a compact and separate group.‡ The following extracts from this chartulary contain all our recorded materials for information concerning the Culdees of Monymusk. The opening document affords evidence of their existence about the year 1131.

No. 2.—*Carta Rogeri comitis de Bouchan.* A. D. circ. 1170.

Rogerus comes de Bouchan tam presentibus quam futuris salutem. Notum sit *etc.* me dedisse *etc.* Keledeis de Munimusc quolibet anno de Foedarg xx. modios de grano ordeicio et x. cudros casei, et de Foleyt xx. cudros casei et iv. modios de grano ordei et multonem, in perpetuam elemosinam sicut Gartenach§ avus meus illis predictam elemosinam dedit et concessit, atque pretaxata asportari infra festum Omnium Sanctorum ad Munimusc. Testibus.‖

No. 3.—*Carta Gilcristi comitis de Marr Keledeis de Munimusc.* A. D. 1199-1207.

Noverit *etc.* me dedisse *etc.* Deo et sancte Marie de Munimusc et Keledeis ibidem servientibus *etc.* ecclesiam de Loychel cum omnibus decimis *etc.*, et cum illa dimidia dauach terre tota in qua sita est ecclesia, libera ab omni exaccione et servicio seculari sicut sunt decime et cetere oblaciones altaris, *etc.*¶

No. 4.—*Carta Johannis Aberdonensis ecclesie ministri Canonicis de Munimusc de ecclesia de Loychel.* A. D. 1199-1207.

Omnibus *etc.* Johannes *etc.* Noverit universitas vestra nos ad presentacionem et peticionem

---

* Printed in "Collections for a History of the Shires of Aberdeen and Banff" (Spalding Club), p. 171.

† Scotorum Historiæ, lib. xii., fol. 258 *b* (ed. Par. 1575).

‡ Registrum Prioratus S. Andree, pp. 362-376. Most of them are reprinted in the Collections, &c., of Aberdeen and Banff, pp. 172-178. It is to be regretted that the scribe who copied these charters into the Register has omitted all the attestations, and thus deprived them of an important chronological element.

§ Probably Gartnait, son of Cainnech, husband of Ete daughter of Gillemichel, whom the Book of Deir records to have granted Petmeccobrig to the abbey of Deir in 1131.

‖ Registrum Prioratus S. Andree, p. 370; Collections for History of Aberdeen, vol. i., p. 172.

¶ Registrum Prioratus S. Andree, p. 373; Collections for History of Aberdeen, vol. i., p. 602.

Gilcrist comitis de Marr dedisse *etc.* Deo et ecclesie beate Marie de Munimusc et Canonicis qui Keledei dicuntur ibidem Deo servientibus et servituris ecclesiam de Loychel, *etc.* *

No. 5.—*Confirmacio ejusdem episcopi eisdem Canonicis.* A. D. 1199–1207.

Noverint *etc.* nos concessisse *etc.* donacionem illam quam G. comes de Marr donavit cenobio suo quod construxit apud Munimusc in ecclesia sancte Marie in qua Keledei ante fuerunt, scilicet ecclesiam de Loychel, cum terris et pertinenciis suis, ecclesiam de Ruchauen *etc.*, ecclesiam de Inuernochcin *etc.* Volumus etiam et concedimus ut prefatum cenobium et fratres ibidem commorantes nulli domo subjecti sint vel alicui faciant subjectionem nisi nobis *etc.*†

No. 6.—*Confirmacio ejusdem episcopi eisdem Canonicis.* A. D. 1199–1207.

Universis *etc.* Johannes *etc.* Sciatis nos ad presentacionem Gilcrist comitis de Marr dedisse *etc.* Canonicis de Munimusc *etc.*, ecclesiam de Afford cum dimidia dauach terre ad ecclesiam ipsam pertinente, in qua sita est ecclesia *etc.*‡

No. 7.—*Bulla Innocentii III. de confirmacione.* A. D. 1199–1216.

Innocentius episcopus *etc.*, dilecti in Domino filii vestris justis postulacionibus grato concurrentes assensu, locum vestrum et personas in eo Domino famulantes, cum omnibus bonis tam ecclesiasticis quam mundanis *etc.*, sub beati Petri et nostra protectione suscipimus *etc.* ac omnes terras possessiones et alia bona a nobili viro Gilcrist comite de Marr in elemosinam domui vestre concessa, et ecclesias sancti Andree de Afford, sancti Marnoci de Loychel, et sancte Marie de Nemoth *etc.* confirmamus *etc.*§

No. 8.—*Carta Willelmi Sancti Andree episcopi.* A. D. 1202–1214.

Omnibus *etc.* nos dedisse *etc.* sancte Marie et Canonicis de Munimusc *etc.* pro anima regis Willelmi *etc.* ecclesiam de Kege *etc.*‖

No. 9.—*Carta Thome hostiarii domini Regis de ecclesia de Afford.* A. D. 1207–1227.

Omnibus *etc.* Thomas *etc.* Noveritis universi me *etc.* dedisse *etc.* Deo et ecclesie beate Virginis de Munimusc, et Canonicis ibidem *etc.* ecclesiam de Afford cum omnibus ad eam juste pertinentibus *etc.*¶

---

* Registrum Prioratus S. Andree, p. 374 ; Collections for History of Aberdeen, vol. i., p. 603.
† Registrum Prioratus S. Andree, p. 374 ; Collections for History of Aberdeen, vol. i., p. 173.
‡ Registrum Prioratus S. Andree, p. 375 ; Collections for History of Aberdeen, vol. i., p. 588.
§ Registrum Prioratus S. Andree, p. 375 ; Collections for History of Aberdeen, vol. i., p. 173.
‖ Registrum Prioratus S. Andree, p. 366 ; Collections for History of Aberdeen, vol. i., p. 619.
¶ Registrum Prioratus S. Andree, p. 365 ; Collections for History of Aberdeen, vol. i., p. 589.

No. 10.—*Confirmacio Ade Aberdonensis episcopi de eadem ecclesia.* A. D. 1207–1227.

Adam *etc.* Noverit *etc.* nos ad presentacionem Thome hostiarii domini Regis dedisse *etc.* Deo et ecclesie beate Marie de Munimusc et Canonicis ibidem Deo servientibus *etc.* ecclesiam de Afford *etc.**

No. 11.—*Confirmacio Thome Hostiarii Regis de ordeo et caseo de Outhirheyclt.* A. D. 1207–1233.

Omnibus *etc.* Thomas *etc.* Sciatis me concessisse *etc.* elemosinam quam avus meus et mater mea dederunt Keledeis de Munimusc, scilicet x. bollas ordei, et x. petras casei de Outhirheyclt; et ita quod ille qui tenebit terram predicte elemosine transmittet has predictas bollas ordei et petras casei usque ad domum predictorum Keledeorum ad festum sancti Martini. Teste W. abbate de Sancta Cruce.†

No. 12.—*Carta Colini Hostiarii.*

Sciant *etc.* quod ego Colinus Hostiarius‡ dedi *etc.* ecclesie beate Marie de Munimusc et Canonicis ibidem *etc.* totam dimidiam dauach terre in qua sita est ecclesia de Loychel *etc.*§

No. 13.—*Carta Philippi de Monte Fichett de eadem.*

Omnibus *etc.* Philippus de Monte Fichett et Anna uxor, filia et heres domini Colini Hostiarii defuncti, *etc.* Noverit *etc.* nos *etc.* dedisse *etc.* ecclesie beate Marie de Munimusc et Canonicis ibidem *etc.* totum jus *etc.* in quadam dimidia dauach terre in qua sita est ecclesia de Loychel, *etc.*‖

No. 14.—*Confirmacio convencionis inter W. episcopum Sancti Andree et Keledeos de Munimusc.*¶ A. D. 1211.

A. de Melros et W. de Driburg abbates, et Robertus archidiaconus Glasguensis, omnibus has litteras etc. Litteras domini pape Innocentii [tercii] in hec verba suscepimus: Innocentius, servus servorum Dei dilectis filiis de Melros et de Driburg abbatibus, Sancti Andree et Glasguensis diocesium, et archidiacono Glasguensi, salutem et apostolicam benedictionem. Venerabilis fratris nostri

---

* Registrum Prioratus S. Andree, p. 365.

† Registrum Prioratus S. Andree, p. 369; Collections for History of Aberdeen, vol. i., p. 174.

‡ Colyn Ostiarius witnesses a charter of Alan Ostiarius, 1232–3. (Regist. Vet. de Aberbroth., No. 128, p. 91.)

§ Registrum Prioratus S. Andree, p. 363; Collections for History of Aberdeen, vol. i., p. 604.

‖ Registrum Prioratus S. Andree, p. 364; Collections for History of Aberdeen, vol. i., p. 605.

¶ Two ancient copies of this valuable record are preserved—one in the Registrum Prioratus S. Andree, from which the above is printed; the other in the Registrum Episcopatus Aberdonensis, which is not quite so correct in its style, but which is more complete, as supplying a hiatus in the other copy, and furnishing the names of the attesting witnesses. It has also a different title, which is curious as showing the use of the word *Kildey* in the fourteenth century: "Commissio impetrata per dominum episcopum Sancti Andree contra destruentes hospitalia aut in aliam naturam convertentes, et specialiter ad reformandum hospitale sive Kildey de Monymuske et processus super eodem" (Registr. Aberdonense, vol. ii., p. 264).

T

Sancti Andree episcopi recepimus queremoniam quod Keledei* quidam qui se Canonicos gerunt, et quidam alii Aberdonensis dyocesis infra villam de Munimusc pertinentem ad ipsum quandam cano-nicam† regularem eodem renitente construere contra justiciam non formidant, in ecclesie sue pre-judicium et gravamen. Quocirca discrecioni vestre per apostolica scripta mandamus quatinus par-tibus convocatis et auditis hinc inde propositis quod canonicum fuerit appellacione postposita statuatis, facientes quod statueritis per censuram ecclesiasticam firmiter observari. Testes autem qui fuerint nominati si se gratia odio vel timore subtraxerint post districcionem eandem appellacione remota cogatis veritati testimonium perhibere, nullis literis veritati et justicie prejudicantibus a sede apostolica impetratis. Quod si non omnes hiis exequendis potueritis interesse, duo vestrum nichilominus ea exequantur. Datum Laterani x. Kal. Aprilis, pontificatus nostri anno xiii. Harum auctoritate partibus in presentia nostra constitutis, ita inter dominum W[illelmum] episcopum Sancti Andree et Keldeos de Munimusc de consensu archidiaconorum suorum et capituli sui Sancti Andree amicabiliter convenit : scilicet quod dominus episcopus Sancti Andree concessit ut iidem Keledei decetero unum habeant refectorium, et unum dormitorium in communi, et unum oratorium sine cimiterio : ita quod corpora Keldeorum et clericorum sive laycorum cum eis commorancium in cymiterio parochialis ecclesie de Munimusc ecclesiasticam recipiant sepulturam, ita libere sicut hucusque solent sepeliri, salvo in omnibus jure matricis ecclesie. Erunt autem ibi duodecim Keledei, et tercius decimus Bricius, quem ipsi Keledei presentabunt domino episcopo Sancti Andree, ut sit magister vel prior eorum. Eo autem cedente vel decedente, Keledei de conKeledeis suis tres eligent de communi assensu eorum, et eos episcopo Sancti Andree quicunque fuerit pre-sentabunt, ut pro voluntate et dispositione sua episcopus Sancti Andree de tribus assumat unum qui prioratum sive qui magistratum‡ habeat, et eidem tamquam fundatori domus Keledeorum fide-litatem faciat. Et in electione prioris vel magistri Keledeorum ita fiet imperpetuum, hoc adjecto quod non licebit eisdem Keledeis vitam seu ordinem monacorum vel canonicorum fratrum§ sine assensu ejusdem episcopi vel successorum suorum ibidem profiteri inperpetuum, nec numerum Kele-deorum prenominatum excedere. Cedente vero vel decedente aliquo Keledeorum libere poterunt alium substituere usque ad numerum prenominatum ; ita quod quilibet Keledeus presente episcopo Sancti Andree, vel eo qui per eum ad hoc fuerit deputatus, jurabit quod predictam compositionem fideliter et sine dolo et malo ingenio quantum in eo est tenebit et servabit. Predicti vero Keledei dimidiam carucatam terre Eglismenythok nomine quam ex donacione Roberti bone memorie epis-copi Sancti Andree habuerunt adeo libere integre et quiete ut eam a tempore ejusdem R. episcopi usque ad hec tempora possederunt, de cetero possidebunt inperpetuum. Habebunt etiam quartam partem ovencionum que in communi conferuntur Keledeis, clericis, persis, et ferdys,‖ ab hiis qui ibidem sepulturam eligunt, et partem que eos contingit de communi elemosina que dicitur sauch-barian, et partem que eos contingit de beneficio quod dicitur thonneom tharmund,¶ libere et quiete, juxta quod ab antiquis temporibus retro usque ad hec tempora habuerunt, salvo in omnibus jure

---

* Here, and elsewhere throughout the instrument, the Aberdeen copy reads *Küldei.*

† *Canoniam.*—Regist. Aberdon. Canonica sometimes signifies "Canonicorum collegium," or "Ecclesia collegiata."

‡ See note †, p. 8 *supra.*   § *Regularium.*—Regist. Aberdon.

‖ *Spersis et ferdis.*—Regist. Aberdon.   ¶ *Thonneom thraumund.*—Regist. Aberdon.

persone et matricis ecclesie. Terras autem quas iidem Keledei ex concessione Gilcrist comitis de Marr sine assensu predicti episcopi,* scilicet Dolbethok et Fornathy, resignaverunt in manu ejusdem episcopi, ita quod de cetero nichil juris vendicabunt in eis nisi de concesione sua vel successorum suorum. Promiserunt eciam firmiter quod de cetero nullas terras que ad episcopum Sancti Andree noscuntur pertinere, ex dono ipsius comitis [vel alterius, sine assensu ipsius] episcopi Sancti Andree de cetero re[cipient, nec aliquid facient] quod cedit in prejudicium dignitatis sue, libertatis ecclesie Sancti Andree, vel in detrimentum ecclesie parochialis de Munimusc. Cum autem contigerit episcopum Sancti Andree venire apud Munemusc, predicti Kelledei recipient ipsum cum processione sollempniter. Dominus eciam Willelmus episcopus Sancti Andree promisit pro se et successoribus suis quod eosdem Keledeos juvabunt et manutenebunt tamquam suos. Ut autem hec composicio futuris perpetua temporibus rata et illibata perseveret, presentis scripti munimine, et tam sigillorum nostrorum quam sigillorum parcium apposicione, et juramento Bricii et Andree Keledeorum, pro se et suis conKeledeis interposito, est confirmata. [Hiis] testibus : [Thoma priore S. Andree, magistro Laurencio archdiacono Laudonie, Petro, Edwardo, Galfrido, capellanis episcopi Sancti Andree, Gervasio de Geafle, Roberto de Haya, magistro Stephano, magistro Adam Ouide, et magistro Michaele, et magistro Petro de Driburch, clericis episcopi Sancti Andree, magistro Bricio de Monymuske, et multis aliis.].†

No. 15.—*Mandatum Willelmi S. Andree episcopi de fratribus de Munimusc.* A. D. 1202–1233.

Willelmus *etc.* Certum est quod hii qui obtentu religionis seculum relinquentes habitum suscipiunt regularem et professionis emittunt votum, revertendi ad communes hominum conversaciones aditum sibi precludunt et regressum. *Etc.* Eapropter dilectorum filiorum nostrorum Prioris et Keldeorum de Munimusc justis supplicationibus inclinati, universitati vestre per presentia scripta precipiendo mandamus quatinus nullum de fratribus predicti loci qui habitum religionis susceperint ibidem et professionem fecerint, sine licencia et litteris commendaticiis predictorum Prioris et Keledeorum ad commorandum inter vos vel communicandum presumatis admittere, set pocius ipsum habeatis tanquam ethnicum et publicanum, donec penitentia ductus quam tocius ad domum propriam et confratres revertatur, super transgressionibus suis plenius satisfacturus, et juxta instituciones regule ipsorum canonicam recepturus disciplinam. Valete.‡

No. 16.—*Carta Duncani comitis de Mar de ecclesia de Loychel.* A. D. 1214–1234.

Duncanus *etc.* Notum facio me dedisse *etc.* sancte Marie de Munimusc et Keledeis sive Canonicis ibidem *etc.* ecclesiam de Loychel *etc.* et cum tota illa dimidia dauach in qua sita est ecclesia *etc.* pro anima *etc.* Willelmi regis *etc.* et pro anima patris mei M. Morgrund et matris mee Agnetis *etc.*§

---

* *Episcopi receperunt.*—Regist. Aberdon.

† Registr. Priorat. S. Andree, p. 370 ; Registr. Episcopat. Aberdonens., vol. ii. p. 264 ; Collections for Hist. of Aberdeen, vol. i., p. 174 ; Jamieson's History of the Culdees, p. 397.

‡ Registrum Prioratus S. Andree, p. 368 ; Collections for Hist. of Aberdeen, vol. i., p. 176.

§ Registrum Prioratus S. Andree, p. 362 ; Collections for Hist. of Aberdeen, vol. i., p. 603.

No. 17.—*Litera Regis Alexandri de eadem ecclesia.* A. D. 1214–1249.

Alexander *etc.* Sciant *etc.* quod cum pax formata esset *etc.* inter Duncanum filium Morgrun comitem de Marr ex una parte et David filium comitis ex altera *etc.* uterque illorum contulit ecclesiam de Loychel *etc.* sancte Marie de Munimusc et Canonicis ibidem Deo servientibus *etc.**

No. 18.—*Carta Duncani Comitis de Marr de ecclesia de Kindrouch.*† A. D. 1228–1239.

Omnibus *etc.* Duncanus *etc.* notum facimus nos dedisse *etc.* sancte Marie de Munimusc et Canonicis ibidem Deo servientibus *etc.* ecclesiam sancti Andree de Kindrouch *etc.* et cum una acra terre in Aucatendregen ex altera parte amnis que vocatur Alien, *etc.*‡

No. 19.—*Confirmacio Gilberti Aberdonensis episcopi de eadem ecclesia.* A. D. 1228–1239.

Omnibus *etc.* Gilbertus *etc.* Noverit *etc.* nos ad presentacionem nobilis viri domini Duncani comitis de Marr dedisse *etc.* sancte Marie de Munimusc et Canonicis ibidem *etc.* ecclesiam Sancti Andree de Kindrouch *etc.* cum una acra terre in Auchatendregen ex altera parte amnis que vocatur Alien *etc.*§

No. 20.—*Confirmacio Gilberti Aberdonensis episcopi de ecclesia de Kege.* A. D. 1228–1239.

Universis *etc.* Noverit *etc.* nos ad presentacionem *etc.* Willelmi Dei gracia episcopi Sancti Andree dedisse *etc.* ecclesie de Munimusc et Canonicis ibidem Deo servientibus *etc.* ecclesiam de Kege *etc.*‖

No. 21.—*Carta David episcopi Sancti Andree de Dolbethoc.* A. D. 1239–1245.

Omnibus *etc.* David *etc.* Noverit *etc.* nos *etc.* dedisse *etc.* Priori de Munimusc et Canonicis ibidem *etc.* Dolbethoc *etc.*, in liberam puram et perpetuam elemosinam ad sustentacionem pauperum et peregrinorum ibidem confluencium, *etc.* teste A. de Malkaruistun.¶

---

* Registrum Prioratus S. Andree, p. 363; Collections for History of Aberdeen, vol. i., p. 604.

† It is said of S. Regulus and his company that, leaving Monichi, now Monikie in Forfar, they "transierunt montana, seu Moneth, et venerunt ad locum qui vocabatur Doldencha, nunc autem dictus Chondrochedalvan." (Historia B. Reguli, Pinkerton, Enquiry, i., p. 460.) This last name is the Kindrouch of the charter, with the name of the river, then called *Alien*, attached to it, the compound signifying "Bridge-end of Alien." Kindrocht is the old parochial name of Braemar in the union of Crathie, and the church stood near Castletown, on the east of the Clunie Water, which enters the Dee from the south. *Alien* or *Aivan* is the ancient name of the Clunie, and Aucatendregen [i. e. *Achadh-an-draoighen*, "field of the thorn"], now Auchindrain, is situated on its east bank.

‡ Registrum Prioratus S. Andree, p. 367; Collections for History of Aberdeen, vol. ii., p. 86.

§ Registrum Prioratus S. Andree, p. 368; Collections for History of Aberdeen, vol. ii., p. 86.

‖ Registrum Prioratus S. Andree, p. 367.

¶ Registrum Prioratus S. Andree, p. 369; Collections for History of Aberdeen, vol. i., p. 177.

No. 22.—*Confirmacio Innocencii IV. Priori et Conventui de Munimusc.* [A.D. 1245.]

Innocentius *etc.* Priori et conventui de Munimusc ordinis sancti Augustini* *etc.* sancti Andree de Afford, sancti Mernoci de Loychel, sancti Diaconiani de Kege, sancti Andree de Kindrocht ecclesias, *etc.* vobis *etc.* confirmamus.†

S.—RECORDS OF MUTHILL.

No. 1.—The existence of Keledei at the comparatively obscure church of Muthill is learned, indirectly, from the attestations to some episcopal charters preserved in chartularies of Cambuskenneth and Northberwic. The priory of Cambuskenneth, near Stirling, was founded for Regular Canons in 1147. A transumpt of its charters, which were suffering from the effects of damp, was made under the Great Seal in 1535, which volume, as well as the charters themselves, has perished. But a transcript made by Mac Farlan in the year 1738 is fortunately in existence, and is preserved in the Advocates' Library at Edinburgh, under the mark 35. 3. 7. A collection of the charters of the Cistercian Nunnery of North Berwick was printed by the Bannatyne Club, under the able editorship of Cosmo Innes, Esq., under the title "Carte Monialium de Northberwic." 4to, Edinb.: 1847.

No. 2.—*Confirmacio de Login per Simeonem episcopum Dunblanensem.* A.D. circ. 1178.

Universis *etc.* Simeon Dei gratia Dunblainensis episcopus salutem. Sciant *etc.* nos concessisse *etc.* monialibus in Nortberwic *etc.* ecclesiam de Login Atheren *etc.* Hiis testibus, Jonatha archidiacono, Thoma decano, Malpol priore Keledeorum de Mothel,‡ Michaele persona de Mothel, Johanne persona de Kilbride, Gregorio persona de Tulibodevin, Pol fratre ejusdem Gregorii, Malcolmo capellano nostro, Sithach et Malcolmo Keledeis de Mothel, Waltero clerico comitis Dunecani.§

No. 3.—*Kyncardin ecclesie confirmatio.* A.D. circ. 1190.

W.‖ Dei gracia episcopus Dumblanensis *etc.* Sciant *etc.* nos concessisse *etc.* Deo et ecclesie

* It would appear that the Keledei of this church had from the commencement of the century been endeavouring to reform their discipline; and their efforts eventuated in the abandonment of their ancient name, and the adoption of the rule of regular canons of St. Augustin. The date of the present instrument proves that Robert Gordon is wrong in referring the change to the year 1300. See Collect. for Hist. of Aberdeen, vol. i., p. 169.

† Regist. Priorat. S. Andree, p. 372; Collections for History of Aberdeen, vol. i., p. 171.

‡ The names of the Culdee witnesses to this charter are printed, but not accurately, in Crawford's Officers of State, p. 6.

§ Carte de Northberwic, No. 5, p. 6.

‖ Keith places this bishop William after Jonathan, named in next charter. But as this instrument implies that it was executed in the reign of William the Lyon, and as the Prior and Parson of Mothel, who attest it, are the same as in last instrument, while different names appear to their offices in the next, his order has been departed from in the present instance. See Dalrymple, Histor. Collect., p. 275.

sancte Marie de Cambuskynneth *etc.* ecclesiam de Kyncardyn cum capellis suis et decimis *etc.* Tenendam *etc.* sicut carta domini regis Willelmi testatur, *etc.* Hiis testibus, Archidiacono Jonatha,* capellano meo Cormac, Malpol priore Keldeorum, Persona de Mothel Michaele, et ejus capellano Machbeth, magistro Symone medico, Martino senescallo, Ricardo capellano comitis, et Johanne cancellario comitis, Henrico capellano, Malis persona de Dunblan, Beano magistro de Dunblan, Ysaac, Michaele clerico persona de Logyn, Matheo capellano de Tulibody, Malcolmo persona de Insula, Matholem, Abraham fratre persone de Kincardin, Simone de Tulibody, et filio ejus Matheo, Symone persona de Alweth.†

No. 4.—*Confirmacio ecclesie de Tulibody.* A. D. circ. 1200.

Jonathas Dei gracia episcopus Dumblanensis *etc.* Sciant *etc.* nos concessisse *etc.* Deo et ecclesie sancte Marie de Cambuskynneth *etc.* ecclesiam de Tulibody, et ecclesiam de Tulicultry, et ecclesiam de Kincardin cum capellis *etc.* Testibus hiis, Priore Malgegill Moethill, Priore Malys de Insula effren,‡ Moricio capellano nostro, Gillecrist capellano nostro, Patricio filio Gillemanthacb capellano nostro, Gillemichell persona de Moethel, magistro Henrico clerico domini episcopi, I. Dunkeldensis, Gilleheshoc filio Johannis de Clechenes, Willielmo de Bennyn, Henrico Pinnum.§

No. 5.—*Confirmacio ecclesie de Logy.* A. D. circ. 1214.

Universis *etc.* Abraham Dei gracia Dunblanensis episcopus salutem. Sciant *etc.* nos concessisse *etc.* sanctimonialibus de Northberewich *etc.* ecclesiam de Login Athran *etc.* Hiis testibus, Gileberto archidiacono, Malkirg priore Kelledeorum de Mothle, Durando canonico de Scone, Willelmo capellano domini episcopi, Luca clerico ejusdem, Michahele canonico de insula sancti Columbe.‖

T.—RECORDS OF MONIFIETH.

No. 1.—*Carta Malcolmi comitis de Anegus de Abthein de Monifoth.* A. D. circ. 1220.

Sciant omnes *etc.* quod Ego Malcolmus Comes de Anegus dedi et concessi *etc.* Nicholao** filio Bricii†† Sacerdotis de Kerimure et heredibus suis in feudo et hereditate totam terram de Abthein de

---

* The inversion of the name and office both here and further on seems to indicate some inaccuracy in the transcription of Mylne's or Macfarlane's copy.

† Registrum de Cambuskenneth (orig. fol. 80), transcript, pp. 152, 153.

‡ That is, ᴵᴺᴵᴾ ᴼᴵᴾᴾᴺᴱᴺᴺ, "the Island of Masses," pronounced *Inchaffray*, and latinized *Insula missarum.*

§ Registrum de Cambuskenneth (orig. fol. 168), transcript, pp. 296, 297.

*‖ Carte de Northberwic, No. 11, pp. 11, 12.

** This Nicholas is styled *Abbas de Monifodh.* in No. 8 *infra.*

†† This Bricius was chaplain to Gillecrist Earl of Angus in 1201, and is sometimes styled *persona* and *capelianus de Kerimor.*

Munifeth.* Tenendam sibi et heredibus suis de me et heredibus meis libere et quiete plenarie et honorifice ex omni exactione et exercitu et consuetudine seculari, salvo communi auxilio domini Regis. *Etc.*†

No. 2.—*Carta Matildis Comitisse de Anegus de Abthein de Monifoth.* A. D. circ. 1242.

Sciant *etc.* quod Ego Matildis comitissa de Anegus in legitima potestate viduitatis mee existens concessi *etc.* Nicholao filio Bricii sacerdotis de Kerimure et heredibus suis totam terram de Abthein de Munifeit, *etc.* Ita libere *etc.* sicut in carta domini M. bone memorie dudum comitis de Anegus patris mei supradicto N. inde collata liberius *etc.* continetur, *etc.* Testibus *etc.* domino Willelmo vicario de Monifeit, *etc.*‡

Broughty Ferry.

No. 3.—*Carta M. Comitisse de Anegus de terra de Portincrag et piscaria et terre in territorio de Kerimor.* A. D. circ. 1242.

Testibus, domino G. de Haya, domino Johanne de Haya, domino W. de Haya, domino Nigello de Mubray, domino W. juvene de Haya, domino Malcolmo de Haya, domino Roberto filio Warnebaldi, Bricio persona de Kerimor, Willelmo vicario de Monifodh, Nicholao Abbate de Monifodh, Johanne Blundo, et Galfrido fratre ejus, Adam de Haliburtonia, et aliis.§

No. 4.—*Carta M. Comitisse de Anegus de terra quam Keledei tenuerunt.* A. D. circ. 1242.

Omnibus etc., Matildis comitissa de Anegus *etc.*, Noverit universitas vestra me in legittima potestate viduitatis mee existentem *etc.*, dedisse *etc.* ecclesie sancti Thome de Aberbrothoc *etc.*, totam terram ex australi parte ecclesie de Monifodh, quam Kelledei tenuerunt in vita patris mei cum toto crofto ex orientali parte ejusdem ecclesie, in liberam puram et perpetuam elemosinam, cum communi pastura et aisiamento petarii hominibus in dicta terra manentibus. Tenendam et habendam libere quiete plenarie *etc.* ‖

No. 5.—*Carta territorii de Monefuth.* A. D. 1310.

Omnibus etc., Michael de Monifuth dompnus Abbathanie ejusdem, *etc.* Noverit *etc.* me et heredes meos teneri *etc.* domino abbati de Aberbrothoc *etc.* in sex solidis et octo denariis *etc.* pro tofto et crofto que ab eis ad foedofirmam teneo in territorio predicte Abbathanie de Monifoth, *etc.*¶

---

* Gillecrist Earl of Angus, about 1202, granted the church of Monifod to St. Thomas's of Arbroath; and among the witnesses is a layman, *Mauricius Abbas de Abireloth,* who ranks after the clergy of all classes. (Regist. Vetus de Aberbrothoc, No. 39, p. 29; see *ibid.* Nos. 41, 43, pp. 30, 31.) Abiriot is a parish in Forfarshire, adjoining Arbroath on the south-west.

† Registrum Vetus de Aberbrothoc, Appendix, No. 4, p. 330.

§ Ibid., No. 114, p. 81.   ‡ Ibid., No. 5, p. 331.

¶ Ibid., No. 323, p. 278.   ‖ Ibid., No. 115, p. 82; see also Preface, p. xxiv.

U.—THE COLIDEI OF YORK.

Deinde* ad Eboracum declinans [Rex Ethelstanus], in ecclesia beati Petri, ibidem diu et devote precibus insistens, se et viagium Deo et beatæ Mariæ, ac beato Petro et sanctis omnibus, humiliter commendabat. Supplicans ministris dictæ ecclesiæ, adtunc dicti Colidei, quatinus pro eo, et expeditione sua devote precarentur; promittens, quod si prospere rediret, ecclesiam illam Eboraci, et ministros ejus digne honoraret. . . . .

Idemque rex Athelstanus deinde redeundo de Scotia, ut præfertur, dum in civitate Eboraci fuerat, et in ecclesia beati Petri ibidem Deo et beato Petro gratias reddiderat, quod sanus et incolumis victor ad propria redisset; videns in dicta ecclesia Eboraci viros sanctæ vitæ, et conversationis honestæ, dictos adtunc Colideos, qui multos sustentabant pauperes, et modicum habebant unde viverent, concessit Deo et beato Petro, et Colideis prædictis, et eorum successoribus imperpetuum, ut melius possent sustinere pauperes confluentes, hospitalitatem tenere, et exercere alia opera pietatis; de qualibet caruca arante in episcopatu Eboraci unam travam bladi anno Domini DCCCC.XXXVI. quæ usque in præsentem diem dicitur Petercorne; cujusmodi et travas, reges tunc temporis potuerunt sacris locis, ex sua regalitate concedere et assignare; et nihilominus, ex concensu incolarum episcopatus Eboraci, rex habuit: travas prædictas sibi et successoribus suis; sic quod exterminaret lupos patriam devastantes; erat siquidem in diœcesi Eboracensi tanta, adtunc, multitudo luporum quod omnes fere villanorum bestias devorârunt. Quibus lupis per prædictum Ethelstanum devastatis, ac processu temporis, dictis Colideis possessionatis, largitione fidelium, et maxime per Thomam seniorem, cui rex Willielmus conquestor episcopatum prædictum contulit, in festo Pentecostes anno Domini 1069. Qui . . . Thomas ecclesiam Eboracensem construxit, et clericos ejusdem multipliciter ditavit.

Ipsi Colidei erexerunt seu fundârunt in civitate Eboraci, in quodam vasto loco ad regem pertinente (et quam ad erectionem idem rex dedit eis, una cum supradictis travis), quoddam hospitale sive manseolum pauperibus ad ipsam civitatem confluentibus: quibus et pauperibus ibidem accedentibus, assignârunt imperpetuum travas prædictas; ipsisque pauperibus, pro ipsorum meliori gubernatione et jurium suorum, in dictis travis salvatione dicti Colidei, sive clerici, unum ex seipsis præfecerunt. Ipseque Willielmus Conquestor ad preces Thomæ archiepiscopi prædicti, nedum donationem factam dictarum travarum hospitali prædicto, per ipsos Colideos, sive clericos, confirmavit; sed etiam ex prærogativa ipsius, qui Conquestor fuerat, pro majori securitate ipsius, dedit ex habundanti, dictas travas prædicto hospitali.

Willielmusque Rufus filius Conquestoris prædicti, rex immediate succedens, fundavit seu

---

* The above was first printed by Dugdale from the " Registrum Cartarum et Munimentorum Hospitalis Sancti Leonardi Eboraci," preserved in the Cottonian Library, Nero D. III. It is described as " one of the finest Manuscripts of its kind, written upon 241 leaves of vellum of the largest size: apparently written about the time of Henry the Fifth."—Monast. Anglican., vol. vi., part ii., p. 607 (Lond. 1846). An abstract is given in English in Drake's Eboracum, p. 332.

mutavit situm dicti hospitalis in locum regium, ubi nunc situatur, ut patet per multas domos adhuc stantes in dicto hospitali, quæ olim erant regiis usibus deputatæ; et dedit et confirmavit dictas travas hospitali prædicto, sicut fecit pater ejus Conquestor. Ipsum vero hospitale, a tempore primæ erectionis sive fundationis suæ, usque ad tempus regis Stephani, dicebatur Hospitale Sancti Petri; et usque in præsens sigillum commune ipsius continet in circumferentia " Sigillum Hospitalis Sancti Petri Eboraci." Ipse vero Stephanus construxit in dicto hospitali quandam ecclesiam in honore sancti Leonardi, et extunc, in antea, dictum est Hospitale Sancti Leonardi. Ipsique Colidei, a dicto anno Domini DCCCCXXXVI. fere per centum annos, tenuerunt, et pacifice possiderunt travas prædictas, usque quo illas concesserunt dicto hospitali, prout superius narratur.*

In 1294, Walter de Langton, Master of St. Leonard's Hospital, drew up a code of regulations for the better ordering of this house,† in which there are many points of resemblance to the ruder and less methodical provisions of the Irish Rule of the Céli-dé.

* Monasticon Anglicanum, vol. vi., part ii., pp. 608, 609 (Lond. 1846).
† Printed in the Monasticon Anglicanum, vol. vi., part ii., p. 610 (Lond. 1846)

———————

POSTSCRIPT.—In the Life of St. Findan, published by Goldastus (Rer. Alamannicar. Scriptores, vol. i., p. 318, Francof, 1606), there occurs the following sentence:—Ⲁⲓⲛⲙⲛⲉ ⲓⲗⲁⲟ ⲟⲥⲩⲣ ⲓⲛ ⲛⲁⲓⲟⲥⲏⲓ ⲛⲓ ⲗⲟⲛⲅⲉ ⲥⲟⲗⲟⲛⲅⲉ ⲥⲉⲗⲉⲃⲉ ⲡⲉⲙⲩⲥ ⲛⲟ ⲣⲉⲛ ⲣⲁ ⲣⲣⲩⲓⲥⲏⲓⲩ,—" Abstinence by day and night: you must not eat until the céle-dé eats before you, or a man under religious rules" (cap. 10, p. 322). St. Fintan, the patron saint of Augia Rheni, or Rheinau, who was a native of the province of Leinster, flourished in the year 800; and his life was compiled not long after, so that the foregoing passage may be regarded as containing one of the earliest examples on record of the term céle-dé. It purports to have been communicated to the saint during his sojourn in Switzerland, and was committed to writing in that country by some one who was conversant with the Irish language, and who seems to have understood the term as denoting a religious order.

At p. 42, line 5, *for* Edmund *read* Ethelred.
At p. 55, *note* ‡, *for* 8, 9, 11, 17–21 *read* 5, 14, 16.
At p. 73, line 22, *for* indoctrined *read* indoctrinated.

INDEX.

Goldastus, Rer. Alamann. Script., cited, 145.

Goodall, in Keith, cited, 71 ; his preface to Fordun's Scotichronicon, 72.

Gowrie, formerly Gobriat, 45.

ᵹᚱᚪᛞ, gradus, 95 ; ᵹᚱᚪᛞ ᚢᚪᚱᚪᛚ, 91.

Graduale, in Culdee library, 131.

Gregory, St., the Great, respect of the Irish for, 2 ; works of, cited, 64.

Gruoch filia Bodhe, 52, 125, 126.

ᵹᚱᚢᚳᚾ, 85.

Guaire Aidhne, 78.

HAND, going to the, 87. *See* Laim.

Henry. *See* Silgrave.

Herbert, Algernon, on the Culdees, 75, 125..

Heremitæ, keledei, 52, 123, 126, 128.

Herenachs, 95, 97.

Hertylpool, John, 101.

Hieronymus, St., cited, 64.

Hilary, or Elair, St., 21.

Holstenius, Codex Regularum, 5. *See* Brockie.

Horæ. *See* Hours.

Hospitals, of keledei, 38, 144.

Hours, ecclesiastical, ᚳᚱᚪᚳᚪ, *see* ᛗᚪᚳᚪᛁᚾ, ᚳᛖᛁᚱᚳ, ᚾᚩᛁᚾ, ᛖᚱᚱᚪᚱᚳᚪᛁᚾ, ᛁᚪᚱᛗᛖᛁᚱᚷᛁ.

Hurkyndorath, or Auchterderran, 128, 129.

Hy, or Ia, ecclesiastics of, 50, 51, 81 ; célidé of, 81.

ᛁᚪᚱᛗᛖᛁᚱᚷᛁ, nocturns, 89, 90.

ᛁᛒᚪᛁᚱᚳ ᚳᚢᛁᚱᚱ Cᚱᛁᚱᚳ, 93.

ᛁᚱᛁᚢᚱᚾ, infernus, 92.

Immolo, to offer, 132.

ᛁᛗᚾᚪ, hymns, 95.

ᛁᛗᚱᛁᚳᚾ, 92.

Inchaffray, ᛁᚾᛁᚱ-ᚩᛁᚱᚱᚱᛖᚾᚾ, 142.

Inchenebo, or Monahincha, 22.

Inchmurahat, 130.

Inchmurthach, near St. Andrews, 130.

ᛁᚾᛒᚢᛒ, 94.

Inis-Cathaigh, 25.

Inis-Locha-Cre, 21.

Innes, Cosmo, on the Culdees of St. Andrews and Brechin, 75, 76 ; his Registrum de Aberbrothoc, 76, 132 ; his Registrum de Brechin, 132 ; his Registrum de Dunfermelyn, 75 ; his Registrum S. Andreæ, 75; his Carta de Northberwic, 76, 141 ; his Scotland in the Middle Ages, 77, 131.

Innes, Thomas, Civil and Eccl. Hist. of, 71 ; Critical Essay of, 35, 132.

Innse-Gall, 81.

Inquisitions of Ulster, 23, 24.

Insula, or Hy, Keledei of, 81.

Insula-effren, Inchaffray, 142.

Interment of Keledei, 55, 113, 138.

Interpretationes dictionum, 131.

Inventio at Down, 12.

Invergowrie River, 45.

Invernythy, 133.

Iona. *See* Hy.

Ireland, desertion of, condemned, 91.

Irishmen in Fife, 126, 130.

Iseal Chiarain, 19, 20, 80.

JAMIESON, Dr. John, Historical Account of the Culdees, 74, 125, 131, 139.

Jocelin, Vita S. Kentegerni, 27.

John, St., styled céledei, 2, 79.

John, bishop of Aberdeen, 135.

John, prior of St. Andrews, 132.

Judex magnus in Scotia, 130.

KATENES, Caithness, Keledei of, 32.

Kege, church of, 136, 141.

Keith, Scottish Bishops, 131, 141.

Kelde, 43. *See* Keledei.

Keldei, 134, 139 ; a late form of Keledei, 131.

Kéledé. *See* Céle-dé.

Keledei, of Scotland, at Abernethy, 54, 133 ; at Brechin, 32, 43, 119 ; at Dornoch, 32, 48 ; at Dunblane, 32, 46 ; at Hy, 32, 50 ; at Lis-

X 2

Saint Andrews, formerly Cill-Righmonaigh, 33; ancient constitution of, 38; keledei of, 32, 75, 107–117, their character, 107, 109, their depression, 110, 114–117; early bishops of, 35, 128; Robert bishop of, 30, 39, later bishops of, 40, 55; endowed at Lochleven, 125; reduced to Saxon discipline, 36; priory of regular canons of, 37, 39, 109–117; church of the Holy Trinity of, 41, 55; St. Mary's of, 41, afterwards called Kirkheugh, 41; Magnum Registrum of, 35, description of, 37; Liber Chartarum of, 40, 47, 54, 74, 128, 129, 131, 135–137, 139–141, fac-similes of portions of, 131, charters of Lochleven entered in, 124.

Saint Leonard's of York, 58.

Salinagium, 126.

Salomonis libri tres, 131.

Salvianus Massiliensis cited, 64.

Saran filius Sodelne, 130.

Sare, or Servan, St., 124.

Sachapn, Saturni dies, Saturday, 86, 89.

Saturday. See Sachapn.

Saturday Review. See Stokes, Whitley.

Sauchbaria, 138.

Saxon influence on the Scottish church, 36.

Saxum Hibernensium, 52, 126.

Scalacronica, referred to, 32.

Scattery Island, 25.

Schools at Abernethy, 128.

Scone, church of, 33.

Sconyn, or Sconie, church of, 128, 130.

Scotland, early institutions of, borrowed from Ireland, 26; Irish saints commemorated in. See Barr, Boniface, Columba, Moluoc; hagiology of, 34; keledei of, 24; episcopi Scottorum, 109, 128; early bishops of, 133; ancient and modern sees of, 30.

Scripture, Holy, 90.

Sea-wanderings of Snedgus, 80.

Selann, a measure, 85, 86, 88.

Selden, John, on the Culdees, 69.

Σεμνόθεοι, 68.

Senan, St., of Scattery, 25.

Sententiarum collectio, 131.

Serb, or Servanus, St., account of, 124. See Servanus.

Serf, St., 53. See Servanus.

Servanus, St., account of, 124; legend of, 34; MS. Life of, 124; alleged founder of the Culdees, 124; his church of Culros, 72, of Lochleven, 51, 52, 53, 124, 125.

Servus Dei, origin of the term, 1; early examples of, 64; borrowed by the Irish, 3.

Seven portions of altar oblations, 39.

Seven years' probation, 87.

Shaw, Lachlan, History of Moray, 62.

Shinan mac Girrigin, St., 25.

Sibbald, Sir Robert, History of Fife, 70, 114.

Silgrave, Henry of, his Catalogue, cited, 32, 43, 46, 48, 49, 50.

Simon, bishop of Dunblane, 134.

Sithach, keledeus, 57, 141.

Skinner, bishop, Eccles. History of Scotland, 72.

Slechtain, flecto, 83; genuflexion, 90.

Sliabh nOchel, or Ochill Hills, 124.

Sligo, célidé of, 2, 82.

Sloʒaꝺach, meaning of, 130.

Slogadadh, dux episcopi, 129.

Smith, Dr. John, Life of St. Columba, 73.

Sodelbh, or Pulcheria, 130.

Soen, dux, 129.

Soépaꝺ eclaiṗi Ꝺé, 93.

Soipchele, meaning of, 66.

Sollaman, solemnitas, 94. See Ꝑṗimꝑollaman.

Soul-friend. See Ɑnmchaṗa.

Spalding Club. See Robertson, Joseph.

Spelman, Sir Henry, Glossary of, cited, 24, 68.

Speris et Ferdis, 138.

Spotiswood, Abp., History of the Church of Scotland, 69.

Srath-Hirenn, Culros in, 124.

Staff of St. Moluoc, 49.

Y

Also published by Llanerch:

THE ANNALS OF CLONMACNOISE, a facsimile reprint.

THE ANNALS OF TIGERNACH, a facsimile reprint from the pages of *Revue Celtique*.

THE HIGH CROSSES OF IRELAND by J. Romilly Allen, a facsimile reprint from the author's Early Christian Symbolism.

THE VOYAGE OF BRAN, translated by Kuno Meyer.

THE LIFE OF ST. GALL by Maude Joynt.

Write to the publishers for a complete list of 100+ small-press editions and facsimile reprints: LLANERCH PUBLISHERS, FELINFACH, LAMPETER, DYFED, SA48 8PJ.